The
—— Pedagogy of God ——

The
—— Pedagogy of God ——

Its Centrality in Catechesis and Catechist Formation

—— EDITED BY ——

Caroline Farey

Waltraud Linnig

Sr. M. Johanna Paruch FSGM

EMMAUS
ROAD
PUBLISHING

Steubenville, Ohio

www.emmausroad.org

Emmaus Road Publishing
1468 Parkview Circle
Steubenville, Ohio 43952

Library of Congress Number: 2011931372
ISBN: 978-1-931018-72-2

Cover design and layout by Julie Davis, General Glyphics, Inc., Dallas, Texas (www.glyphnet.com)

Contents

Preface

This book, arising from an international catechetical conference held in Rome in 2009, examines what the Church, in her recent documents on catechesis, understands by "the pedagogy of God" and what the relationship is of this pedagogy to the discipline and practice of catechesis and to catechist formation. We hope that this volume will be particularly useful for catechetical leaders in the Church. The language of "the pedagogy of God" is not very familiar to many of us. As a result, it is not yet significantly influencing our approach to catechetics or our formation programs for catechists. Yet it is crucial. The pedagogy of God provides a framework for understanding the nature and purpose of catechesis: a close examination of the Congregation for the Clergy's *General Directory for Catechesis* (1997) and of John Paul II's *Catechesi Tradendae* (1979), in particular, enables us to see that this pedagogy provides us with universally valid principles that are the necessary foundations for the communication of Revelation. This focus upon the pedagogy of God is rooted in the current renewal of catechesis proposed by the Church. The retrieval of this concept is a key part of the more general theological *ressourcement* following the Second Vatican Council.

In this book, the central features of this pedagogy are traced, including some of the scriptural roots of the concept and its patristic development. The relationship of God's pedagogy to catechetical formation is explored and implications are then traced into the concrete areas of doctrinal and moral formation, formation in prayer, sacramental and liturgical formation, and Christian initiation. Particular chapters focus upon implications of the pedagogy of God for the catechetical methods we employ and for the catechist's understanding of his or her own vocation.

Where it seemed appropriate, the original style of a conference paper or address has been maintained. In other cases, some adjustments have been made to adapt the paper given at the Conference for this publication.

Many have collaborated on this project. The translation work by Anne Harriss, Anne St. John-Hall and Bernard Farrell-Roberts has been invaluable; and the work of Colleen Rainone at Franciscan University of Steubenville, with her kindly and patient reminders and proofreading of the text, has facilitated much of the process for completion. May this book serve the coming of God's Kingdom as Christ was born of Mary in Bethlehem.

Abbreviations

The following abbreviations are used for the books of the Bible cited in the text:

Gen.	Genesis	Sir.	Sirach
Ex.	Exodus	Isa.	Isaiah
Lev.	Leviticus	Jer.	Jeremiah
Num.	Numbers	Lam.	Lamentations
Deut.	Deuteronomy	Bar.	Baruch
Josh.	Joshua	Ezek.	Ezekiel
Judg.	Judges	Dan.	Daniel
1 Sam.	1 Samuel	Hos.	Hosea
2 Sam.	2 Samuel	Joel	Joel
1 Kings	1 Kings	Am.	Amos
2 Kings	2 Kings	Jon.	Jonah
1 Chr.	1 Chronicles	Mic.	Micah
2 Chr.	2 Chronicles	Zeph.	Zephaniah
Ezra.	Ezra	Zech.	Zechariah
Neh.	Nehemiah	Mal.	Malachi
Tob.	Tobit	Mt.	Matthew
Jdt.	Judith	Mk.	Mark
Esth.	Esther	Lk.	Luke
1 Macc.	1 Maccabees	Jn.	John
2 Macc.	2 Maccabees	Acts	Acts of the Apostles
Job	Job	Rom.	Romans
Ps.	Psalms	1 Cor.	1 Corinthians
Prov.	Proverbs	2 Cor.	2 Corinthians
Eccl.	Ecclesiastes	Gal.	Galatians
Song	Song of Songs	Eph.	Ephesians
Wis.	Wisdom	Phil.	Philippians

Col.	Colossians		Jas.	James
1 Thess.	1 Thessalonians		1 Pet.	1 Peter
2 Thess.	2 Thessalonians		2 Pet.	2 Peter
1 Tim.	1 Timothy		1 Jn.	1 John
2 Tim.	2 Timothy		2 Jn.	2 John
Titus.	Titus		3 Jn.	3 John
Philem.	Philemon		Jude	Jude
Heb.	Hebrews		Rev.	Revelation

THE FOLLOWING ABBREVIATIONS ARE USED
FOR OTHER WORKS CITED IN THE TEXT

AA Second Vatican Council, Decree on the Apostolate of Lay People (*Apostolicam Actuositatem*), November 18, 1965

AG Second Vatican Council, Decree on the Church's Missionary Activity (*Ad Gentes Divinitus*), December 7, 1965

Catechism The Holy See, *Catechism of the Catholic Church*, Definitive Edition, 1997

CD Second Vatican Council, Decree on the Pastoral Office of Bishops in the Church (*Christus Dominus*), October 28, 1965

CI Spanish Bishops' Conference, *Christian Initiation: Reflections and Orientations*, 1997

CIC The Holy See, *Code of Canon Law*, 1983

CL John Paul II, On the Vocation and Mission of the Lay Faithful (*Christifidelis Laici*), December 30, 1988

CT John Paul II, On Catechesis in Our Time (*Catechesi Tradendae*), October 16, 1979

DS Denzinger-Schonmetzer, *Enchiridion Symbolorum, definitionum et declarationum de rebus fidei et morum (1965)*

DV Second Vatican Council, Dogmatic Constitution on Divine Revelation (*Dei Verbum*), November 18, 1965

EN Paul VI, Evangelization in the Modern World (*Evangelii Nuntiandi*), December 8, 1975

FR	John Paul II, Faith and Reason (*Fides et Ratio*), September 14, 1988
GCD	Congregation for the Clergy, *General Catechetical Directory*, 1971
GDC	Congregation for the Clergy, *General Directory for Catechesis*, August 11, 1997
GE	Second Vatican Council, Declaration on Christian Education (*Gravissimum Educationis*), October 28, 1965
GS	Second Vatican Council, Pastoral Constitution on the Church in the Modern World (*Gaudium et Spes*), December 7, 1965
Instruction	Congregation for the Doctrine of the Faith, Instruction on the Ecclesial Vocation of the Theologian, May 24, 1990
LG	Second Vatican Council, Dogmatic Constitution on the Church (*Lumen Gentium*), November 21, 1964
OT	Second Vatican Council, Decree on the Training of Priests (*Optatam Totius*), October 28, 1965
PDV	John Paul II, I Will Give You Shepherds (*Pastores Dabo Vobis*), 1992
PG	J.P. Migne, ed., *Patrologia Graeca*, (Paris, 1857–1866)
PL	J.P. Migne, ed., *Patrologia Latina*, (Paris, 1841–1855)
PO	Second Vatican Council, Decree on the Ministry and Life of Priests (*Presbyterorum Ordinis*), December 7, 1965
RCIA	The Holy See, *Rite of Christian Initiation of Adults*
SC	Second Vatican Council, Constitution on the Sacred Liturgy (*Sacrosanctum Concilium*), December 4, 1963
SCG	Saint Thomas Aquinas, *Summa Contra Gentiles*
ST	Saint Thomas Aquinas, *Summa Theologiae*
USCCB	United States Conference of Catholic Bishops

Introduction

Msgr. Paul Watson

The most important reason for understanding divine pedagogy is, as the *General Directory for Catechesis* makes clear, that the pedagogy of God is both the source and the model for what is known as the pedagogy of the Faith. In other words, it is from God Himself that the Church has learned how to communicate and teach in such a way that an individual not only gains wisdom and knowledge of the Faith, but also is personally liberated and transformed by this knowledge, entering into a personal relationship with God Himself—a dialogue in which the person allows him or herself to be guided by God (GDC 139). The divine pedagogy begins in the Old Testament and reaches its zenith and perfection in the person of Jesus Christ.

In his words, signs and works during his brief but intense life, the disciples had direct experience of the fundamental traits of the "pedagogy of Jesus," and recorded them in the Gospels: ... Inviting his disciples to follow him unreservedly and without regret, Christ passed on to them his pedagogy of faith. (GDC 140)

While the practice of catechesis today certainly draws upon modern wisdom and pedagogical methods, it is the pedagogy of God Himself that must really determine the practice of teaching and passing on the Faith. The process of transmitting divine Revelation is *radically* different from the ordinary human means of teaching and communicating. God's pedagogy is first and foremost a work of grace, since God is primarily communicating Himself. The *GDC* speaks of this communication as a dialogue of salvation or redemption. The effect of Revelation is that God liberates the human person from the "bonds of evils and attracts him to himself by bonds of love" (GDC 139). This transforming effect is the product both of God's creative and redemptive love and His condescension in accommodating Himself to the situation of humankind—"to the diverse ages and life situations."

While the pedagogy of God is unique as a result of the transforming power of grace, the GDC insists that there can be no opposition or separation from the pedagogical action of man. It is significant to notice the various words the GDC uses to describe the relationship between the pedagogy of God and the pedagogy of man—it asks that there be no confusion, separation, or opposition. These words are strongly reminiscent of the words describing the relationship between the divine and human natures in the incarnate Person of the Word—Jesus Christ. The implication is that Jesus Christ Himself is the complete revelation of the pedagogy of God. Jesus is the Master Pedagogue in whom both divine and human pedagogy are joined—without confusion, separation, or opposition. This means that our catechetical methodology can never simply be a matter of adopting modern pedagogical models. It must always judge and adapt them in the light of Jesus. The catechist must, therefore, be prepared to immerse him or herself in the Gospels—reflecting on the encounters between Jesus and His disciples, between Jesus and the many others whom He leads to faith.

UNITED WITH CHRIST

Thus far we have been speaking of the pedagogy of God as the model for our own pedagogy or catechesis. When we speak of models, we usually imply that we have something to imitate—a pattern already established which we then follow. However, the relationship between the pedagogy of God and the practice of the catechist is much more profound. Catechesis is the *means* by which God's pedagogy is made present, here and now. We need to understand the teaching of the Second Vatican Council on the nature of the Church, especially the teaching in the Dogmatic Constitution of the Church (*Lumen Gentium*). The Council teaches that *the Church is, in Christ, in the nature of a sacrament* (see LG 1). In other words, the Church is not simply a gathering of those who profess to follow Jesus; the Church is a mystery (*mysterion* was the original word in Greek from which the word *sacramentum* is a Latin translation). The Church shares in and continues the very mystery of the Incarnation. This is the reason that the first chapter of *Lumen Gentium* expounds, using various biblical images, the relationship between Christ and the Church. The most profound image is that of the body. The Body of Christ is, like Christ Himself, a reality both divine and human:

> The society structured with hierarchical organs and the Mystical
> Body of Christ, are not to be considered as two realities, nor are the

visible assembly and the spiritual community, nor the earthly Church and the Church enriched with heavenly things; rather they form one complex reality which coalesces from a divine and a human element. For this reason, by no weak analogy, it is compared to the mystery of the incarnate Word. (*LG* 8)

Here is a teaching of immense depth and importance. It is not, of course, a new teaching of Vatican II. It is rooted in the New Testament and in the patristic interpretations of the Scriptures. It is, however, a teaching that needs to be highlighted and stressed again today. It is typical to find many today speaking of the Church in language that derives more from sociology and the language of politics. The result is that, while still using the theological language of the Body of Christ, in practice the profound significance of the sacramental nature of the Church is largely lost to sight.

The Church is sacramental insofar as she is both the sign and the effective presence of the saving mystery of Christ. She *is* the continuing presence of Christ in the world, albeit a visible organization made up of sinful human beings. The divine element is precisely the mystical Body of Christ endowed with all the qualities, virtues, and power of Christ (*Lumen Gentium* describes these as "heavenly gifts"). Traditional theology has used the concept of *communicatio idiomatum* to describe the communication of the divine qualities of the Second Person of the Trinity to the human nature of Christ. In the same way, there is a *communicatio idiomatum* between the person of Christ and the Church. The Church shares in and perpetuates in time and space the qualities of Christ. Hence His salvific activity is continued in the actions (especially the sacraments) of the Church. His virtues are incarnated in each person in the Church through the gifts of the Spirit. His word is made present in the announcement of the Gospel, in the teaching of the Faith and in the ministry of consolation and healing that is the very stuff of the life of the Church.

The *General Directory for Catechesis* takes this general teaching about the relationship between Christ and the Church and applies it specifically to the Church's mission of catechesis, stating: "From her very beginnings the Church, which 'in Christ, is in the nature of a Sacrament,' has lived her mission as a visible and actual continuation of the pedagogy of the Father and of the Son, 'as our Mother is also the educator of our faith'" (GDC 141). Thus, the Church does not so much imitate the divine pedagogy as continue it, making it present in the world. The catechist, as a member of the Church, and indeed, a representative of the Church, is also the means by which the divine pedagogy continues and is effectively present. This, of course, has tremendous implications for the catechist, both with regard to the goals of catechetical activity, since the goals are precisely those of divine pedagogy (liberation of the catechumen from bonds of evil and attraction to God Himself by bonds of love), and with regard to the personal formation and preparation of the catechist—nothing short of personal conformity to the Master, Jesus Christ, and of incarnating, in each and every particular situation, Christ the Teacher.

It is worth noticing at this point something in the *General Directory for Catechesis* that, at first, seems unusual. The first chapter of Part III, entitled "The Pedagogy of God, source and model of the pedagogy of the faith," has various subsections which speak of the "pedagogy of God" and "the pedagogy of Christ" but, perhaps strangely, inserts "the pedagogy of the Church" before the section "Divine pedagogy, action of the Holy Spirit in every Christian." This clearly reflects the importance of what we have already said above about the nature of the Church and the nature of the Church's pedagogy. It appears that the GDC wishes to emphasize that the Church is continuing the pedagogy of Christ. The Spirit's role is in fact, through His gifts and His activity, to conform the Church to Christ, and indeed, to conform the individual disciple in such a way that the disciple's activity continues the pedagogical and redeeming mission of Christ. Hence, we can say that ultimately the pedagogy of God is the sending (the mission) of the Son and the Spirit, for the purpose of bringing humanity into communion, into participation in the divine life.

THE CHARACTERISTICS OF DIVINE PEDAGOGY

The primary characteristic of divine pedagogy is that it is progressive. As the *Catechism* states: "God communicates himself to man gradually. He prepares him to welcome by stages the supernatural Revelation that is to culminate in the person and mission of the incarnate Word, Jesus Christ" (*Catechism*, no. 53). The *Catechism* takes up the idea of Saint Irenaeus that God and man had to become accustomed to one another. Blessed John Henry Newman expressed the same idea and indicated that it was because of sin that humankind needed gradually to be introduced to God—sin determines even the manner of the Incarnation:

He once had meant to come on earth in heavenly glory, but we sinned; and then He could not safely visit us, except with a shrouded radiance and a bedimmed Majesty, for He was God. So He came Himself in weakness, not in power.[1]

---

[1] John Henry Newman, "The Glories of Mary for the Sake of Her Son," Discourse 17 in *Discourses to Mixed Congregations*, available at http://www.newmanreader.org/works/discourses/discourse17.html.

It was not only in the Incarnation that God chose to communicate with humanity slowly and in stages. The whole history of salvation, especially in the Old Testament, is testimony to this gradual unfolding of Revelation. God in His loving condescension accommodates Himself to the human condition. Principally, it was through transforming "events in the life of his people into lessons of wisdom" that God thus adapted Himself "to the diverse ages and life situations" (GDC 139). And so the events of Israel's history become pregnant with divine meaning and are the vehicles of the divine pedagogy. God progressively reveals Himself and His purpose for humanity through the historical events of Israel and the key characters who play a role in shaping that history, figures such as Abraham, Isaac, Jacob, Joseph, Moses, David, Elijah and the other prophets. Many other individuals, too, form the backbone of the history, each with their limitations and foibles, each within a particular context, but their lives and the events in which they are involved are transformed by God's participation in them into divine pedagogy—at once partial in terms of the whole Revelation of God and yet containing within them the essence of that fullness finally revealed in the coming of Jesus.

This understanding of the history of salvation is the basis for the Catholic tradition of the spiritual reading of Scripture and for the Church's insistence that Scripture be read as a unity. The Fathers of the Church saw Christ hidden within the events and persons of the Old Testament. This remains today the reason that we continue to read the Old Testament and proclaim it in the liturgy. In the Church's practice of catechesis, which, as we have seen, is a continuation of divine pedagogy, the principle of gradual and progressive Revelation is respected through the practice of narrating the history of salvation and especially through relating this history to the liturgical events that make up the process of Christian Initiation, a succession of sacred events with divine power and meaning.

DIVINE PEDAGOGY AND THE LAW

God's adaptation of Himself to the human condition also has the purpose of revealing that human condition. Divine pedagogy has the aim of revealing the slavery to sin in the human heart and at the same time, through God's grace, of liberating and transforming the heart so as to make it capable of communion with Himself. Here we touch another important element of divine pedagogy—the Law.

In his *Letter to the Galatians*, Saint Paul describes the Law as a "pedagogue or guardian." The people of Galatia were pagans. They had no knowledge of the religion and history of Israel, no knowledge of the Old Testament. During the evangelization of Galatia, emissaries arrived from Antioch demanding that the Galatians be instructed in the Old Testament. The question for Paul was whether access to the Divine Teacher was now direct—does it now require passage through the Old Testament? The Greek word "paidagogos," which we translate as "pedagogue," did not refer to a teacher but rather to the slave who took the young child to the teacher, then led the child safely home again. The Law, according to Paul, performed the function of the "paidagogos," leading the people of Israel on a journey, forming them to be capable of being taught by God. The journey through the wilderness of forty years was a very slow process. It was a kind of pilgrimage of formation. The Law embodied this formation, while it became interiorized in the people. The focus here is on *interiorization*. The Law only achieves its purpose if it becomes interiorized. This interior process is the work of grace, a divine activity in the human mind and heart. *Par excellence*, it was the prophets who emphasized this interiorizing of the Law and Covenant, and who castigated those "who honor me with their lips, while their hearts are far from me." The Psalms, too, were seen as exemplaries—articulations of a heart transformed by God and as a result reflecting a heart that is in communion with God. Once again, we touch upon the reason why the Old Testament, in this case the Psalms, is so much part of our liturgy today, especially the Divine Office.

So what was Paul's answer to the question? Do we still need the Old Testament and the Law? In one sense, no. The Law performed the function of a guardian until the individual came in contact with the Divine Teacher. Now the New Law, the Law of the Gospel, is the grace of the Holy Spirit, who brings us to the Divine Teacher, Christ, and "makes known to you all that is mine" (Jn. 16:15), and all that belongs to Jesus is from the Father. In the new dispensation, the divine pedagogy takes place as we learn to live in the Spirit, and in the Spirit learn to come to Jesus, to put our faith in Him and learn from Him how to order the use of grace in our lives. Through our union with Christ, our lives, our actions, and our words become the fruit of grace—not the mere following of a law. We have in fact returned to the earlier point made about our Christian lives in which the goal is conformity to the image of Christ. Docility to the Holy Spirit in our lives, whether it is in moments of darkness or enlightenment, is the goal of moral formation or development. Again, it is a process of interior transformation, cooperating with the action of the Spirit, conforming us to Christ and leading us to share in Christ's filial relationship with the Father.

In another sense Paul answers, "yes," to the role of the Law. The Law cannot justify us, cannot transform us or make us capable of communion with God. And yet it functions as a revelation of our sinful condition and indeed continues to function as a pedagogue in the sense that the Law (in particular, the Decalogue) leads us to Christ, and is by Christ deepened and made fully capable of being interiorized by the grace of the Spirit. Saint Irenaeus says,

The Lord prescribed love towards God and taught justice towards neighbour, so that man would be neither unjust, nor unworthy of God. Thus, through the Decalogue, God prepared man to become his friend and to live in harmony with his neighbour. ...The words of the Decalogue remain likewise for us Christians. Far from being abolished, they have received amplification and development from the fact of the coming of the Lord in the flesh.[2]

This aspect of the divine pedagogy teaches us the importance of moral development in our catechesis, yet it reminds us that only the divine action can touch the heart from the inside. This is the way of grace. The Decalogue serves the action of the Holy Spirit. The Church (as mother) must do as God does. In the formation and education of the child, the father and mother act in collaboration. So, the Father (through the mission of the Son and the Spirit) and the mother (the Church) act together in gracing the catechumen so that the heart is transformed and conformed to Christ.

Summing up so far, our exploration of the divine pedagogy as source and model for our own catechesis has led us to recognize the goal of catechesis (communion with the Trinity) and also God's method of progressive and staged revelation and transformation through the events of salvation history, and through the Law, which is now seen as the precursor of the new law of the Spirit, which does not abolish the Law but deepens and transforms it in Christ. This divine pedagogy is continued in the Church in the progressive handing over (traditio) of the Creed (Part One of the Catechism), in the redemptive events of the Church's liturgical life (Part Two of the Catechism) and in the moral development of the catechumen in the new life of the Spirit (Part Three of the Catechism).

THE DIVINE PEDAGOGY AND PRAYER

The divine pedagogy is a "dialogue of salvation between God and the person" (GDC 143). Our pedagogy of faith, equally, is more than either *information* or *formation*: it is ultimately a leading of the person into intimacy with God. And so we arrive at

---

2   Saint Irenaeus, *Adversus hareses* 4, 16, 3–4; PG 7/1, 1017–1018. See *Catechism*, no. 2063.

the matter of prayer as an integral part of catechesis. As Part Four of the *Catechism* makes clear, prayer is essentially our entry into the filial prayer of Jesus. In this, it is Jesus Himself who is the Master Pedagogue and it is the Spirit who makes us capable: inspiring us to respond in faith to the thirst of God (manifested by Jesus' thirst on the Cross) for human beings to come to Him. In the *Catechism*, preceding Part 4 on Christian Prayer, there is a miniature from the Monastery of Dionysius on Mount Athos, showing Christ praying to the Father and Saint Peter turning to the others and pointing to Jesus as the Master and the way of Christian prayer.

The divine pedagogy of prayer also includes the Old Testament prefigurements—Abraham, Noah, Moses, David, and Elijah—while in the new dispensation, after the Divine Master Himself, there is Mary and the cloud of witnesses, the saints. Prayer is a response to God's call and involves embracing and contemplating the whole truth of God and profoundly grasping the spiritual reality thus communicated by God.[3] For the catechist to serve this end of divine pedagogy, it is vital that he or she also be a witness, in other words, someone who knows personally the manner in which God teaches us, knowing both the consolations of prayer as well as the battle; who knows that dryness in prayer reveals that faith is both light and obscurity, and in times of the latter we are called to humble and persevering vigilance, with the Holy Spirit praying in us in "sighs too deep for words" (Rom. 8:26). According to the *Catechism*, it is above all the Lord's Prayer that conforms us to the filial prayer of Jesus. When the petitions of the Our Father truly express the desires of our heart, then will the image of Christ have come to maturity in us.

---

3   See *Catechism*, no. 2651.

PART 1

Preliminary Considerations

1

The Key to Christian Pedagogy

Cardinal Antonio Cañizares Llovera

This is the translated text of the cardinal's homily given to the participants of the Conference on the Pedagogy of God and Catechesis in the Basilica of Saint Peter, at the tomb of Saint John Chrysostom, on July 7, 2009.

With affection, great joy, and sincere admiration, greetings to each and every participant in this event. The Church thanks you for dedicating time and part of your lives to Christian education. You have clearly understood that Christian education is the best investment in the future that we can make today. It is without doubt the Holy Spirit who drives forward this fundamental work in the life of the Church and the world.

The need for Christian education is heightened in a situation like ours: with insufficiently evangelized adults and young Christians, who are frequently separated from the practice of their faith and on occasion abandon that faith; with important shortcomings in Christian initiation; and with children, in growing numbers, who have not reached religious awakening. Dedicate yourselves to it apostolically with evangelical zeal; respond with a type of education that makes the Gospel of Jesus Christ joyfully present, in whom is revealed the truth of God and man inseparable from each other since the Incarnation.

There is an urgent need today to promote education with a religious depth that leads to a real and effective meeting with, and experience of, the living God, following in His way of life and in His engagement with mankind. It is necessary to provide an unambiguous Christian teaching, fully integrating the essential elements of faith and Christian morality, clear in the presentation of the living substance of the Gospel and of Christian life or morality. Let us never succumb to the temptation to reduce Christian education to a vague religious awareness or a mere anodyne introduction to a series of values or ideals that do not reach the depths of the heart of man, incapable of newly conforming him to the will of God. Never, amongst us, should education be reduced to a blurred announcement of Jesus Christ that represents something other than Jesus Himself in person (that which has been called "the cause of Jesus," or an ideal together with some attractive values).

It is clear that only a Christian education that engenders and that leads the believer to a personal encounter with Christ, is able to give sense and hope to man. Like Apostle John, we unceasingly discover that it is only when "that which we have seen and heard about the word of life" (cf. 1 Jn. 1:1) is communicated—Jesus Christ in person and present in His Church—that children, youth, and adults enter into communion with us, into this living experience that unites us to the whole Church, which was founded on the faith of the apostles. For this reason the knowledge of and the encounter with the living Son of God made man is at the center and foundation of our Christian education. There is no other. This is the root of all its originality. We are not proposing yet another religion or an ethical model of life with a set of ideals, empty of sense and without strength, because it has been stripped of its personal encounter with Jesus Christ. We propose "that which happened to us on the road" (cf. Lk. 24:35) and that which has filled us with hope. We announce that "we have seen, we have found the Lord" (cf. Jn. 1:41), or that He has come out to meet us in our lives. Just as Andrew and John did for Simon, or Philip for Bartholomew, when others who have had experience of Him lead us to His side, they communicate the real and true experience: joyful and encouraging, illuminating and giving meaning and strength to our lives.

This demands of us that we reclaim a Christian education that engenders the knowledge and living experience of the Gospel of Jesus. Educators, of which I am one, cannot be anything other than participating witnesses and providers of truth in the testimony of the ecclesial community.

If just a doctrinal or a moral issue were in question, there would be no need for us to be witnesses, but as we are dealing with one Person, one single event, the Christian educative task necessarily demands of us on the one hand that we give testimony, and on the other an education that leads to this witness.

In this sense, the words of Saint John in his first letter, "we are declaring to you what we have seen and heard, so that you too may be in communion with us" (cf. 1 Jn. 1:3), are emblematic and entirely enlightening, demanding of Christian education, and reminding us that the education we provide must be authentically Christian and eminently personal and personalizing.

All this, in turn, tells us that we need to live a real ecclesial integration and communion, because Christ is only found in the Church, and our witness is only possible in light of our communion with the experience that is in the Church. Christian education, beginning in the founding experience of the Church and leading back to her, must be an act and a fact of the Christian community itself. Only in the Church and in cordial communion, real, affective and effective with her, is it possible to have education able to form new men and women of truth: Christians, joyful to be so, who witness to a new life and who have learnt the art of living the new truth of a person who brings Jesus Christ to others, expressing this with freedom and joy.

Loving the Church as Christ loved it—invigorated by the sense and the pride of belonging to her—strengthening our communion with her, strongly experiencing the Church and feeling part of her, living the grateful joy of the gift of being part of the Church and having her as mother, are fundamental and essential for our Christian education to be true. These actions and experiences guarantee that our education will make it possible for a new humanity to arise, made up of men and women renewed by the new message of the Gospel.

Christian education leads us to enter into a new universe, into a history that precedes us, into a new people. It immerses us in the history, tradition, and life of this people, of this family with its convictions, with its customs, with its language, with all that constitutes this new humanity, this new work of God. Christian education is the apprenticeship of life; catechesis is the apprenticeship and initiation in every aspect of the life of this family. The less solid the social environment, as is often the case today, the more one needs a Christian education to help one identify with the memory of this family, which is none other than the Church. This is the key to Christian pedagogy, inseparable from that pedagogy which God brings about in humanity, and that we must learn. May God grant us this grace.

Translated by Bernard Farrell-Roberts

2

An Original Pedagogy
for Catechesis

Petroc Willey

We examine here what the Church, in her recent documents on catechesis,
understands by the notion of "the pedagogy of God," and what the relation-
ship is of this pedagogy to the discipline of catechesis. We will see that a
close examination of the Congregation for the Clergy's General Directory
for Catechesis (1997) and of John Paul II's Catechesi Tradendae (1979), in
particular, enables us to identify and specify the distinctive subject discipline
of catechesis through offering a set of universally valid principles which pro-
vide necessary foundations for the communication of Revelation (that is, for
catechesis).

THE *GENERAL DIRECTORY FOR CATECHESIS*

The notion of "the pedagogy of God" lies at the center of one of the most recent documents of the universal Magisterium on catechesis published by the Congregation
for the Clergy, the *General Directory for Catechesis* (1997). It is a concept also found in
the earlier *General Catechetical Directory*, published in 1971, shortly after the Second
Vatican Council; in John Paul II's Apostolic Exhortation *Catechesi Tradendae*
(1979), and in the *Catechism of the Catholic Church* (1992 and 1997). While the
term "the pedagogy of God" has been emerging more and more strongly within the
Church's catechetical literature, it is not itself a term which has a strong, or obvious,
history of use within Catholic writings on religious education or catechesis;[1] and

---

1 Thomas Groome, for example, discussing the *GDC*'s new emphasis on the pedagogy of God, describes it as a
   "rather amazing proposal" that the concept of the pedagogy of God should function as the source and model of

therefore, it is intriguing to examine this phenomenon of the retrieval of a concept which had deep significance during the patristic period in particular. The interest lying behind this retrieval is not antiquarianism or nostalgia. The Church does not simply look back to a "pure" or better period in the past, which must now be reinstated. The role of the Magisterium is to discern in what ways the Tradition may be fruitful and provide a rich source of life in the new situations of the present day. The Church is not looking to provide some wooden return to the past. Rather, she delves into the past as a rich seam of inspiration and application for the present. This is what is meant by the often-repeated concept of "reading the signs of the times"; "the Church seeks to discover the meaning of the present situation within the perspective of the history of salvation" (GDC 32). One can view the current interest in the notion, therefore, as part of the more general theological *ressourcement* following the Second Vatican Council.[2]

A restoration, a recovery, is currently taking place in the area of the transmission of the Faith, a restoration in which the concept of the "pedagogy of God" has a pivotal role to play. The documents of the Magisterium, we have noted, have been putting this understanding in place. The *General Directory for Catechesis* has identified, as the primary difficulty facing catechesis today, that catechists do not yet have a full understanding of "the conception of catechesis as a school of faith, an initiation and apprenticeship in the entire Christian life" (GDC 30). Other difficulties are then listed following this one: lack of attention to the foundational place of Tradition; lack of integration between catechesis and liturgy; various lacunae (gaps) in doctrinal presentations, and so on. At the heart of these problems, however—and

the pedagogy of faith ("Total Catechesis/Religious Education: A Vision for Now and Always," in T. Groome and H.D. Dorrell, *Hopes and Horizons* [Mahwah, NJ: Paulist Press, 2003], 26). The term as such does not appear in a number of the other Magisterium writings on catechesis and education since the Second Vatican Council. It is not used in the Council's document on education, *Gravissimum Educationis* (1965), or in the *Rite of Christian Initiation* (1972), the republication of which re-established the concept of the adult catechumenate at the heart of developments in catechesis, or in the International Council for Catechesis' document, *Adult Catechesis in the Christian Community* (1990). Nor does it appear in any of the major documents focused on schools and education from the Congregation for Catholic Education: *The Catholic School* (1977), *Lay Catholics in Schools: Witnesses to Faith* (1982), *The Religious Dimension of Education in a Catholic School* (1988), or *The Catholic School on the Threshold of the Third Millennium* (1997), or in Pope Paul VI's Apostolic Exhortation *Evangelii Nuntiandi* (1976). Nonetheless, the understanding of education presented in these documents can assist in the interpretation of the term, since the corpus represents a coherent understanding of education. The neglect of any explicit use of the concept "pedagogy of God" in a number of the Church's educational writings can explain why some commentators writing on the *General Directory for Catechesis* omit to identify and highlight the significance of its use (for example, B.L. Marthaler, "Measuring Success in Catechetical Programs," *America* vol. 181, 9, 22–26. Two documents of the Council which provide background for our understanding are the Dogmatic Constitution on Divine Revelation, *Dei Verbum* (1965), and the Decree on Missionary Activity, *Ad Gentes* (1965).

2 On the theme of *ressourcement* in relation to catechetics see J. Ratzinger and C. Schönborn, *Introduction to the Catechism of the Catholic Church* (San Francisco: Ignatius Press, 1994), 11–15, and M. D'Ambrosio, "*Ressourcement* Theology, *Aggiornamento* and the Hermeneutics of Tradition," *Communio* 18, Winter 1991.

therefore at the center of the restoration which needs to be put in place—lies the question of catechesis as a "school of faith" embracing the *entire* Christian life. It is here that we find the crucial place of the pedagogy of God.

The *ressourcement*, in which the Church is participating in the area of cat-echesis, is the retrieval of the Patristic concept of a distinctive Christian *paideia* in order for the Church's work of catechesis to "be a true and proper school of Christian pedagogy" (GDC 33).[3] The term "εν Χριστω παιδέια," "Christian *paideia*," or "Christian education," first appears in Clement's *Epistle to the Romans*, around AD 96. The term *paideia* derives from the Greek word for a child, *pais*, and was used in ancient Greek civilization to denote the Greek understanding of education. In his classic work on the Greek *paideia*, Werner Jaeger wrote of how difficult it is to translate.

> It is impossible to avoid bringing in modern expressions like *civilization, culture, tradition, literature,* or *education*. But none of them really covers what the Greeks meant by *paideia*. Each of them is confined to one aspect of it: they cannot take in the same field as the Greek concept unless we employ them all together.[4]

The Greek understanding of *paideia* included both the aim of this education—the development of the whole of a culture—and also the process of education, the inculturation of a person into the developing heritage of society, which was transmitted from generation to generation. When the Church speaks of a Christian "education" or "pedagogy," therefore, she encompasses within these terms both aims and processes.

This ancient Greek understanding was then taken over into the classical Roman system of education. "It was not even a case of imitating; it was on the whole a pure and simple transfer."[5] Classical Rome took over the Greek conception of the *paideia* wholesale; the Greek *paideia* was the prototype; it was now transferred into the Latin-speaking world of the Romans.

---

3   See Marrou's classic account of ancient educational philosophy and practice, *A History of Education in Antiquity* (London: Sheed and Ward, 1956), 314. The original French text was published in 1948, as *Histoire de l'Education dans l'Antiquité* (Paris: Editions du Seuil).

4   *Paideia: The Ideals of Greek Culture*, 3 volumes, trans. G. Highet, 2nd Edition (Oxford: Oxford University Press, 1939) vol. 1, Preface, 5. This seminal work provides an extended treatment of Greek culture and education. In a later work, *Early Christianity and Greek Paideia* (Cambridge: Harvard University Press, 1965), Jaeger explains how the Greek ideal was subsequently taken up and developed in the light of Christian doctrine and life, so that the ancient Christian educational concept of the *paideia* evolved.

5   Marrou, *A History of Education in Antiquity*, 265.

It was upon this heritage that, in the early centuries, Christianity developed its own catechetical schools, with its own distinctive philosophy of education and curriculum.[6] The Church saw her educational system as the crowning of the ancient concept of the *paideia*. In this unique form of education the Church understood it to be divine Revelation itself which formed the basis for the path of practical formation. It is God's Revelation that is transmitted and received as the way of life to be followed. Within the patristic tradition it was especially, but not exclusively, the Alexandrian writers and thinkers who developed the unique concept of the Christian *paideia*. They drew from the central Greek philosophical tradition on education the notion of the formation of the whole person within culture and united this to key Christian doctrines; especially the central doctrines of God as Blessed Trinity and the of the Divine Persons as a relational unity; the doctrine of the human person as made in the image of Christ, the divine Son; and of the work of grace and redemption undertaken by the joint "missions" of the Son and the Spirit in the restoration of each human person in the Body of Christ, in the image and likeness of God.

The restoration of the person in the Christian *paideia*, therefore, is understood to be an education of the whole person—involving the senses, body, intellect, heart, passions, will, and spirit—with an appreciation of the interplay between the different elements of the personality.[7]

This Christian *paideia*, this "school of faith," is not to be understood as confined to the development of new institutions. It concerns the transformation of the whole of culture and a complete way of life. There were certainly identifiable catechetical schools in which the Faith was taught. We know, for example, that Augustine wrote his treatise *De Doctrina Christiana* for his Cathedral school in Hippo in North Africa. Nonetheless, whilst there were central places of learning,

---

6   It is not true to say, therefore, that "the Church never developed any Christian form of education." (A.H.M. Jones, *The Decline of the Ancient World* [New York: Longman Publishing Group, 1975], 351). Jones is referring to the Christianity of the first few centuries, but even at this time we find the distinctive forms of Christian education emerging. For a careful analysis of educational terms used in classical Roman works, especially Cicero and Quintilian, and the paralleling of these in Augustine's understanding of education, see E. Kevane, "De Doctrina Christiana: A Treatise on Christian Education," *Recherches Augustiniennes* 4 (1966), 97–133, and his "*Translatio imperii*: Augustine's *De Doctrina Christiana* and the Classical *Paideia*," *Studia Patristica* XIV (Berlin: Akademie-Verlag 1976), 446–460.

7   It is an understanding that Arthur and Nicholls argee is central also to the educational thought of Newman: "It is this concept of *paedeia* that Newman took from the classical philosophers and Greek Fathers of the early Church and it runs through all his work. ... It is Newman's achievement to have combined the humane tradition of the Ancient Greeks with the religious traditions of the Greek and Latin Fathers, particularly Saint Augustine." (James Arthur and Guy Nicholls, *John Henry Newman: Continuum Library of Educational Thought*, vol. 8 [London: Continuun 2007], 90). Newman writes of this uniting of Greek ideals with Christian revelation in *The Idea of a University*: "the grace stored in Jerusalem, and the gifts which radiate from Athens, are made over and concentrated in Rome. This is true as a matter of history." (London: Longmans Green, 1947), 231.

"school" also needs to be thought of as a metaphor in the Christian tradition for speaking about the whole of the Christian life. It is a "school" in the way that we might speak about a "school of philosophy."

The Church is asking for a return to the richer sense that the word "doctrine" originally had. Derived from the Latin "*doctrina*," the word originally covered not only the content of what was taught, but also the process of teaching and handing on this content. As Kevane demonstrates, in writers such as Cicero and Quintilian, "*doctrina*" is used as the direct translation for *paideia*,[8] so that when Augustine came to title his work on the content and the transmission of the Faith, *De Doctrina Christiana*, he was consciously building on this heritage.

. Broad sense of School

It is in this broad educational sense that the monastery is described as a "school" by Benedict, with the monk as a student in the school. In the Prologue to his *Rule*, Benedict famously writes, "Therefore we intend to establish a school for the Lord's service (*dominici schola servitii*)."[9] The image of the monastery as a school for the Lord's service is introduced at the very beginning of the Prologue to the *Rule*, which consciously mirrors Wisdom literature in its opening: "Listen carefully, my son, to the master's instructions, and attend to them with the ear of your heart. This is advice from a father who loves you; welcome it, and faithfully put it into practice."[10] The monastery is the place for learning the teaching of the Lord and also for learning how to live such teachings; it is the place in which "the Lord waits for us to translate into action, as we should, his holy teachings."[11] There is no need to judge from Benedict's use of the term that Christianity subscribed to the view that only a spiritual elite, the monks, have access to this "school."[12] The Christian tradition does not focus in some exclusive way upon the monastery as the "true" school, even

---

8   See E. Kevane, "*Translatio imperii*: Augustine's *De Doctrina Christiana* and the Classical *Paideia*," *Studia Patristica* XIV, 458. In classical Latin "The root meaning of *doctrina* is the activity of teaching." (*Ibid.* 459). Kevane draws attention, for example, to Quintilian who speaks of *orbis ille doctrinae* which the Greeks call *Enkylion paideian*. (*Institutio oratoria* I, 10, 1). See further, B.L. Gildersleeve and G. Lodge, *Gildersleeve's Latin Grammar*, 3rd Edition (New York: Heath, 1894), 124–125.

9   See *Rule of St. Benedict*, Prologue 45. See also *RB 80 The Rule of St Benedict in Latin and English*, ed. T. Fry OSB (Collegeville: The Liturgical Press, 1981), 13. The image is used by others of the monastery. For example, see Stephen Harding, describing Citeaux, *Exordium coenobii et ordinis Cisterciensis*, 17, PL 166: 1508.

10 Compare Prov 1:8; 4:1, 10, 20; 6:20. It is also possible that at this point, and in the opening sections of the Prologue, Benedict is drawing upon ancient baptismal catecheses for his material. For a discussion of this possible source see A. de Vogüé and J. Neufville, eds., *La Règle de saint Benoît* (Pairs: Les Éditions du Cerf, 1971–1972), 4, 42–48.

11 *Rule of St. Benedict*, Prologue 35.

12 Contra R.A. Blacketer, *The School of God: Pedagogy and Rhetoric in Calvin's Interpretation of Deuteronomy* (Dordrecht: Springer, 2006), 46. In the West, for example, under the renaissance in Christian education initiated by Charlemagne, and centered around the Palatine School organized by Alcuin, monastic education was typically provided both for *schola claustri* (those intending to enter religious life) and *schola exterior* (those who would be returning to other occupations and vocations).

if some writings were to see a more intense focus upon the Lord's educational activity there. The Christian school is for everyone. No one is debarred from it, except through sin. The image of the whole of the Christian life as constituting a "school" in which one is taught by God Himself is common, for example, in the writings of Augustine,[13] and is used by Rupert of Deutz and Alain of Lille.[14] It is found in the Protestant as well as the Catholic Tradition; so, for example, Calvin writes that every Christian is *"escolier en son Eglise."*[15] The Church is a community of disciples, of learners, following in the Way. Within the school it is crucial to note that there are teachers, or catechists, who play a vital role in assisting the whole community in its learning.[16]

In this school of God, the learning that can be found is of a different quality compared to the earthly knowledge and wisdom that can be gained elsewhere. Paul contrasts the divine wisdom that is available in the Christian school with the learning available from the Greeks—even the highest learning from human philosophy must be counted as mere foolishness.[17] Christianity offers a new, higher and salvific learning. We can use the work of Saint Thomas Aquinas to understand how the Christian tradition has seen this notion of a "higher" kind of knowledge that, in its turn, requires a distinctive kind of "school." Saint Thomas describes four different kinds of light: the light by which we see things using our senses; the intellectual light by which we understand things and gain insight into them; the highest light of all—the divine light which enables us to see God in heaven; and then, standing between intellectual knowing and the direct vision of God, what Saint Thomas calls the "prophetic light"—a distinctive kind of knowing of those mysteries that God reveals to us, and the response to which is the obedience of faith from us.[18] Catechesis has to do with the transmission of what is revealed to us in the prophetic light: God Himself, in the mysteries of the Faith, making up what the Church describes as the precious "Deposit of Faith."

The Church holds, then, that there are distinct "orders" of knowledge.[19] On the one hand, we have sense knowledge and intellectual knowledge: both of these forms of knowledge have their source in creation—in reason and the senses. Then

---

13 See *De Doctrina Christiana* 4.5.7; also *Sermo* 98:3, *PL* 38:592.

14 For details, see Blacketer, *The School of God*, 38–40.

15 Sermon on Ps. 48:9–15, cited in Blacketer, *The School of God*, 30.

16 If the Church is a "school," then the domestic Church is the domestic school. This helps us to understand the irreplaceable role of parents in education, in the Christian domestic *paideia*.

17 See 1 Cor. 1:17–25.

18 Saint Thomas work is found in *ST* 2a 2ae q.171, art. 2.

19 See the Constitution of Vatican Council I, *Dei Filius*, DS 3015, 3041–3043.

there is a different order of knowledge, which has its origin in the gift of faith, given directly by God, and which has for its object the mysteries of God Himself. The pedagogy of God is concerned with the principles needed to transmit the knowledge and understanding, which God gives through the "prophetic light." The *General Directory for Catechesis*, therefore, sees catechesis as one form within the ministry of the Word of God. The Word of God, it explains, "transmits Revelation, through the Church, by using human words" (GDC 50).[20] The "of God" here is a reference to God as the living source of this Word: God is the subject who is speaking, communicating His Revelation to His creatures. The light of faith is needed to hear and to respond to this Word.

So much for the general *ressourcement* being sought. Central to this idea of the Christian "school of faith" is the striking notion of the pedagogy of God. Since it is primarily a *conceptual framework* and understanding of the term which we are seeking, rather than simply an understanding of its historical development, we will focus our exposition and examination of the concept of the pedagogy of God on the fullest treatment of the pedagogy of God in relation to catechesis, which is found in the *General Directory for Catechesis*; and so we turn our attention to this document.

The *General Directory for Catechesis* is structured in five parts, together with a preface and introduction. The third part (paragraphs 137–166) is titled "The Pedagogy of the Faith." This part is, in turn, divided into two chapters, together with a brief introduction (paragraphs 137–138). The first chapter is titled "Pedagogy of God, source and model of the pedagogy of the faith" (paragraphs 137–147), while the second is "Elements of Methodology" (paragraphs 148–166).

Regarding the weight and significance of this third part of the document, we may note that the Introduction to the *Directory* distinguishes between those parts of the document that have greater importance and are "universally valid" and those parts which offer guidelines which alter according to time, place, and circumstances. The chapter on the pedagogy of God belongs firmly in the former category.

> It is evident that not all parts of the Directory have the same importance. Those dealing with Divine Revelation, the nature of catechesis, the criteria governing the proclamation of the Gospel message are universally valid. Those, however, referring to present circumstances, to methodology and to the manner of adapting catechesis to diverse

---

20 The other "forms" of the Word of God are the primary proclamation of the Faith, liturgy, and theology. In all of these, God speaks His Word, uniting it to human words and actions (see GDC 51–52).

age groups and cultural contexts are to be understood rather as indications or guidelines. (GDC 10)

This distinction reveals the "universally valid" parts of the *Directory* to be, therefore:

- Part 1: "Catechesis in the Church's Mission of Evangelization." This part places catechesis firmly within the Church's mission of evangelization, following especially the treatment of catechesis within Paul VI's *Evangelii nuntiandi*, with "evangelization" being understood in the broadest sense of "the carrying forth of the Good News to every sector of the human race so that by its strength it may enter into the hearts of men and renew the human race,"[21] and therefore encompassing the elements of proclamation, witness, teaching, the celebration of the sacraments, and the love of neighbor, even while the rich and complex reality of evangelization always resists any definition less than that of the overall mission of the Church.[22]

- Part 2: "The Gospel Message." This part focuses upon the nature and aims of catechesis and upon the content of the Catholic faith, that which is the subject matter of catechesis. The GDC highlights the central place of the *Catechism of the Catholic Church* as the most recent reference point for catechesis and for handing on the Faith in the contemporary world.

- Part 3: Chapter 1, "The Pedagogy of God, source and model of the Pedagogy of the Faith." This sets out for us the pedagogy of God the Father, the pedagogy of the Incarnate Son, the pedagogy of the Church, and finally the pedagogy of "the Holy Spirit in every Christian." This chapter then goes on to examine the implications of this pedagogy for catechesis.

PEDAGOGY, CONTENT, AND METHOD DISTINGUISHED

It is clear that the document moves to the level of "guidelines" and "indications" after this chapter, since the second chapter of the Third Part concerns methodology and especially the "diversity of methods in catechesis." This second chapter specifically distinguishes between what it terms "methods" of transmitting the Catholic faith, which are to be adapted to particular circumstances, and "the pedagogy of God." It says,

---

21 *EN* 18, highlighted in *GDC* 46.
22 On this, see especially *EN* 14–18 and *GDC* 46–48.

The Church, in transmitting the faith, does not have a particular method nor any single method. Rather, she discerns contemporary methods in the light of the pedagogy of God and uses with liberty "everything that is true, everything that is noble, everything that is good and pure, everything that we love and honor and everything that can be thought virtuous or worthy of praise" (Phil. 4:8). (GDC 148)

The following parts of the *Directory*, parts four and five, are concerned with different ages, groups, and cultural and social contexts within which catechesis is delivered, as well as catechesis in "the particular Church."

We can see from this overview of the structure and contents of the *Directory*, then, that the document very clearly distinguishes between:

- the universally valid concept of the *pedagogy of God*, which it describes as the "source and model of the pedagogy of the faith," and
- *methods of catechizing*, which differ according to a number of factors including age, intellectual and spiritual maturity, cultural background, and so on. The document teaches that catechetical methods are to be evaluated in the light of this pedagogy of God.

This distinction makes it clear that when the Church uses the phrase "pedagogy of God" in this document, the reference is not to a method for teaching, but rather to a more overarching concept by which methods for teaching can themselves be evaluated. This distinction between "pedagogy" and "methodology" is also made clear in the preface, in a reference to the earlier *General Catechetical Directory* of 1971. The preface speaks of that document as one which "has oriented the particular churches in their renewal of catechesis and has acted as a point of reference for content and pedagogy as well as for methodology" (GDC 2). Interestingly, it makes a distinction between three concepts: content, pedagogy, and methodology. This makes it clear that "pedagogy" is being understood in this teaching document neither as an aspect of the content of the Faith, which is handed on in catechesis, nor as a method of handing faith on.[23] It appears to stand between content and method, more by way of *overarching principles of transmission that govern the nature of catechesis precisely as transmission of the Faith*. Located at the center of the *General Directory for Catechesis*,

---

23 The assimilation of the notion of pedagogy to that of methodology is said in the *Directory* to be one of the difficulties under which the Church has been laboring, as she has been attempting to retrieve a richer and more holistic understanding of the notion of the transmission of the Faith. The recent period of catechetical activity is judged to have been one in which there has been "excessive insistence on the value of method and techniques" at the expense of attention given to the "demands and to the originality of that pedagogy which is proper to the faith" (GDC 30).

the pedagogy of God acts almost as a bridge, uniting the first parts on the nature and content of catechesis to the latter parts on the particular methods to be used for specific churches, groups, and situations. Necessarily, these principles are themselves *universally valid*, since they govern the transmission of the Faith in catechesis in any and every situation.

While we have not examined yet the precise relationship of pedagogy to content on the one hand, or to methods on the other, we can see already the significant point, that is, that the Church is claiming to have a specific set of principles that govern and overarch catechetical processes. We will see that these pedagogical principles are held to flow from the Faith itself.

DIVINE PEDAGOGY AS GOVERNING INSPIRATION

Turning now to a more detailed examination of the paragraphs in this third part of the *Directory*, what is made clear is that the pedagogical principles to be used in catechesis take their direct inspiration from what God has revealed about His pedagogical action with regard to mankind. This is an important point upon which to be clear: the pedagogical principles which are to be used as a point for evaluation of methods in education and in catechesis have as their source the *divine activity in history*. Catechetical methodology is to be placed within the context, not of a set of self-justifying principles, but within what Christian Revelation has identified as an account of God's own activity. "Catechesis, as communication of divine Revelation, is radically inspired by the pedagogy of God, as displayed in Christ and in the Church" (GDC 143). The *Directory* refers us to *Catechesi Tradendae* for a fuller statement on this point:

> The irreducible originality of Christian identity has for corollary and condition no less original a pedagogy of the faith. ... Throughout sacred history, especially in the Gospel, God himself used a pedagogy that must continue to be a model for the pedagogy of faith.[24]

The "originality" of the pedagogy in the sense of the uniqueness of the pedagogy will occupy us in a moment. For now, our interest is in the fact that the ultimate reference point for understanding the notion of the pedagogy of God in catechesis is the pedagogy of God in history. When the term "pedagogy of God" is encountered in catechetical documents, it might appear that the reference is simply to a set of principles or ideals, against which catechetical activity might be measured

24 CT 58; see reference in *GDC* 144.

and evaluated. And indeed it can be accepted that the pedagogy of God can be translated into principles, which can then be studied for an understanding of how they apply to catechesis. Nonetheless, the ultimate reference point is not to these principles in themselves but to the ongoing divine activity in history, which these principles then attempt to identify and enshrine.[25]

This understanding of catechetical practice, taking its reference point from God Himself and His activity, is consistent with the way in which the Church teaches that human life and activity as a whole have the divine life as their point of reference: "You shall be holy; for I the Lord your God am holy"; "be perfect, as your heavenly Father is perfect."[26] The doctrinal basis for this is contained in the teaching of the human person as made "in" the image and likeness of God, with this being understood as an ongoing making and re-making by the two "hands" of the divine Son and Spirit, under whose redeeming and sanctifying activity human persons are brought to share in that final unity and wholeness for which God destined His creation, sharing in the life of the Blessed Trinity itself.[27]

The *Directory* thus refers us to the concrete events of God's own activity, describing this as a "pedagogy":

> God, in his greatness, uses a pedagogy to reveal himself to the human person: he uses human events and words to communicate his plan; he does so progressively and in stages, so as to draw even closer to man. God, in fact, operates in such a manner that man comes to knowledge of his salvific plan by means of the events of salvation history and the inspired words which accompany and explain them.[28]

God's activity is being presented as educational in character. It is to be understood as a pedagogy. Catechesis, as an education in the Faith, is being asked to take this

---

25 For the argument that the *Catechism of the Catholic Church* enshrines such a restored understanding, and for an exploration of the "catechetical keys," which can be put in place to enable the practice of catechetics to participate in this vision and to foster it in catechetical settings, see P. de Cointet, B. Morgan and P. Willey, *The Catechism of the Catholic Church and the Craft of Catechesis* (San Francisco: Ignatius Press, 2008).

26 Lev. 19:2; Mt. 5:48. Catholic moral teaching understands the Christian life as a sharing in the life of Christ. See, for example, L. Melina, *Sharing in Christ's Virtues* (Washington, D.C.: Catholic University of America Press, 2001).

27 For an account of this doctrinal basis see *Catechism*, no. 703–706 for the image of the two "hands" of the Father, an image taken from Saint Irenaeus; *Catechism*, no. 758–769 for this understanding of salvation as a communion with the divine life brought about through a "convocation" of men in Christ; *Catechism*, no. 1701–1709 for the explanation of man made in the image of God and for this as the grounding of a new life in Christ and in the Holy Spirit; and see also *Catechism*, no. 516–521 for the mystery of the Son of God sharing in the "stages" of human life so as to enable each human person to share in the stages of the life of the divine Person of the Incarnate Son.

28 *GDC* 38, referring to *Catechism*, nos. 53 and 122, to *DV* 15, *CT* 58, *CL* 61, and also to the work of Saint Irenaeus of Lyons in *Adversus haereses* III, 20, 2.

divine educational activity as its point of reference. Just as in matters of faith, it is in the divine realities themselves that we believe rather than in the formulas, which express those realities; so in this catechetical process, it is *the divine activity itself with which catechesis is concerned* rather than simply principles that express this activity. Nonetheless, the principles that express this divine activity allow us to investigate and understand it better so as to be able to collaborate with it.[29] As we shall see, this point concerning the divine personal center of our understanding of pedagogy impacts directly on how we conceive of the relationship between catechists and those being catechized.

THE ORIGINALITY OF THE PEDAGOGY

We can return now to the paragraph we cited from *Catechesi Tradendae* in order to identify a further point, this time concerning the notion of the "originality" of the pedagogy which is asked for in catechesis:

> The irreducible originality of Christian identity has for corollary and condition no less original a pedagogy of the faith. … Throughout sacred history, especially in the Gospel, God himself used a pedagogy that must continue to be a model for the pedagogy of faith. (*CT* 58)

Pope John Paul II writes of the "original" pedagogy of the Faith being inseparable from the "irreducible originality" of Christian identity. "Identity" always has to do with essence, and so here John Paul is finding the originality of the pedagogy of the Faith in the "essence" of the Faith itself.[30] The word "originality" is also pointing us back to the notion of *origins*—not so much in the sense of historical origins, but the transcendent origin of the Faith. The pedagogy to be used in the transmission of the Faith, like the Faith itself, has its source and vitality from God Himself.[31]

This particular paragraph of *Catechesi Tradendae* is especially concerned to explore the possible contribution of other academic disciplines to a Catholic understanding of pedagogy in catechesis. John Paul writes in this paragraph of the concept of "pedagogy" understood in a broader sense, as concerning the "science" of education. "Among the many prestigious sciences of man that are nowadays making

---

29 On this point about faith, see Saint Thomas Aquinas, *ST* 2a 2ae, 1, 2, ad 2.

30 This originality, therefore, can be found in aspects of *methodology* in catechesis as well. John Paul provides an example in the area of memorization. While all educational activity employs memorization to some extent, John Paul invites catechists to "put this faculty back into use in an intelligent and even an original way in catechesis" (*CT* 55). He specifically mentions the Christian understanding of "memorial" as something that can inspire catechists when approaching this area.

31 On this point, see P. de Cointet et al., *The Catechism of the Catholic Church and the Craft of Catechesis*, p. xiv.

immense advances, pedagogy is certainly one of the most important." What he is speaking about, then, is the academic discipline of education, and he highlights the many developments that have been taking place in this area, "with varying degrees of success."

The central point he wishes to make is that *there must be a specific pedagogy used in catechesis*:

> Account must always be taken of the absolute originality of faith. Pedagogy of faith is not a question of transmitting human knowledge, even of the highest kind; it is a question of communicating God's revelation in its entirety. (CT 58)

The reason adduced for this need for a specific pedagogy, a specific Christian "science" of catechesis, is because catechesis is to communicate "God's revelation in its entirety." This distinctive character of catechesis as a unique kind of educational activity generates the need for a distinct pedagogy.[32]

We can see that the potential contribution from other sciences to the discipline of catechesis is acknowledged. No judgment is made *pro* or *contra* any particular contribution.[33] Rather, John Paul's concern is to make the clear claim that catechesis is a discipline in its own right, drawing upon its own set of criteria, with its own "original pedagogy," so that an understanding of this can henceforth enable an appropriate evaluation of, and use of, other academic disciplines.

John Paul, in *Catechesi Tradendae*, was wanting both to acknowledge the possibility of a contribution to this pedagogy from a range of associated disciplines in the natural and human sciences (biology, psychology and, sociology are explicitly mentioned, and there is an earlier mention of political science)[34] and also to urge the need for an evaluation of such contributions against the "originality of the

---

32 The 1971 *General Catechetical Directory* had made this point when it taught, "Now, however, after the consummation of revelation, the Church has the obligation of sharing the entire mystery of our salvation in Christ with the people to be instructed. Mindful of the pedagogy used by God, she too uses a pedagogy, a new one, however, one that corresponds to the new demands of his message" (33). The pedagogy to be used clearly flows from the "obligation of sharing the entire mystery of our salvation in Christ."

33 The *Directory*, similarly, prescinds from any particular judgment in these matters, while affirming, again, that in general the human sciences should be employed *in so far* as they can authentically be used in the service of communication of the Faith. See GDC 242–244, which deals with the place of the human sciences both in the communication of the Faith and in the formation of catechists.

34 In *Catechesi Tradendae* 52, John Paul writes of "the danger and the temptation to mix catechetical teaching unduly with overt or masked ideological views, especially political and social ones, or with personal political options." Although he is speaking here of dangers to an accurate and balanced presentation of the *content* of the Faith, the question of ideologies affecting transmission of the Faith is implied in the paragraph: "it is on the basis of revelation that catechesis will try to set its course, revelation as transmitted by the universal Magisterium of the Church, in its solemn or ordinary form."

faith." The classic contributions to catechesis and religious education from Piaget, Kohlberg, Goldman, Chomsky, Fowler, and others is thereby acknowledged, and at the same time a requirement is set in place to provide an evaluation of these conceptual and disciplinary frameworks against a pedagogy that is inspired by the need to communicate God's Revelation in its entirety.[35]

Let us summarize these findings. We have seen that the Church's contemporary catechetical documents have been putting in place, as a part of the overall *ressourcement*, a renewed understanding of catechesis as a "school of faith" embracing the entire Christian life for the formation of the person within a unique, original pedagogy. Within this renewed concept of the Christian *paideia*, the Church has provided *a central place for the notion of the pedagogy of God*. This is not to be identified simply as an interest in methodology, to be set alongside the content of the Faith. Rather, *"pedagogy" indicates a set of universally valid principles* which can themselves provide the criteria for an evaluation of possible methods and for the contribution of various sciences, since the pedagogy of God specifies that which marks out catechesis as a discipline worthy of study in its own right. We have also seen that *these catechetical principles themselves have their source in the activity of God in history*.

---

35 The *General Directory for Catechesis* notes briefly, in the same vein, "Thus the catechist knows and avails of the contribution of the sciences of education, understood always in a Christian sense" (GDC 147). There is both a positive acknowledgement and also a reminder for the need to make an evaluation of what is offered.

3

The Pedagogue and the Teacher

Petroc Willey

The pedagogy of God provides an original pedagogy for the craft[1] of cat-echetical communication. In this craft, God appears both as Teacher and as Pedagogue, supporting and elevating the teaching and learning of catechists and of catechumens.

TEACHING, LEARNING, AND COMMUNICATION

Catechesis is the communication of God's Revelation,[2] a communication that requires an attention to the *content* of what is transmitted and also to the twin activities of *teaching* and of *learning*. Over and above the processes of human teaching and learning the catecheti-cal documents of the Church are interested both in ways in which God Himself teaches, revealed above all in Jesus Christ, who has a "unique title to the name of 'Teacher,'"[3] and also to ways in which God enables His creatures to receive Revelation, to learn what He has to teach them.

Catechesis, taking its inspiration from God's pedagogy, is therefore to be understood not simply as the art of teaching, but the art or craft of *communication*, of transmission, encompassing both teaching and learning. Thus, treating of cat-echetical formation, the *General Directory for Catechesis* says succinctly, "the purpose of formation, therefore, is to make the catechist capable of communicating" (GDC

---

1 On catechesis as a craft to which one is apprenticed and which is to be practiced, see P. de Cointet, B. Morgan and P. Willey, *The Catechism of the Catholic Church and the Craft of Catechesis* (San Francisco: Ignatius Press, 2008), 1–23.

2 See CT 58.

3 In *Catechesi Tradendae*, John Paul draws attention to the "nearly fifty places" in the Gospels where this title is given to Jesus or claimed by Him (see CT 8 and footnotes 20–24). He also notes that the portrayal of Christ as teacher is prominent in early iconography.

235).[4] In his or her formation, then, the catechist is helped to be attentive to skills of teaching and also to awareness of the processes of learning.

In relation to the twin themes of teaching and learning, the documents of the Church in speaking of catechesis, emphasize sometimes one aspect and sometimes the other. In one section of *Catechesi Tradendae*, therefore, we find John Paul writing of catechesis as a learner-led process: "catechizing is in a way to lead a person to study this mystery [of Christ] in all its dimensions" (CT 5), while in other sections he speaks of catechesis in terms of teaching and instruction.[5] Speaking of the Gospels, for example, John Paul writes that they "display with varying degrees of clarity a catechetical structure." He then adds, by way of explanation, "Saint Matthew's account has indeed been called the catechist's gospel, and Saint Mark's the catechumen's gospel" (CT 11). John Paul is noting that the perspectives of teacher and of learner, of catechist and catechumen, are put before us in the different Gospels. Catechesis, then, is a discipline concerned with both teaching and learning. Catechesis is both, since it is communication and transmission. It concerns the one who communicates, that which is communicated, and the one who receives the communication. Catechesis is necessarily attentive to all of these dimensions. It takes an interest in how we teach, what the sources are for our teaching, how we learn, and what are the sources for our learning.

We can find a confirmation of this significant point in the presentation of the pedagogy of the Faith in Part Three of the *General Directory for Catechesis*. Here we find two significant points: firstly, that a *distinction is drawn between the roles of pedagogue and of teacher or catechist*; and secondly, that *the catechist or teacher role is placed within a wider context of a pedagogy, which embraces both teaching and learning.*

SCRIPTURAL UNDERSTANDING

We can begin our exploration of the significance of the distinction drawn between the roles of teacher and of pedagogue by looking at the chapter in the *General Directory for Catechesis* on the pedagogy of God, which opens with a quotation from the *Letter to the Hebrews*: "God is treating you as sons; for what son is there whom his father does not discipline?" (Heb. 12:7, in GDC 139). We shall find that this quotation leads us directly to the role of the pedagogue.

---

4   The GDC cites from the 1971 *General Catechetical Directory*, "the summit and center of catechetical formation lies in an aptitude and ability to communicate the Gospel message" (GCD 111).

5   So, for instance, "the image of Christ the Teacher was stamped on the spirit of the Twelve and of the first disciples" (CT 10), and "[the apostles] transmitted to their successors the task of teaching" (CT 11).

Two notes are struck here through this unexpected opening quotation, both of which might seem to sit uneasily with contemporary catechetical practice: first of all, there is a strong filial context—it is an *education for sonship* which is placed at the beginning of this account of pedagogy; and secondly, there appears to be a *focus on discipline* at the heart of the relationship between father and son.[6]

For an understanding of why the authors of the *Directory* might have selected this starting point for its treatment of pedagogy it is necessary to turn to the Scriptures and to the ancient educational practice upon which the Scriptures were drawing for their account of God's pedagogy.

Examining the quotation more closely, we can note that the word in Hebrews 12:7, which is rendered in English as "discipline," is the Greek *paideuei*, παιδεύει. It is a word that links us directly to the scriptural notion of pedagogy. The whole of the passage in this chapter from Hebrews, in fact, uses a range of words linked to the verb *paideuo* (παιδεύω), meaning "to bring up, to train, or to instruct." Associated with this verb are a number of nouns: paideia (παιδεία), meaning upbringing, training, or instruction;[7] *paideutes* (παιδευτής), an instructor; and finally, *paidagogos* (παιδαγωγός), one who is a custodian, guide, or pedagogue. The underlying root for all of these words is *pais* (παις), child. All are associated, therefore, with the education of children.[8] The *General Directory for Catechesis* has selected a particularly

---

6 The importance of discipline is reaffirmed in a subsequent paragraph in this chapter from the *Directory*. The section examining the pedagogical action of the Holy Spirit in the lives of Christians opens with a citation from Psalm 94:12, "Blessed is the man whom thou dost chasten, O Lord, and whom thou dost teach out of thy law" (see GDC 142). Perhaps because of the difficult connotations of this notion of discipline the references are dropped from the United States Conference of Catholic Bishops' *National Directory for Catechesis* (Fort Wayne, IN: Our Sunday Visitor, 2005). One of the unintended side-effects of this exclusion, however, as we shall see, is to render less accessible the important distinction between teaching and pedagogy which the *General Directory for Catechesis* was making.

7 Although the word is not used by Homer, we find the noun παιδεία as early as the 6th century BC, in the sense of education and instruction (see D. Fürst, "παιδεύω," in *The New International Dictionary of New Testament Theology*, ed C. Brown [Exeter: The Paternoster Press, 1978, vol. 3], 775). The emphasis in the scriptural use of these related terms is on *instruction through discipline*. For details of scriptural use, see W.F. Arndt and F.W. Gincrinch, *A Greek-English Lexicon of the New Testament and other Early Christian Literature*, 4th revised edition (Cambridge: Cambridge University Press, 1952), 608. We can see the strong link between education and discipline in that the Hebrew noun "mûsār" has a double meaning of both instruction and also correction or chastisement. In the Septuagint the Greek παιδεία is often used as the translation for "mûsār," while the verb παιδεύω often translates the Hebrew verb "yāsar," meaning to chastise, discipline, or correct. So the "mûsār YHWH" (Deut.11:2) is the guidance, and also the chastisement of God, the educational and disciplinary dealings of the Lord in history. The concept of "mûsār YHWH" is taken up in the *Letter to the Ephesians* where it appears as the guidance offered to parents to bring up their children in the παιδεία κηριου, the "paideia kyriou," the discipline and instruction of the Lord (Eph. 6:4). It is mainly in the Wisdom literature that we find these terms "mûsār" and "yāsar," especially in the Book of Proverbs, in the Psalms, and in Ecclesiasticus. This link between education and punishment was not unique, of course, to the Hebrews; Marrou cites texts from ancient Egyptian practice which parallel this approach (see H. Marrou, *A History of Education in Antiquity*, xvi–xvii).

8 In fact, the verb and noun were both extended in later times to cover adult education as well (see D. Fürst, "παιδεύω," in *The New International Dictionary of New Testament Theology*, 775), so that our term "pedagogy" typically is taken to apply to both child and adult-related educational practices.

appropriate point to begin its presentation on the pedagogy of God since this passage from Hebrews uses derivatives from this word group no less than eight times.
The whole of this passage is of interest to us:

> And have you forgotten the exhortation which addresses you as
> sons?—
>> "My son, do not regard lightly the discipline of the Lord
>> (παιδείας κυριου),
>> nor lose courage when you are punished by him.
>> For the Lord disciplines (παιδεύεί) him whom he loves,
>> and chastises every son whom he receives."
>
> It is for discipline (παιδείαν) that you have to endure. God is treating
> you as sons; for what son is there whom his father does not discipline
> (παιδεύεί)? If you are left without discipline (παιδείας), in which all
> have participated, then you are illegitimate children and not sons.
> Besides this, we have had earthly fathers to discipline (παιδευτας)
> us and we respected them. Shall we not much more be subject to the
> Father of spirits and live? For they disciplined (επαιδεύον) us for a
> short time at their pleasure, but he disciplines us for our good, that
> we may share his holiness. For the moment all discipline (παιδεία)
> seems painful rather than pleasant; later it yields the peaceful fruit of
> righteousness to those who have been trained by it. (Heb. 12:5–11)

One can see the themes of sonship and discipline prominent in this passage. As we
have noted, it is, one might suppose, a strange point from which to begin a presentation on the pedagogy of God that needs to provide the inspiration for the "exercise"
of catechesis (GDC 138).

A second significant use of terms in Scripture drawn from this word
group is found in Paul's *Letter to the Galatians*, where Paul writes of the purpose
of the Mosaic Law within God's economy of redemption. He describes the Law
as a παιδαγωγός—a custodian, guide, or pedagogue: "the law was our custodian
(παιδαγωγός) until Christ came, that we might be justified by faith. But now that
faith has come, we are no longer under a custodian (παιδαγωγόν); for in Christ
Jesus you are all sons of God, through faith" (Gal. 3:24–25).[9]

---

9 παιδαγωγός is taken from the Greek παις (child) and αγωγός (custodian). Paul's argument continues in Gal.
4:1–7, using the related analogy of being like a son in a patrician household.

One set of words in the New Testament, then, is connected with "pedagogy," a group of words signifying the training and instruction of children, and including here the ancient role of the pedagogue.

In addition to the range of words linked to the verb παιδεύω, there is a second set of words in the New Testament, this time derivatives of διδάσκω, to teach. Here we find διδάσκαλος, "a teacher" and διδαχή, meaning "teaching," or "doctrine."[10] The Pauline letters make it clear that teaching was regarded as a specific charism in the early Christian communities, and we therefore find "teacher" included in the lists of such charisms in the *Letter to the Romans* 12:6–8 and in the *Letter to the Ephesians* 4:11–12. While some are called to be prophets, administrators, servers, or exhorters, for example, others are specifically called to the ministry of teacher. From the beginning, teachers of the Faith clearly played a central role in the early Christian community. The high value placed on the role of the teacher in the Christian community is a reflection of Jewish sources and tradition.[11] This in turn is a reflection of the fact that Judaism is rooted in the conviction that God has revealed Himself to His people, and that this Revelation is to be handed on; it is to be taught and learned and is to form the basis for personal and social life.[12] Those responsible for the transmission of this Revelation were accorded a position of great respect. In the first place this meant the parents, for the family was seen as the center of education and formation. The family was supported, from exilic times onwards, by synagogue-based education, led by the "Rabbi," the Hebrew term for "teacher."[13] Rabbis gathered students around them and communities of learners were formed under these teachers.

10 See, for instance, 1 Cor. 12:28–29, Eph. 4:11, and Acts 13:1 where teachers, διδάσκαλοι, are mentioned ranking after apostles and prophets. In the pastoral epistles, 1 Tim. 2:7 and 2 Tim. 1:11, we can see "teacher" being linked with, and differentiated from, "preacher" and "apostle." Meanwhile, διδαχή is already being used to signify established teaching and doctrine: Rom. 6:17, 16:17; 1 Cor. 14:6; Acts 5:28.

11 In the Greek and Roman ancient world, by contrast, the διδάσκαλος was generally considered a less prestigious position. In the case of elementary teachers in particular it was a "humble, somewhat despised occupation." Elementary teachers were badly paid, and required few qualifications (see H. Marrou, *A History of Education in Antiquity*, 145). It was Diocletian's Edict in AD 301 which at least fixed the "magister's" salary at 50 denarii a month (see H. Marrou, *A History of Education in Antiquity*, 267).

12 "The survival of the Jews and Judaism is in a large measure due to the continuous emphasis, throughout Jewish history, upon the transmission of ideas and practices from old to young and from one generation to another." J. B. Miller, "The Role of Education in Jewish History," in *The Jews: Their History, Culture and Religion*, vol. 2, ed. L. Finklestein (New York: Harper and Row, 1960), 1234.

13 For a good overview of Jewish educational structures during the Old Testament period, see E. Kevane, *Jesus the Divine Teacher: Fullness and Mediator of Biblical Revelation* (New York: Vantage Press, 2003), 82–95. From the period of the Babylonian captivity onwards, in the Jewish Diaspora, "rabbi" was regularly translated by διδάσκαλος. See G. Friedrich and G. Kittel, *Theological Dictionary of the New Testament*, vol. 6, (Grand Rapids, MI: Eerdmans, 1968), 961–965.

In a further development, the concept of the Rabbi and his students was gradually influenced by the Hellenistic notion of the Master with his followers in the great philosophical schools, so that there was an interlinking of the Greek concept of the *paideia* with the Jewish tradition of education. This was the origin of the Hebrew word μαθετης, "disciple,"[14] drawn from the Greek tradition of the philosophical schools. The teacher-disciple relationship found its apex, of course, in Jesus and His circle of the twelve.

In this culminating point in Christ, we can see both the continuity and the distinctive nature of the Christian *paideia* with regard to both the Greek and the Jewish backgrounds. For the Jewish tradition had not taken over the Greek concept without alteration but had ensured that the Rabbi was always understood to be an interpreter and a transmitter of tradition. The Rabbi referred back to Moses through whom the divine Revelation, the Torah, was given. The Jewish tradition therefore places both the teacher and the disciple under the authority of one who is greater than them both. Ultimately, this "greater than" has its source in God, whose Revelation Moses had received and that was now handed on in the Torah.

Jesus' claim to be greater than Moses, to be Himself the point of interpretation of the Torah ("You have heard it said ... But I say to you ...") placed His status as a teacher on a wholly different plane. Jesus is recognized as teaching with an authority far beyond that of the Jewish scribes (see Mt. 7:28). All notions of "teacher" are henceforward to be referred to Him.[15] The Revelation to be transmitted by Christian διδασκαλοι would now be that which had its source and origin in Christ, and they themselves would speak only as His spokesmen. John Paul sums up this catechetical perspective on Christian teaching when he says that, in catechesis, it is Christ who is taught and Christ who teaches: everything "is taught with reference to him," and "anyone else teaches to the extent that he is Christ's spokesman" (CT 6).

It is significant that nowhere does Saint Paul, or any other part of the New Testament, speak of a "charism" to be a pedagogue. We have seen that the Mosaic Law is spoken of as a pedagogue in the *Letter to the Galatians*, and the *Catechism* understands the coming of the *Holy Spirit* as the new Law placed in the heart, so that

---

14 On this see the judgment by Rengstorf in G. Friedrich and G. Kittel, *Theological Dictionary of the New Testament*, vol. 4, (Grand Rapids, MI: Eerdmans, 1980), that with respect to the concept of the "disciple" in Judaism, the "formal dependence of the Rabbinate on Hellenism ... may be taken as certain" (440). For a full picture, see the whole article, 415–460.

15 Mt. 23:8–10 is clearly a key text, when Jesus instructs His disciples not to allow themselves to be called Rabbi, since they had one teacher. Matthew's Gospel reinforces the truth of Jesus' unique position by allowing only Judas, within the circle of the twelve, to retain the title "Rabbi" for Jesus: the other disciples refer to Him as *Kyrie*, Lord. The Teacher of the disciples is the Lord Himself.

the role of pedagogue is then taken by the Holy Spirit.[16] *But no human being is ever given this role.*[17] The charism identified in the early Christian communities is one of teaching rather than pedagogy.

It is not only in Scripture that we find this differentiation of teaching and pedagogy. It is found in the ancient educational world as a whole. The Scriptures are drawing upon ancient educational practice through this notion of pedagogy and some account of this is helpful to a full understanding of the concept.[18] (It is important to note, in addition, that the pedagogue appears not only in ancient Greek and Roman educational practice, but also has a place in Jewish writings of the time.[19])

Essentially, the pedagogue would be the figure—usually a slave—in ancient Greek and Roman households who would be tasked with accompanying the young child to and from school.[20] The pedagogue was not the teacher, but rather the one who led the child to the teacher to receive instruction. Then he would bring the child safely home again. The role of the pedagogue, therefore, was not formal instruction as much as supervision on behalf of the father; and, because the pedagogue represents and acts on behalf of the father, he is a person to whom respect is properly due, alongside the father.[21] The pedagogue was to see to it that the child remained attentive at school and, once home, was to generally supervise the child's behaviour and habits, disciplining the child as needed. The focus of the work of the

---

16 On this point, see the definition of the New Law in *Catechism*, no. 1966 as *"the grace of the Holy Spirit* given to the faithful through grace in Christ" (emphasis in the original), in fulfillment of Jeremiah's prophecy of the coming of the law into the heart (Jer. 31:31–34, see *Catechism*, no. 1965). See also *Catechism*, no. 715, where the fulfillment of this prophecy is linked to the coming of the Spirit at Pentecost.

17 While the notion of pedagogue appears, for early Christians, to be reserved for God and for His Law, we shall see that, according to the *General Directory for Catechesis*, the *Church as a whole* incarnates this role of pedagogue in this time of what the *Catechism* describes as "the age of the Church" (*Catechism*, no. 1076).

18 For a helpful presentation of the meaning of "pedagogue" see N.H. Young, "'παιδαγωγός': The Social Setting of a Pauline Metaphor," *Novum Testamentum* 29 (1987), 150–176. The presence of a pedagogue in a household is associated, socially, with a certain level of privilege—it is the freeborn child who is placed under the tutelage of the slave. In the divine pedagogy, of course, it is the Son who takes the place of the slave in order to raise free children of the Father.

19 The term pedagogue was a loanword in Judaism and in rabbinic literature, and would probably have been known to Paul in that context as well as through ancient educational practice (see W.F. Arndt and F.W. Gincrinch, *A Greek-English Lexicon of the New Testament and other Early Christian Literature*, 608), and so one finds it used, for example, in Josephus' *Antiquities* (1.2.1; 9.6.3; 10.10.1; 18.6.9; 20.8.10). A.T. Hanson suggests a particular Jewish inspiration, in Numbers 11:11–12, as a background to Paul's use of "pedagogue" to describe the Law ("The Origin of Paul's Use of παιδαγωγός for the Law," *Journal for the Study of the New Testament*, 34 (1988), 71–75). While this must be uncertain, it is nonetheless important to appreciate that this term appears within Judaism as well as within the wider ancient world of education (see further, R.N. Longenecker, *Studies in Paul, Exegetical and Theological* (Sheffield: Sheffield Phoenix Press, 2004), 53ff.

20 See, for example, Plutarch, "De liberis educandis," *Moralia*, vol.1 (Cambridge, MA: Harvard University Press, Loeb Classical Library, 1927).

21 See Plutarch, *Lyc.* 17, 1. For this very reason, Plutarch upbraids parents who take lightly the choice of pedagogue. They ought to be men of the finest qualities, as was Phoenix, tutor to Achilles ("De liberis educandis," *Moralia*, vol. 1, 6–7). The need for a careful choice of pedagogue is emphasized also by Quintilian, *Institutio oratoria*, I, 1, 8–11.

pedagogue is, therefore, *the formation of character through a personal relationship with the growing child* and *an integration of those studies learned at school with the virtues and qualities of character expected in the household.* It is the role of the pedagogue to help the child to learn and to put into practice, that which has been given by the teacher.[22] The teacher, on the other hand, teaches, but is *not* the supervisor of the behavior of the child.

In his account of educational practice in the ancient classical world, Marrou explains that, from the classical Hellenistic period onwards, the word "pedagogue" gradually changed its meaning until it came to signify "educator" in a broader sense. It can be difficult for us today to retrieve this earlier understanding of the pedagogue, Marrou suggests, since "we have made the school the decisive factor in education"; whereas, "for the Greeks the decisive factor was the surroundings in which the child grew up—the family with its surroundings and friends."[23] Interestingly, it is in the teaching of the Church that this conviction concerning the family as the key agent for catechesis and education has been retained, where school personnel are regarded as being *in loco parentis*. For this reason, *the pedagogy of God has a particularly strong application in the area of family catechesis.*[24] The family is the original and fundamental learning and teaching community within which the "school of faith" can take root.

A painful aspect, from the child's point of view, could arise with regard to the disciplinary role of the pedagogue. The symbol of the pedagogue in the ancient world was a cane or forked stick.[25] In general, the connection between education and often-painful discipline was an expected one: "No progress without painful effort."[26] Nonetheless, it is important not to exaggerate this aspect. It is the care of

---

22 See H. Marrou, *A History of Education in Antiquity*, 142–149. To some extent the position of the pedagogue picks up the older Homeric figure of the tutor.

23 H. Marrou, *A History of Education in Antiquity*, 221.

24 See P. Willey, "Parents as Primary Educators," in *Theology and Catechesis for the New Millennium*, ed. J. Redford (Dublin: Veritas, 2003), 242–254. Among the numerous texts of the Magisterium on this subject, see *Catechism*, nos. 2221–2231; GE 3, 6; FC 36. The ways in which parents should exercise a pedagogical function for their children, as their "primary educators" is discussed in the patristic period as well; for example by John Chrysostom in "On Vainglory and on How Parents Should Bring up Their Children," in *Christianity and Pagan Culture in the Later Roman Empire*, trans. M.L.W. Laistner (Ithaca: Cornell University Press, 1951).

25 We find the figure of the pedagogue mentioned in Saint Augustine's *Confessions* (I, 19, 30). In the *City of God* (XXI, 14) he recalls his childhood with a certain amount of horror, saying that if there was a choice between returning to childhood or death, surely one would wish to choose the latter! The pedagogue clearly brings deep-seated, painful memories back for Augustine. In Seneca's *De clementia* we find the humanitarian Roman arguing that the pedagogue should not rage at free-born boys (e.g. 1, 14:1–3; 1, 16:3). Plutarch, likewise, urges: use praise and reproof rather than blows ("De liberis educandis," *Moralia*, vol. 1, 12).

26 Aristotle, *Politics*, VIII, 1339a28. The Greek παιδεία comes to signify both education and punishment because of the connection between education and corporal correction.

the child that was the task of the pedagogue and he was necessarily a trusted figure within the household.

We can see the differentiation of the roles of pedagogue and teacher in Plato's *The Laws*, where he speaks of the development of the child:

> He must be bound with many bridles; in the first place, when he gets away from mothers and nurses, he must be under the management of tutors (παιδαγωγόις) on account of his childishness and foolishness; then again, being a freeman, he must be controlled by teachers (διδασκαλοις), no matter what they teach, and by studies; ...[27]

We can see here that the pedagogue typically has the care of very young children, even from the time of infancy—although the pedagogue might sometimes remain with authority over a child until he reached early adolescence. Teachers would begin working with children, likewise, from a young age. The differentiation between pedagogue and teacher, with the understanding that the pedagogue will accompany the child to the teacher, is noted in a 3rd century letter: "so, my son, I urge both you and your pedagogue that you go to a suitable teacher."[28] The notion of leaving behind the authority of both pedagogue and teacher as the child reaches maturity is found in Xenophon, a disciple of Socrates:

> When a boy ceases to be a child and begins to be a lad, others release him from his pedagogue and from his teacher; he is no longer under them, but is allowed to go his own way.[29]

We can see here the echoes of Paul's *Letter to the Galatians*, 3:24–25 and 4:1–7, in which the Law is conceived as a pedagogue for God's people, leading them to Christ. Christ here is being seen, not so much as the teacher to whom the pedagogue leads the growing boy, but as the point of fulfillment, of maturity, so that the boy is released from the tutorship of the Law, from the pedagogue. This movement of the Law leading God's people to Christ is essentially historical; the time before Christ is being seen as a period of being placed under a pedagogue, a period both of preparation and of constraint, as the pedagogue accompanies them to "school," to "teachers" who instruct them. In Paul's thinking, the relationship between the Law

---

27 *The Laws* VII, 808D–E, trans. B. Jowett (Glouchester, UK: Dodo Press, 2007). See also *The Republic* 373C and 467D.

28 *Poxy*, 6.930, cited in Longenecker, *Studies in Paul, Exegetical and Theological*, 55.

29 *Respublica Laededaemoniorum* 3.1. For the Greek text see *Xenophon on Government*, Cambridge Greek and Latin Classics, ed. V.J. Gray (Cambridge: Cambridge University Press, 2007), 79–94.

and Christ is essentially one of moving to a state in which one can claim one's inheritance. The "heir" is able to inherit; he is no longer a child under a tutor, but has been adopted as a son. Law cannot deliver our inheritance. The Law, as pedagogue, does not provide us with fulfillment, but prepares us for it, leads us to our inheritance and makes it possible for us to receive it. The metaphors of educational maturing, of inheritance rights for sons, and of the legal entitlements of adopted children are all brought together in this complex Pauline passage. As we have noted, the whole of Saint Paul's thought and that of the New Testament, involves, in fact, a development of this theme of pedagogy with the coming of Christ and the Spirit, with the Law being fulfilled in Christ, but not abrogated. We shall return to this point when we consider the Trinitarian structure of the section on the pedagogy of God in the *General Directory for Catechesis*.

There is another point of interest for us in this image of the pedagogue. Historically, the oversight of the pedagogue was in the area of physical welfare, and more especially of moral welfare. The association of the role of pedagogue with that of a growing child made it natural that this educational reality should form an image of the way in which the body and the passions need to be governed by rationality. So, for instance, Aristotle, in his treatment of the virtue of temperance, argues that "the appetitive part of us should be ruled by principle, just as a boy should live in obedience to his pedagogue (παιδαγωγόν)."[30] The implications of the pedagogy of God for an understanding of the relationship between the passions and learning is something which needs to occupy us as part of the provision of an adequate anthropological foundation for the pedagogy of God.

We have looked, then, at the way in which the *Directory* is emphasizing that catechesis, as the art of communication of the Faith, is concerned with both teaching and learning, and how these complementary aspects are represented in the two figures of teacher and pedagogue, which we find in the Scriptures and in ancient educational practice. A focus upon the respective roles of teacher and pedagogue has been suggestive for ways in which we might begin to examine how teaching and learning relate to each other. We have also seen the central place given to the role of modelling in the development of character, through the relationship of the growing child to the pedagogue, with the pedagogue standing in the place of the father-figure, as

---

30 *Nicomachean Ethics* 1119b 13–15.

his representative.[31] It is an emphasis on educational development through an individual fostering of children, one by one, rather than a concept of mass education.

DIVINE AND HUMAN AGENCY: THE TRINITY, THE CHURCH, AND THE ROLE OF THE CATECHIST

As well as indicating the twin aspects of learning and teaching, this differentiation between pedagogue and teacher is also relevant for that other crucial relation-in-distinction, between the divine and human roles in catechesis, in the transmission of the Faith. In what sense does the *Directory* understand God Himself to be the Teacher and Pedagogue, and how far does the catechist embrace each of these roles within the work of catechesis? We shall see that the *Directory* is assisting us in identifying a specific role for the catechist as a teacher of the Faith under God the Teacher, while also emphasizing that this teaching role needs to take account of the wider pedagogical environment within which the one being taught is set. This point emerges more clearly if we attend to the Trinitarian structure of the first chapter in part three of the *Directory*.

Divine Agency

The most obvious point about the structuring and the content of this first chapter is that *it is centered upon God*. It is concerned to provide an explanation and an account of God's pedagogy, not simply of human catechetical activity. We noted earlier that the way in which this pedagogical activity provides a "source and model" of the pedagogy of the Faith is not simply by yielding a series of sound principles upon which to base human activity, but by being a permanent point of on-going reference for that human activity.

The sections within this chapter on the pedagogy of God concern, in the first place, paragraphs on the role of each of the persons of the Trinity in the pedagogy, together with a short section on "the pedagogy of the Church." In the light of this starting point, the *Directory* explains that the catechist necessarily emphasizes the "divine initiative" (GDC 143), avoiding any confusion between "the salvific action of God, which is pure grace, with the pedagogical action of man" (GDC 144). Catechesis has this constant reference point to the activity of God: "Catechesis

---

31 It is a model which was taken up in the Christian monastic tradition in particular, through the concept of the "Abba," to whom disciples were attached for their formation. For a broad collection of lives illustrating this development, see B. Ward and N. Russell, *Lives of the Desert Fathers: The Historia Monarcharan in Aegypto*, Cistercian Studies Series no. 34 (London: Mowbray, 1981).

performs the function of disposing men to receive the action of the Holy Spirit and to deepen their conversion" (GCD 22).

The emphasis in catechesis, then, is on the work of God, an emphasis that is found also in the *Catechism of the Catholic Church*. In their introduction to the *Catechism*, Ratzinger and Schönborn stressed, "the primacy in catechesis is to be given to God and his works. Whatever man has to do will always be a response to God and to his works … [T]here is a clear catechetical option, but this choice is not optional: it is self-evident. It simply corresponds to the reality: God is first; grace is first."[32] This point is true both of the weighting and of the ordering of topics in the *Catechism*,[33] and it is also true of the work of catechesis itself, of the educational "handing on" of the Faith. It is true, in other words, of content and also of pedagogy. The work of God has a "primacy" in the communication of the Faith.

This stress on the salvific work of God in the transmission of the Faith highlights the importance of implicit and explicit adverting by the catechist to this work during catechetical sessions. The catechist helps others "to perceive the action of God throughout the formation journey," and catechetical sessions "encourage a climate of listening, of thanksgiving, and of prayer."[34] One can see how this emphasis leads to a strong organic connection being made, both for the catechist and for catechumens, between the presentation of doctrine and an attentiveness to the spiritual life.

Theologically, we understand God to be primary in the transmission of the Faith because, as we have seen, catechesis "is a question of communicating God's Revelation in its entirety" (CT 58). It is not a teaching or transmission of natural knowledge, or of information or theoretical concepts drawn from the world around us, but the communication of that which *God* wishes to reveal. It is "not a question of transmitting human knowledge, even of the highest kind" (CT 58). The teaching comes "from above" (Jn. 3:31). "He who is of the earth belongs to the earth, and of the earth he speaks," but "he whom God has sent utters the words of God" (Jn. 3:31, 34). It is therefore important to appreciate, the *Directory* states, that catechesis therefore has "the never-ending task of finding a language capable of communicating

---

32 J. Ratzinger and C. Schönborn, *Introduction to the Catechism of the Catholic Church* (San Francisco: Ignatius Press 1994), 48–49.

33 "The plan of the CCC is in itself a message," wrote Schönborn (J. Ratzinger and C. Schönborn, *Introduction to the Catechism of the Catholic Church*, 46). For a discussion of the ways in which this weighting and ordering is significant for catechesis, see P. de Cointet et al., *The Catechism of the Catholic Church and the Craft of Catechesis*, 19–22.

34 GDC 145; cf. GCD 10, 22.

the word of God" (*GDC* 146).[35] This, therefore, is the first point: that "the truths that concern the relations between God and man wholly transcend the visible order of things."[36] They belong to "another order of knowledge, which man cannot possibly arrive at by his own powers: the order of divine Revelation."[37]

Then there is a second key point: *Dei Verbum*, the Dogmatic Constitution on Divine Revelation of the Second Vatican Council, made it clear that Revelation is "the act by which God communicates himself in a personal way."[38] Revelation is not only a series of propositions about God, but is God *Himself*, giving Himself to His creatures.[39] "God truly reveals himself as one who desires to communicate himself, making the human person a participant in his divine nature."[40] The fact of the Incarnation, of God becoming flesh to become man's Teacher and Pedagogue, lies at the heart of the originality of the Faith. During the period of the Old Covenant, the Lord upbraided the shepherds of His people: "they had abandoned those for whom they should have cared, and they left in ignorance those whom they ought to have taught."[41] And then the promise follows: "I myself will shepherd my people. I myself will teach them."[42] That God teaches through His creation was not new. That He teaches through conscience was also not new. Both of these points are true, of course, but it is not in these that the originality of the pedagogy of the Faith lies. That man learns through the diligent application of his mind, contemplating the mysteries of the universe through investigation, study, and detailed exploration of the world around him; that he seeks out masters from whom he might learn wisdom: these are ways of learning familiar to us. But they are not new. What is new is that the First Cause of the universe, the Source and End of all things, Wisdom itself, should take flesh and come to teach in history, disciplining a People for Himself in time, having compassion on them, because they were like sheep without a shepherd, and teaching them many things.[43] That is the fullness of God's pedagogy. It is the culmination of a history of gradual Revelation, as God showed Himself to His people.

35 On the implications of this catechesis "from above", see further P. de Cointet et al., *The Catechism of the Catholic Church and the Craft of Catechesis*, 97–100.

36 Pope Pius XII, *Humani generis* (August 12, 1950), 2.

37 *Dei Filius*, DS 3015.

38 GCD 10, referencing *DV* 2. See also GDC 36.

39 On the importance of not dividing the personal and propositional dimensions in catechesis, see P. de Cointet et al., *The Catechism of the Catholic Church and the Craft of Catechesis*, 41–59.

40 GDC 36, referring to 2 Pet. 1:4 and *Catechism*, no. 51–52.

41 See, for example, Jer. 23:1–6; Ezek. 34:1–10; Zech 10:1–11:17.

42 See Is. 40:10–11; Ezek. 34:11–16.

43 Cf. Mk. 6:34.

What is important to note here is first of all that there is an equivalence proposed between content and pedagogy. The content of Revelation *is* God's communication of Himself. God's *Revelation* of Himself is His *gift of Himself.* God reveals not only truths about Himself; He reveals Himself. Secondly, the act of communication, of Revelation, is one of God "making the human person a participant in his divine nature." Revelation is the act of God "enlarging" the human person so as to be able to participate in God's nature. In Revelation, it is the human person who is enabled to undergo change.[44] Saint Paul, drawing upon the image of Revelation as a lifting of the veil by the Spirit, writes of this as a matter of the believer's being "changed from glory into glory."[45] The term "Revelation" is taken from the Greek *apokalypsis,* meaning "to uncover." It is etymologically linked to the Greek word for "veil," *kalumma,* used both for the veil worn by the priest entering God's presence in the Temple, and also of the bridal veil. Drawing especially from the *Book of Exodus* 34:33ff, when Moses covers his face with a veil, Paul writes of the new dispensation arising from the fullness of Revelation having been made available in Christ, so that the veil is now lifted by the Spirit for the Christian believer (2 Cor. 3:7ff). The nuptial dimension of this lifting of the veil of the bride is developed, of course, in the final chapter of the Book of Revelation. It is because Revelation is a communication of a plan "which proceeds from love" (GCD 10) that the "entire Christian life bears the mark of the spousal love of Christ and the Church" (*Catechism,* no. 1617).

If this, therefore, is the essence of catechesis—the teaching of the human person and at the same time the enabling of that person to receive this "word from above," this Revelation from God which is, in fact, the gift of God Himself—then one of the key areas for examination will be a fuller understanding of how God acts in the catechetical process, and a deeper appreciation of human capacities, their preparation and transformation in order to receive this divine communication.

Human Agency

In spite of this primacy accorded to the work of God, human agency in the craft of catechesis is not neglected. After stating that the catechist necessarily emphasizes the "divine initiative," the *Directory* carefully adds: "Neither, however, does it oppose

---

44 Saint Augustine uses the image of thought finding expression in words as a way of explaining that, when God was made flesh, He did not alter: "Our thought is not transformed into sounds; it remains entire in itself and assumes the form of words by means of which it may reach the ears without suffering any deterioration in itself. In the same way the Word of God was made flesh without change that he might dwell among us." (*De Doctrina Christiana,* I, XIII, 12). When Revelation takes place, the change is on the human side, not the divine.

45 2 Cor. 3:16, 18. On the Holy Spirit as the primary agent in conversion, see also *EN* 6–12, 15–16, 31, 49; GCD 12, 16.

them and separate them" (GDC 144). The catechist must not confuse himself with God, but neither is he to be cast aside. In fact, the discussion here identifying and contrasting the respective roles of God and man in the transmission of the Faith must not leave us in any doubt as to the centrality of the person, after God Himself, in the work of catechesis. On the contrary, in the Church's understanding of catechesis, the person is irreplaceable. God is the primary agent in catechesis, but this is not in competition with human agency. God and His creatures are not rivals, needing to divide agency between them. Thomas Aquinas puts it this way:

> An effect that results from a natural cause and from the divine power
> is not attributed partly to God and partly to the natural agent but it
> is completely from both according to different modes, just as the ef-
> fect is entirely attributable to an instrument and also entirely to the
> principal agent.[46]

Because catechesis is to be "inspired" by the pedagogy of God, which is God's personal work in communicating Himself to others, the catechist is necessarily central in echoing[47] this personal transmission of the Faith. "The work of the catechist must be considered of greater importance than the selection of texts and other tools" (GCD 71). The catechist is "essentially a mediator," facilitating "communication between the people and the mystery of God, between subjects amongst themselves, as well as with the community" (GDC 156). *It is the catechist as personal subject that is crucial to the work of catechesis*, acting in such as way as to ensure that "his activities always draw support from faith in the Holy Spirit and from prayer" (GDC 156). The catechist, then, acts truly, but always in relation to the Divine Agent, and always as a facilitator of that primary relationship between God and His people, and between God and each person.

It is instructive to consider here the discussion of the role of the human and divine in teaching in Augustine's *De Doctrina Christiana*.[48] Augustine notes, following the *Letter to the Galatians* in which Paul insists that he was taught directly by God, without any human intermediary,[49] that God does not *need* to teach through men: He "could have given the Gospel to man even though it came not from men nor

---

46 SCG III, 70.

47 "Echo" here indicates the meaning of the word for catechesis used in the New Testament, *katechein*. See *The New International Dictionary of New Testament Theology*, ed. C. Brown (Milton Keynes: Paternoster Press, 1978), 3:771–772.

48 See *De Doctrina Christiana*, IV, XVI, 33.

49 Gal.1:1, 12.

through a man." Nonetheless, argues Augustine, God has *in fact* chosen to use men as His teachers, and he provides numerous citations from the Scriptures to demonstrate this. In the introduction to this work, Augustine had already considered possible objections to what he was going to present and these included the view that one is taught most effectively by divine assistance alone, independent of the normal means of transmitting knowledge and culture.[50] Augustine completely opposes this view and sees in its appeal to some charismatic view of knowledge gained directly from God a simple laziness about the process of education. Augustine argues that one cannot expect to gain an adequate grasp of Christian faith and life apart from the normal apparatus of an educational structure and system. He is committed to the notion of a Christian *paideia*, which he believes must ground a holistic Christian culture. It is through the process of an incarnate, human transmission that God teaches, and not apart from this, except rarely. Those who become confused about this point, Augustine warns, will stop reading books, will stop listening to homilies or the readings at Mass, and will cut themselves off from all possibilities of real learning.[51]

This indispensable and specific role of the catechist as a teacher is made clear in the *Directory* through an apparently counter-intuitive ordering of the initial sections of the first chapter of part three: beginning with the pedagogy of God the Father, and then the pedagogy of the divine Son, the *Directory* places a section on "the pedagogy of the Church" before moving on to the pedagogy of the Holy Spirit, acting in every Christian.[52] Why this ordering of the material? Why, in particular, is the Church placed before the Holy Spirit? And how can this help us to understand the role of the catechist in the catechetical process more clearly?

The central reason has surely to do with the relationship between Mary's motherhood of Christ and her motherhood of the Church.[53] Mary and the Church

---

50 *De Doctrina Christiana*, I, I, 2.

51 See *De Doctrina Christiana*, I, I, 6–7. As one can see from this passage from Augustine, Moran is incorrect in supposing that Augustine's Platonic inheritance, combined with his belief in God as *the* Teacher has led him to disparage the role of human teachers ("Revelation as Teaching-Learning," *Religious Education*, vol. 95, 3 [Summer 2000], 269–284). Augustine asks that catechists avail themselves of the highest skills in communication (*De Doctrina Christiana*, IV, II, 3).

52 The ordering of sections in the pedagogical part of the 2005 United States Conference of Catholic Bishops' *National Directory for Catechesis* follows what one would initially sense to be a more appropriate one, highlighting God's work before that of the Church, and therefore reverses the order of the sections on the pedagogy of the Church and the pedagogy of the Holy Spirit (see 4, 28, 3–4).

53 This is a relationship brought out particularly strikingly in John Donne's poem "Upon the Annunciation and Passion Falling Upon One Day, 1608": "At once a Son is promised her, and gone;/ Gabriel gives Christ to her, He her to John;/ Not fully a mother, She's in orbity [bereavement];/ At once receiver and the legacy." Using one of his favorite geographical concepts, of the map of the globe, Donne describes the unity between the moment of annunciation, of Christ's incarnation in the womb of Mary, and the moment of Christ's entering into death, the

are the "places" where revelation is received in its fullness, and are therefore the *loci* for its full transmission. The section on the pedagogy of the Son makes clear that in the "fullness of time," with a "perfection found in the newness of his Person," we have the fullness of the gift of Revelation (GDC 140). Remembering that the perfection of Revelation is essentially the fulfillment of *the capacity to receive the gift of God*, we have at the Incarnation the fulfilling of Revelation in history in the person of Mary, prepared and made ready for the reception of the divine Son. This is why the historical moment of the Annunciation is the living source for understanding the heart of catechesis.[54] There is a natural movement in the text here, from this historical point of the reception of God's gift of Himself in its fullness in Mary, to the historical birth of the Church, who is both mother and teacher.[55] And so the following paragraph begins,

> From her very beginnings the Church, which "in Christ, is in the nature of a Sacrament" (*LG* 1) has lived her mission as a visible and actual continuation of the pedagogy of the Father and of the Son. She, "as our Mother is also the educator of our faith" (*Catechism*, no. 196). (GDC 141)

The section on the pedagogy of the Church is placed before that describing the pedagogical action of the Holy Spirit in each person because the Church as a whole incarnates the ongoing pedagogy of God, within which the catechist works, and provides the overall context for the animating activity of the Holy Spirit. Catechesis is a specific ministry and work within the whole of the Church's activity and the catechist can take his place securely only within this ecclesial, pedagogical context. *The Church as a whole has this character of being a "sacrament" of the divine pedagogy, of being the "educator of our faith."*

The catechist is not himself tasked with this overall enabling of others to learn, but is rather asked to "be inspired" by this point, this pedagogical context within which he works—to be aware of it and to make those whom he catechizes aware of it. Within this context, *the catechist has a specific role within the "ministry of the Word," of proclaiming and explaining this Word.* The primary role of catechists is

---

lowest point of this condescension of God into created human reality: "Th' abridgement of Christ's story, which makes one—/ As in plain maps, the furthest west is east—/ Of th' angels *Ave*, and *Consummatum Est.*"

54 As P. de Cointet et al., put it, "in this revelation of the condescension, mercy and faithfulness of God, and in the perfection of Mary's response, we see the whole of the craft of catechesis" (*The Catechism of the Catholic Church and the Craft of Catechesis*, ix).

55 So Pope John XXIII, *Mater et Magistra* (1963).

to announce and to teach the Good News. The *Directory* explains that, as a part of His overall pedagogy, God has entrusted "words of instruction and catechesis which are transmitted from generation to generation" (GDC 139), and that the Incarnate Son likewise gave "the undiluted proclamation of the Kingdom of God as the good news of the truth and of the consolation of the Father" (GDC 140). Catechists are those who announce God's saving plan, explaining and fostering understanding of the message, participating in "the school of the word of God" (GDC 142).

God's pedagogy, as we have seen, is broader than this ministry of the Word: it is a whole pedagogy of the salvation of the person. Knowing that God is the Pedagogue, accompanying His people and disciplining them in and through His Church, the catechist is freed to concentrate upon the essential heart of his work. The catechist proclaims Jesus Christ. That is his task. He acts as a spokesman for the divine Teacher, Christ Himself, "enabling Christ to teach with his lips" (CT 6). He does this so as to lead others to faith. But this response of faith, while a fully human act involving the will and the intellect, is ultimately a gift from God.[56] The catechist proclaims so as to assist the Holy Spirit—the divine Pedagogue working in synergy with the Church.

THE ROAD TO EMMAUS AND THE ANNUNCIATION

A study of the post-resurrection story from the Gospel of Luke of the meeting between Christ and His disciples on the road to Emmaus[57] can help us better to understand how this participation in the ministry of the Word—this proclamation and explanation of the Word—is the focus for the catechist's ministry. It is an important narrative from the Gospels to consider in this context since the Emmaus image of Christ's accompanying on the way has often, mistakenly, been taken as a picture for how catechists are to understand their role. It is proposed that they "accompany" those whom they catechize, asking them questions and listening to their story. The Emmaus story is taken as a model, in other words, of catechetical methodology, prioritizing an experiential catechesis that invites those being catechized to begin by "telling their story" as a prelude to any didactic activity by the catechist. Only after this "sharing" of their story by catechumens, it is proposed, may the catechist in turn speak the words of Christ and the proclamation of the Church. Thomas Groome is one of the key religious theorists who interpret the Emmaus account in this way, grounding his distinctive catechetical methodology of

---

56 See *Catechism*, nos. 153–160.
57 Lk. 24:13–35.

five movements of "Shared Praxis in Praxis" in this narrative. The risen Christ, he proposes, is here "the educator *par excellence*," allowing the disciples to "tell the story of their recent experience," in response to which He "recalls a larger Story of which their story is a part." Groome himself does not require that this telling of the larger Story be one faithful to the Tradition of the Church, as definitively interpreted by the Magisterium. In fact, he asserts that any such attempt would be neither desirable nor possible.[58]

But this approach misunderstands the catechist's role, in any case, by assuming that the catechist takes on the role that is given to the Church as a whole. The Emmaus account is concerned with how the Risen Christ is present in this "age" of the Church and of the Spirit, as the *Catechism* describes our time.[59] The narrative makes it clear that the Lord now acts in and with His Church, especially through the sacraments. Christ is the one who walks alongside His people; He accompanies them on "the way."[60] As we have seen, the Church is described in the *Directory* as a "visible and actual continuation of the pedagogy of the Father and of the Son" (GDC 141).

Within this narrative of Emmaus we can indeed identify the specific role of the catechist, communicating the Faith in the name of Christ: this is where Christ "interpreted to them in all the scriptures the things concerning himself" (v. 27). Here we see Christ the Teacher, and the specific role of the catechist tied to the ministry of the Word, explaining how all of the Scriptures have reference to Christ and

---

58 See T.H. Groome, *Christian Religious Education: Sharing Our Story and Vision* (New York: Harper and Row, 1980), 135–138, and then ch. 9, and especially 184–185, 194–195. In the first movement of "Shared Praxis in Praxis," "the *primary* object of reflection is the self who reflects" (185). Among those who follow this broad approach see J. Gallagher, *Soil for the Seed* (Great Wakering, Essex: McCrimmons, 2001), 309–321. Jim Gallagher rightly identifies the usefulness of Michael Paul Gallagher's linking of the Emmaus account to the stages of the catechumenal model as a whole, but he fails to sufficiently distinguish between the "teaching" and "pastoral" roles in this model which would allow room for the systematic catechesis asked for by the Church. For M.P. Gallagher's work on this see his *Struggles of Faith* (Dublin: Columba Press, 1990), 63–65. Liam Kelly, also, prioritizes the "ability to journey, to be a companion ... over the ability to impart doctrinal information." (*Catechesis Revisited: Handing on the Faith Today* (London: Paulist Press, 2000), 114. Writing of the development of catechetical formation in Italy since the Second Vatican Council, Enzo Biemmi contrasts two models of catechetical formation, one a more traditional model focused upon the content of the Faith, and the more recent focused upon an "accompanying" of adults. Here, too, there is a sense that prioritizing the need for a strong pastoral context for catechesis is leading to the partial eclipsing of the handing on of the Deposit of Faith rather than to a proper distinction between roles in the support of catechumens. See E. Biemmi, "La practique de la formation des catéchistes en Italie," in H. Derroitte and D. Palmyre, *Les Nouveaux Catéchistes: leur Formation, leur Compétences, leur Mission* (Bruxelles: Editions Lumen Vitae, 2008), 231–243. For an account of the Emmaus narrative more in harmony with what is being proposed here see E. Kevane, *Jesus the Divine Teacher: Fullness and Mediator of Biblical Revelation* (New York: Vantage Press, 2003), 213–214.

59 *Catechism*, no. 1076.

60 Indeed, of course, He *is* the Way: Jn. 14:6. That the narrative is an account of how Christ is present to the Church in this new age is emphasized by Luke in the repeated reference to what the disciples discovered "on the way" (24:32, 35), reminding readers of the early description of the Christian Church as those who followed "the Way" (see Acts 9:2).

find their fulfillment in Him. Other parts of the narrative highlight different points: Christ's unseen but real presence with His people (v. 15); the need for a conversion of heart and understanding to recognize Him (v. 16); the Paschal Mystery as the fulfillment of the Father's plan (vv. 17–26); His remaining with the Church in and through the Eucharist; and the missionary impetus of the Eucharist (vv. 33–35). Understanding the Emmaus story can help us to focus, then, upon the heart of the work of the catechist precisely as an annunciation and explanation of the Faith, providing the "undiluted proclamation of the Kingdom of God as the good news of the truth and of the consolation of the Father" (GDC 140).

One final, important point needs to be made in this section on the relationship between divine and human agency. It is to reinforce the point that the catechist, in his active proclamation of the Word, is to serve the work of learning the Faith that is being undertaken by the catechumen. The catechist is asked to teach, always aware that what is involved is a sensitivity to the possibilities for learning that lie at the center of the transmission of the Faith. *The teaching is given for the sake of a learning that needs to take place.*[61] Without this orientation, the catechist can begin to "teach," can even "perfect" his teaching style and content, but without any interest in the act of *communication.* The catechist, therefore, is asked to associate himself with the Church as the Mother who enables her members to learn. John Paul writes in *Catechesi Tradendae:* "In our pastoral care we ask ourselves: ... How are we to enable them [children and young people] to know the meaning, the import, the fundamental requirements, the law of love, the promises and the hopes of this Kingdom?" (CT 35). The language is one of "enabling to learn," it is one of assisting, of working sensitively with those being taught so that they may be open to the activity of the pedagogue within their lives. The question with which John Paul is preoccupied is that of how to assist the child to *learn* what is being taught. Put more broadly, catechesis as a whole is to have a "pastoral perspective" (CT 25).

The catechist keeps his focus upon the activity of the divine Pedagogue and upon the catechumen as the one who is being called to respond to that divine work. Clement of Alexandria writes of this gradual inner enlightenment, which is the work of the Holy Spirit in the person:

---

61 Here we can agree with the proposal of Giguère that catechesis moves its focus from the act of teaching to the broader context of the facilitation of learning. He writes, "dans le trinôme classique *traditio-receptio-redditio,* seul le premier terme relève de l'activité du catéchète." (Paul-André Giguère, "Maturité de la foi: concept opérationè ou slogan cosmétique?", *Lumen Vitae* LXIII, 4 (2008), 402.) He argues for a shift in attention towards the interior assent and adherence of the catechumen. This "shift," however, should not be thought of in any sense as a lessening of the work of the catechist as the one who announces and explains the Faith, handing on the Word, but rather as a placing of this catechetical work within the broader pedagogical context of the Church and the Holy Spirit working together in the lives of those being catechized.

As those who try to remove a film that is over their eyes, do not supply to them from without the light which they do not possess, but removing the obstacle from the eyes, leave the pupil free; thus also we who are baptized, having wiped off the sins which obscure the light of the Divine Spirit, have the eye of the spirit free, unimpeded, and full of light, by which alone we contemplate the Divine, the Holy Spirit flowing down to us from above.[62]

It is an inner transformation that is needed. Moreover, it is an inner transformation united to a transformation of the *life* of the person—it is *sin*, and not merely ignorance, which needs to be wiped away for the light of the Spirit to shine through in the person. And this transformation is the work of the Pedagogue.

In this way, the proclamation of the catechist "serves and is included in the 'dialogue of salvation' between God and the person" (GDC 143). Catechists announce and explain the Good News, all the time focused on assisting those being catechized in their reception of the Word, knowing that this is where the heart of their cooperation with the divine Pedagogue lies.

We can see this point about the role of the catechist finding its place within the divine pedagogy through appreciating that the Church teaches that the pedagogy of God is revealed in its fullness at the Annunciation.[63] The Annunciation narrative helps us to remember that the catechist's interest is to be upon the learner who is a "Marian" figure being invited to receive God's gift of Himself. Mary is the figure at the heart of the Annunciation narrative. She is served by the messenger of God, who speaks the words so that the Holy Spirit might enable the Word to be received and conceived in her. A clear emphasis is therefore placed on the learner in the learning process, upon the one who receives the Word in catechesis: "All human education and all real communication require first of all that interior activity be made possible and be stimulated in the one to whom they are directed" (GCD 75). Learning necessarily requires the active participation of the learner. No one can learn *for* another.

---

62 *Paedagogus* I, 6, "The Instructor," *The Ante-Nicene Fathers*, vol II, American Edition, reprinted 1994, eds. A. Roberts and J. Donaldson (Edinburgh: T & T Clark), 207–298.

63 See GDC 140. See also *Catechism*, nos. 484; 494; 721. Because the fullness of time marks the new beginning for the whole of creation, as the eternal God binds Himself to time, the Feast of the Annunciation was, until 1752, in England and the colonies, kept as New Year's Day (see C. Zaleski, "Rare Alignment," *Christian Century* [March 22, 2005], 33).

The notion of active participation can, of course, be misunderstood. Just as a comparable statement with reference to the Liturgy[64] has often been misunderstood to be encouraging merely greater external activity, rather than a more holistic understanding of the need for a greater participation of the person in the work of the Liturgy through the intellect, the body, and the will, so the requirement for the active participation of the catechumen is susceptible to many misunderstandings that would leave such participation at a surface level. What is asked for in the Church's documents on catechesis is not so much more external activity on the part of the catechumen within catechetical settings. Neither is it a focus upon the human ideas, concepts, memories, or experiences of the catechumens. It is not a focus upon the catechumens in and of themselves, as much as attentiveness to their capacities for learning, communion, and relationship with the divine Pedagogue. It is a placing of the catechist's ministry of the word at the service of a "communion," an "intimacy" with Christ, so that Christ can lead the catechumen "to the love of the Father in the Spirit" (CT 5). The catechist's annunciation of the Faith is to assist the person "to open himself to the religious dimension of life" (GDC 147); indeed, to be such as to "move the person to abandon himself 'completely and freely to God' (DV 5): intelligence, will, heart and memory" (GDC 144).[65] One of the roles of the catechist, then, is that of asking the learner to hand himself over into the hands of the Pedagogue, for an "indoctrination," an inner formation in and through doctrine,[66] so that a new seeing, understanding, and acting is made possible through a transformation of attitudes, dispositions, and habits. A dynamic model of an education that is conceptual, emotional, dispositional, and spiritual is put in place.

To sum up: we have seen that the pedagogy of God is primarily concerned with the activity of God as the Pedagogue of the human person. Catechesis takes its "permanent inspiration" (see GDC 137) from this fact, and is therefore an exercise in the "original pedagogy of the faith" (GDC 138). We have seen that the person of the catechist has a crucial role to play within this pedagogy, as he allows the annunciation and explanation of the Faith to be the activity of Christ the divine Teacher speaking with his lips. Finally, we have seen that the activity of teaching is itself orientated towards enabling and assisting the catechumen, the learner, in his appropriation of the Faith, working with the divine Pedagogue of the Holy Spirit, for the sake of a deeper communion with Christ.

---

64 See SC 11.
65 See further GDC 157 and, in the 1971 Directory, 75.
66 See Rom. 6:17 and the τύπος διδαχης.

4

The Pedagogy of God: Aim and Process

Petroc Willey

All educational systems necessarily include the notion of educational aims. It is these that direct the educational processes, provide them with criteria for judgment, and allow one to put in place and evaluate means for achieving those aims or ends. Knowing about our purposes, aims, and goals, enables us to put structures in place to achieve these. The General Directory for Catechesis for this reason focuses upon questions of the aims and ends of catechesis since, it reminds the reader in the introduction, "defects and errors in catechetical material can be avoided only if the nature and end of catechesis … are correctly understood from the outset" (GDC 9). One is an "effective" educator, according to one's own criteria, in so far as one is succeeding in achieving what one considers to be one's educational aims.

CHILDREN OF THE FATHER

The aim of the pedagogy of God is described in the *General Directory for Catechesis* in the following way, drawing upon the Pauline *Letter to the Ephesians*:

> The disciple seeks "to grow in all things towards him, who is the Head, Christ" (Eph. 4:15). The pedagogy of God can be said to be completed when the disciple shall "become the perfect Man, fully mature with the fullness of Christ himself" (Eph. 4:13). (GDC 142)

This image of the "perfect Man" is a reference, of course, to Christ Himself. God's education of His people is complete when they come to realize the fullness of their stature in Christ.

This notion of the goal of development could easily be misunderstood to be no more than a picture of the Aristotelian model of the perfectly virtuous and self-sufficient person, grown to full maturity, and now with a Christian orientation through the reference to Christ as the model of just such a person. But the model that the *Directory* is using, drawn from the patristic understanding of the Christian *paideia*, is distinctive in a number of ways.

In the first place, of course, what is most distinctive is indeed *the reference to Christ*. But, as we will see in the section in which we treat of the stages of the pedagogy of God in history, Christ is not being posited simply as a "model" of perfection for our imitation, although He is this as well. More deeply, we are being asked to "grow up" into the one who first "came down," who condescended to come among us, who followed the downward stages of our fall into error and the bitter effects of sin, in order that He might lead us up out from our unlikeness, into which we had fallen, to our true image. "Christ experienced all the stages of life, thereby giving communion with God to all men."[1] He takes us into His body so that we might be brought up into His fullness. Augustine has the figure of Christ saying to His disciples: "you are to come through me, to arrive at me, and to remain in me."[2] We are being asked to grow into the image of Christ only with the assistance of grace and of our union with Christ in Baptism.

In the second place, therefore, *this growing up into Christ is an ecclesial reality*. The stages of development do not culminate in an image of an *individual* "ideal man," in the sense of an adult human being, perfected in his personal, moral, or spiritual life. Christ, as the "perfect man", is primarily an image of *relationship*, of the Head to the members to the body, and of the members of the body each to the other. The picture of maturity is one of mutual relationship, with each part "working properly" so that the whole body "upbuilds itself in love" (Eph. 4:16). The passage from Ephesians in which the concept appears is concerned with the development of the whole Body of Christ into "the fullness of Christ" (Eph. 4:13). This culmination of development in a relationship is an organic image of a "group," or a "body" of people in relationship to God. Through membership in the Body of Christ each person's individual aims and goals are transcended in a wider set of ends: as members of Christ, they participate in *His life* and therefore in *His ends*.[3]

---

1 Saint Irenaeus, *Adversus haereses* 3, 18, 7: PG 7, 1, 937.

2 *De Doctrina Christiana*, I, XXXIV, 38.

3 On this point see C.H. Dodd, *Gospel and Law: The Relation of Faith and Ethics in Early Christianity* (New York: Columbia University Press, 1951), 34–36. On the distinction between the Body of Christ and collectives, and the

Thirdly, building upon what we have seen so far, the image provided in Ephesians is that of the whole "body," with Christ as the Head, related to the "one God and Father of us all, who is above all and through all and in all" (Eph. 4:6). The image is one of the relationship of this "body" as *children of God to their Father*. We can see this especially clearly when we set it alongside the other statements concerning the aim of the pedagogy of God made in this section in the *Directory*. Thus we see that the *Directory* calls the divine pedagogy the "action of the Holy Spirit in every Christian" (GDC 142), encouraging a "filial encounter with God" (GDC 143), bringing people to their happiness and fulfillment as free children of the Father. The divine pedagogy "causes the person to grow progressively and patiently towards the maturity of a free son" (GDC 139). Catechesis is a "journey" towards the Father (GDC 143). On this journey, the Holy Spirit makes the Church youthful. Thus *Lumen Gentium* teaches:

> The Spirit dwells in the Church and in the hearts of the faithful, as in a temple (cf. 1 Cor. 3:16; 6:19). In them he prays on their behalf and bears witness to the fact they are adopted sons (cf. Gal. 4:6; Rom 8:15–16 and 26). … By the power of the Gospel He makes the Church keep the freshness of youth. (*LG* 4)

The work of the Holy Spirit is to maintain the youthfulness of the Church, its child-likeness. Within a Catholic understanding, moreover, it is Mary, mother and model of the Church, who is the youngest creature of all. Because of her immaculate conception, the French novelist, George Bernarnos calls her "younger than sin, younger than the race from which she sprang, and though a mother, by grace, Mother of all grace, our little youngest sister."[4]

We have seen that in the ancient world the pedagogue was the figure in Greek and Roman households who would be tasked by the father of the household with supervising the child's behavior and habits on behalf of the parents, disciplining the child as needed. *The pedagogue acts in order to support the filial relationship with the father.* In his work, *Paedagogus*, Clement of Alexandria makes the connections for us: "That, then, pedagogy is the training of children is clear from the word

---

way in which this union in the Body protects the value of each individual person, see C.S. Lewis, "Membership," *Fern-seed and Elephants and other Essays on Christianity*, ed. W. Hooper (London: Collins, 1975), 11–25.

4 *The Diary of a Country Priest*, trans. P. Morris (London: Collins, 1977), 181. "In Mary, God puts a check on the law of degradation and decline" (J. Saward, "The Pedagogy of Péguy," *The Chesterton Review*, vol. XIX, 3 [August 1993], 369).

itself. It remains for us to consider the children whom scripture points to; then to give the Pedagogue charge of them. We are the children."[5]

The work of catechesis, then, can be conceived as being for the sake of enabling the development of this mature childlikeness in the one Body of Christ, childlikeness before the Father. Saint Paul, in his *Letter to the Romans*, emphasizes to his readers that the Father has sent the Spirit of His Son into their hearts to make them His children (Rom. 8:15–16). The life of grace is thus conceived as a sharing in the Sonship of Christ—in the knowledge and love of the Father for the Son and in the returning loving knowledge of the Son for the Father. Christians live in the Holy Spirit, who is their mutual joy.[6]

This view of the end of education stands in contrast to some aspects of the classical view, in which the mature *adult* is the standard for education. Marrou in fact argues that what he terms the "barbaric severity" of the schools, which typified so much education in the classical world, was a result of the view that the education of the child was only for the sake of the grown adult, without the child being valued for his own sake.[7] The whole point of education was "to teach the child to transcend himself."[8] There is, it is true, a transcendence asked of the person within the pedagogy of God, for the sake of the other, but this is better conceived as of one of *the maturing of the child*, or as a development from "childishness" to "childlikeness."

FROM CHILDISHNESS TO CHILDLIKENESS

When the *General Directory for Catechesis* speaks about the goal as being one of sonship, or childlikeness, it is not meaning to downplay the idea of human growth and maturity, of course, but rather to specify the *kind* of maturity which the Church is seeking to support through catechesis. It wants the notion of Christian maturity to be accurately understood. It is not to be thought of in terms of autonomy and self-reliance. Rather, what is to be sought is a mature dependence—the "maturity of a free son."

The image of the "child," and the associated image of the "pedagogue," have a double reference in Scripture, for they can, in fact, indicate states of either immaturity and of authentic maturity. We have already noted that in the *Letter to the*

---

5 *Paedagogus* bk. 1.5, "The Instructor," *The Ante-Nicene Fathers*, vol. II, American Edition, reprinted 1994, eds. A. Roberts and J. Donaldson (Edinburgh: T & T Clark), 207–298.

6 See *ST* 2a 2ae q. 45 art. 4. Saint Thomas explains that we are called to participate in the Wisdom of God, who is the eternal Son. In reaching and sharing in perfect Wisdom, "man attains to the sonship of God."

7 On this see H. Marrou, *A History of Education in Antiquity*, 218–220.

8 Marrou, *A History of Education in Antiquity*, 219.

Galatians, with its reference to the Law as a pedagogue, the theme of moving from the position of a child to that of an adult is a prominent one.

Paul, for example, employed images of childhood to indicate a lack of maturity in the Christian life. He referred to the Corinthian Christians as young children who were learning their first letters. So he writes in his *First Letter to the Corinthians* of the need for the brethren to learn "not to go beyond what is written" (1 Cor. 4:6). The image Paul is using here is that of a small child learning to trace the letters of the alphabet, carefully writing over the faint outline of the letters to learn their shape. Paul is asking the Christians in Corinth to consider themselves young children, copying him in each respect, and not straying off the outline of their "letters."[9] The ambiguity involved in this use of "child" imagery is clear. It entails a criticism of the Corinthian's comparative lack of maturity, as well as a positive call to obedience and discipleship.[10]

A striking image of learning in childhood is also found in the Book of Isaiah, with a depiction of Israel as a babe or a young child needing to be fed small morsels of knowledge at a time:

> Whom will he teach knowledge,
> and to whom will he explain the message?
> Those who are weaned from the milk,
> those taken from the breast?
> For it is precept upon precept,
> precept upon precept,
> line upon line, line upon line,
> here a little, there a little. (Isa. 28:9–10)

The capacity for learning is limited in young children; they can receive only so much. When it comes to learning doctrine, Calvin suggests, in a commentary on this passage, God has to "chew every word and syllable for us."[11] Cicero makes a similar injunction regarding the teaching of young children: teachers should chew up what is to be learned, as nurses feeding babies. The keynote for learning with young children is to make the morsels small and also to be persistent.[12] This image is picked up

9 For a use of this image see also Plato: *Protagoras* 326D, and for Paul's use here see Ronald L. Tyler, "First Corinthians 4:6 and Hellenistic Pedagogy," *Catholic Biblical Quarterly* vol. 60, I (January 1998), 97–103. The practice is also recommended in Quintilian, *Institutio oratoria*, I, 1, 2, 7.

10 See also 1 Cor 3:1–2; 4:14–15 and 13:11 for similar use.

11 R.A. Blacketer, *The School of God: Pedagogy and Rhetoric in Calvin's Interpretation of Deuteronomy* (Dordrecht, Netherlands: Springer, 2006), 59; cf. also 83–87.

12 *De Oratore*, trans. E.W. Sutton and H. Rackham, Loeb edition (Cambridge: Harvard, 1948), 2:39, 162.

by Saint Augustine, however, and transformed in the light of the Christian doctrine of the Incarnation; for Christ became a little child like this precisely out of love for man's helplessness. Augustine allows this very immaturity to be seen as a revelation of Christ's love for His people:

> [Christ] became a little child in the midst of us [and] like a nurse cherishing her children. For is it a pleasure to lisp shortened and broken words, unless love incites us? And yet men desire to have infants to whom they have to do that kind of service; and it is a sweeter thing to a mother to put small morsels of masticated food into her little son's mouth than to eat up and devour larger pieces herself.[13]

The immature child is a point of attraction for the loving mother; so also, Augustine suggests, is the immature people of God an attraction to the Father who loves what He has created and sends the divine Son to take on the form of the fallen image in order to restore it.

We see here the important theme of the "condescension" of God, which plays so significant a part in the notion of the pedagogy of God.[14] This is the point that, out of love, the infinite God "condescends" to dwell with His creatures. He reaches down to their level, in order to lift them to His own. In a striking section of *De Catechizandis Rudibus*, Augustine argues that intelligence animated by love naturally delights in descending "to the lowest objects." Catechesis is intelligent activity animated by love, and as such makes the riches of Revelation available to the lowest level. Inspired by the pedagogy of God, the catechist makes the Good News of salvation accessible to every person.

The image of the child is also used positively in the Scriptures, to indicate the perfection of Christian maturity. That the child can be such a positive image flows, of course, from its Christological use. At the climax of the pedagogy of God it is the *Son* who appears.[15] The Father has given us "the All Who is His Son."[16] "The Son" is therefore a characteristic self-appellation by Jesus, just as "Abba," "Father" is His characteristic address to God.[17] Jesus is the "Little Child, God eternal" (*Catechism*, no. 525), and to become a child is the condition for entering the

---

13 *De Catechizandis Rudibus*, 10:15.

14 See GDC 131, especially note 40 and 146; also *DV* 13.

15 See Heb. 1:1–2.

16 Saint John of the Cross, *The Ascent of Mount Carmel* 2, 22, 4, in *The Collected Works of St John of the Cross*, trans. K. Kavanaugh OCD and O. Rodriguez OCD (Washington, DC: Institute of Carmelite Studies 1979), 180.

17 For Son and Father brought together, see Matt. 11:27 and also 21:34–38; 24:36.

Kingdom of this Child (see *Catechism*, no. 526).[18] The child as an ideal, therefore, is not to be misunderstood as an encouragement to childishness, but rather as the fostering of childlikeness in imitation of the divine Child and as a result of sharing in His filial relationship with the Father.

We find a good example of this positive use of the notion of "child" to signify Christian maturity in Clement of Alexandria's *Paedagogus*. Clement spends much time explaining and justifying the ideal of childlikeness as the goal of a Christian education.[19] The youth of the Christian springs from the union he has with the incorruptible Word:

> The new people are called young, having learned the new blessings;
> and we have the exuberance of life's morning prime in this youth
> which knows no old age; in which we are always growing to maturity
> in intelligence, are always young, always mild, always new.[20]

This focus on childlikeness does not exclude for him a proper awareness, also, of the notion of the mature person as the final aim of catechesis. In particular, he is concerned to defend Christians against the charge of an immaturity in their thinking. He asks rhetorically: do we think of ourselves as children, because of the "childish and contemptible character of our education"? Clement answers the critics who would suppose this to be the case by reference to Baptism since it is through Baptism that Christians receive the light of the knowledge of God: "Straightway, on our regeneration, we attained that perfection after which we aspired. For we were illuminated, which is to know God."[21]   *Childlike*

The childlikeness, then, flows from the Christian's unity with the Word of Life in Baptism, which renews their youth. And with this youthfulness are a number of the qualities of the child that a Christian education should also seek to engender. Indeed, Clement maintains this focus on the ongoing importance of childlike qualities by associating them with Christ as a *Child*-Pedagogue. "And how shall not the discipline of this child be perfect, which extends to us, leading as a schoolmaster us as children, who are his little ones?"[22]

---

18 Significantly, the final image of Christ in His Kingdom is of a *lamb* (see Rev. 19:7, 9).

19 Clement, *Paedagogus*, bk 1, *passim*. Note, for example, the long excursus on the figurative meanings of "child" and the associated discussions on feeding with "milk" and with "meat." The purpose of these investigations into the Scriptures and their use of these terms is to establish the connections between "child" and "innocence" on the one hand and "child" and "maturity" on the other.

20 *Paedagogus* I, 5.

21 *Paedagogus* I, 6. Cf. *Catechism*, no. 1216 and references.

22 *Paedagogus* I, 5.

In the first place, then, Clement writes of the ideal of childlikeness in relation to the central Christian Revelation of God as Father and of the adoption of Christians as children of this Father. The Pedagogue leads us ever more deeply into the realization of this central relationship we have with God as our Father. In its description of the life of prayer, the *Catechism* recommends the childlike qualities expressed by the Greek word, *"parrhesia"*:[23] "straightforward simplicity, filial trust, joyous assurance, humble boldness, the certainty of being loved" (*Catechism*, no. 2778). This, the *Catechism* calls a "characteristically Christian expression," and it follows the new state of being into which Christians are introduced through the gift of the Spirit. The redemptive work of God leads to a new possibility of relationship with the Father, which springs from a union with the divine Son and the coming of the Spirit. "The new man, reborn and restored to his God by grace, says first of all, 'Father!' because he has now begun to be a son."[24]

Quite apart from Revelation, Clement also focuses on the intrinsic positive qualities of children, and especially of their openness to learning, as well as their trust, simplicity, and guilelessness. These stand out as more general virtues within a religious framework of convictions concerning God as Creator and Sustainer, and within the Christian doctrine of Providence.[25]

A key characteristic in catechesis, emphasized in both the *Directory* and the *Catechism*, which is needed in order to enable this development of the mature child, is the notion of a *catechesis of filial trust*. The *Catechism* speaks of "the great school" of trust (*Catechism*, no. 305). Catechists seek to educate their hearers into a deeper and more profound sense of trust. Catechesis is given for the sake of a growth in the relationship between the Lord and His people, so that the person can "abandon himself 'completely and freely to God' (*DV* 5): intelligence, will, heart and memory" (*GDC* 144).

Trust is needed by the catechumen in the development of this relationship precisely because "the discipline and instruction of the Lord" (Eph. 6:4) takes place within this context of a fallen human nature and fallen creation. "Out of heaven he let you hear his voice, that he might discipline you" (Deut. 4:36). Because of sin, the

---

23 See Eph. 3:12.

24 Saint Cyprian, *De Dom. Orat.* 9, PL 4, 541. This sonship is adoptive rather than natural. Jesus consistently distinguished His Sonship from that of the disciples. See Mt. 5:48; 6:8–9; 7:21; Lk. 11:13; Jn. 20:17).

25 For an extended treatment of the theme of childlikeness in the Christian life, especially as it is manifested in the saints, see J. Saward, *The Way of the Lamb: The Spirit of Childhood and the End of the Age* (Edinburgh: T & T Clark, 1999).

Lord walks "contrary" to His people.[26] But this disciplining is always for our good, since it is given in order to overcome the work of sin in us, which distances us from our true fulfillment: life with the Lord. A catechesis on God's self-sufficiency, His freedom from needs, and His perfection is important here since it is a guarantee of His goodness. Aquinas puts it in this way:

> To act out of need indicates that an agent is imperfect, that its nature
> is to act but also to undergo. This is not fitting for God. And so God
> alone is completely free, because God acts not for his own gain but
> solely from his own goodness.[27]

Because God has no other reason for acting except to bring His creatures to perfection and fulfillment, catechists are able to assure their hearers that times of testing are aspects of an overall process of assisting people in a deepening movement of entrusting themselves to their Creator and Preserver.[28] In *Paedagogus*, Clement uses a medical analogy for the way in which the Pedagogue treats His disciples. The bones of humanity, in its fallen state, are broken. "Society had to be reset."[29] The work of resetting the broken limbs belongs to the divine Pedagogue; that is not the role of the catechist.[30] But the catechist can assist the healing process by explaining *why* this work of disciplining humanity is necessary, providing an understanding of God's purpose and loving design in creation and redemption; and offering examples of conversion and holiness, highlighting the happiness of the saints in order to give hope. In other words, the catechist can help others to understand the divine mercy at work.

> Truly, to help a person to encounter God, which is the task of the
> catechist, means to emphasize above all the relationship that the per-

---

26 See Lev. 26:18, 28. This "contrariness" is best understood, as it was by Charles Williams, as the human antagonism towards the good, flowing from sin. Sin introduces the falsity of a perverted view of the Good—that is, of Being—in which it is seen and experienced as contrary to one's good. "They know evil; that is, they know the good of fact as repugnant to them." For a discussion of Williams' views, see D. Sayers, "Charles Williams: A Poet's Critic," in *The Poetry of Search and the Poetry of Statement* (London: Victor Gollancz, 1963), 69–90.

27 *ST* 1a q. 44 art, 4 ad.1.

28 Cf. Deut. 8:1–6.

29 H. Ritter, "The Christian Schools of Alexandria," *The Dublin Review*, London, vol. III, no.6 (July–Oct. 1864), 302. Clement is not original in this analogy. We find the Stoic philosopher Epictetus describing the philosopher's lecture room as a hospital (*The Discourses of Epictetus*, ed. C. Gill [London: Everyman, 1995], 3, 23, 30).

30 Augustine's wise strictures on the boundaries that need to be set around human discipline are worth consulting. It is a good lesson in humility when we find ourselves sinning in our attempts to correct the sin of others, "when we find it easier to respond to the sinner's anger with our own anger than to the sinner's misery with our mercy" (*Commentary on Galatians*, trans. E. Plumer, 57.5, and see 224–227).

son has with God so that he can make it his own and allow himself
to be guided by God. (GDC 139)

The catechist can point to the goodness of the Lord's disciplining education in its
overall purpose, which is to educate the whole person into a renewed, deepened relationship with God for the sake of each person's perfect and everlasting happiness.
This purpose governs the content and the methods of the whole of God's pedagogy.

There is a rich and nuanced discussion in the Christian tradition, then, of
themes of child and adult in relation to the aims of education, with a concomitant
analysis of the differences between a true childlikeness and a mere childishness on
the one hand, and of a mature adulthood and a mere "growing up" on the other. The
Christian tradition fosters the ideal of the child, understood in a Christological and
ecclesial sense, as the end of education. The historical figure of the pedagogue, as we
have seen, focuses upon the training of the child's character and this indicates for
us a broad understanding to the meaning of education, incorporating intellectual
formation within a broader "training" of the person.

THE PROCESS: PROGRESSIVE AND IN STAGES

One of the accented features in the presentation of the pedagogy of God in the
Directory is that it is progressive and takes place in stages. The two key references
concerning this point are worth citing here. The first is from the *Catechism*:

> [The divine plan of Revelation] involves a specific divine pedagogy:
> God communicates himself to man gradually. He prepares him to
> welcome by stages the supernatural Revelation that is to culmi-
> nate in the person and mission of the incarnate Word, Jesus Christ.
> (*Catechism*, no. 53)

This first citation is followed first by a reference to Saint Irenaeus, who in *Adversus
haereses* speaks of God and man becoming "accustomed" to one another throughout
history until this culminates in the Incarnation, and then secondly by a presentation of the "stages" of Revelation in history, leading up to the fullness of Revelation
in Christ.

The second citation is found in the *General Directory for Catechesis*:

> God, in his greatness, uses a pedagogy to reveal himself to the human
> person: he uses human events and words to communicate his plan;

he does so progressively and in stages (*Catechism*, no. 54–64), so as to draw even closer to man. God, in fact, operates in such a manner that man comes to knowledge of his salvific plan by means of the events of salvation history and the inspired words which accompany and explain them. (*GDC* 38)

As with the first citation, the notion of progression and of a pedagogy taking place by "stages" appears to be tied especially to the events of salvation history. God's pedagogy points towards the historical fact of the Incarnation—this makes sense of the fact that the next heading in the *Directory* concerns Christ "mediator and fullness of Revelation" (*GDC* 40).

The *Directory* returns on other occasions to the notion of progressiveness, especially in its section on the pedagogy of God, where it stresses that a catechesis inspired by this pedagogy will "accept the principle of progressiveness in Revelation" (*GDC* 143), and will "promote a progressive and coherent synthesis" between each person's adherence to God (*fides qua*) and the content of what is transmitted (*fides quae*) (*GDC* 144). These two references appear to broaden the concept of progressiveness to include a specific catechetical interest in the ways in which the communication of the Faith is received in concrete terms by each person: catechetical presentations, inspired by the pedagogy of God, need to take into account the notion of a "progressive" presentation of content.

Having looked at the content and immediate context of these references to the pedagogy of God, let us turn now to unpack their meaning in more detail.

NATURAL STAGES AND CATECHETICAL STAGES

In one respect, the model being presented here, of a pedagogy that is developmental and in stages, might appear to be simply mirroring the natural growth of the person, from the growing child to adulthood. John Paul certainly uses this image in *Catechesi Tradendae*:

From infancy until the threshold of maturity, catechesis is thus a permanent school of the faith and follows the major stages of life, like a beacon lighting the path of the child, the adolescent and the young person. (*CT* 39)

The "short prayers that the child learns to lisp" are seen as "the start of a loving dialogue" with God that continues throughout life and that reaches its climax in adulthood, where we find "the principal form of catechesis, because it is addressed to persons who have the greatest responsibilities and the capacity to live the Christian message in its fully developed form" (CT 36 and 43). For this reason, the *General Directory for Catechesis*, like its 1971 predecessor, spends much time in the consideration of the ways in which catechesis needs to be adapted for and presented to differing age groups.

In this picture of catechesis accompanying the person through the different stages of natural development, catechesis functions in a way similar to the picture presented of the sacraments in the *Catechism*:

> The seven sacraments touch all the stages and all the important moments of Christian life: they give birth and increase, healing and mission to the Christian's life of faith. There is thus a certain resemblance between the stages of natural life and the stages of the spiritual life.[31]

There are several advantages in taking this to be the basic hermeneutic for understanding the gradual approach in the pedagogy of God.

Firstly, in so far as this is the picture of the development of catechesis, it coheres well, in principle, with contemporary models of psychological and educational development, which can provide the natural adjunct and human foundations for this growth. The work of educational theorists is often presented in terms of the development through various "stages," which can be conceived as either simply descriptive or else to some extent prescriptive also, guiding notions of development towards implicit and explicit goals. So, for example, Piaget set out cognitive stages of development in his *Science of Education and the Psychology of the Child*, upon which Kohlberg constructed his own stages of moral development. In the specific area of religious education, in *Readiness for Religion* and *Religious Thinking from Childhood to Adolescence*, Goldman claimed to have identified a series of developmental stages through which the growing religious understanding of the child must pass, while James Fowler's *Stages of Faith* offers a series of steps which, he proposes, can be used both to guide and to understand development in the spiritual life.[32]

---

31 *Catechism*, no. 1210, referencing for support Saint Thomas Aquinas, ST 3a, 65, 1.

32 It is not the intention of this paper to offer an evaluation of these major, and well-known, models of staged cognitive, moral, religious, and spiritual development. It is enough to note that in terms of empirical evidence to support or refute the theories, and at the conceptual level, the approaches of each of these theorists is debated. As we saw earlier, one of the arguments in *Catechesi Tradendae* is precisely that an evaluation of these conceptual and disciplinary frameworks needs to be made against a pedagogy which is inspired by the need to communicate God's Revelation in its entirety.

Secondly, it is necessarily the case that all educational philosophies pay attention to what they understand to be the most appropriate models for developing intellectual, moral and personal virtues and abilities, with each stage building upon the one before after its successful mastery. Thus, for example, Aristotle outlined a progressive education rooted in his anthropology which understood the intellectual development of the person to be both the most challenging to achieve well and the highest in order of value. His educational stages begin with the training of the body; move onto the education of character; and culminate in the intellectual formation of the person.[33]

Thirdly, this understanding also harmonizes with the Catholic theological principle of grace building upon nature: God's pedagogy, working in progressive stages of Revelation, would build upon and work alongside the natural stages in the development of the child.

Finally, this understanding of what the Church means by the progressive nature of the pedagogy of God, which is to provide the inspiration for catechesis, would also appear to make sense of the insistence that adult catechesis is where the central emphasis of the Church's work in this area needs to be directed. The gradual natural stages of growth of the person, culminating in adulthood, would be paralleled by a catechesis that supported the growing child and adolescent until it reached the mature catechetical "form" of an adult catechesis.

Attractive though this understanding is, there are also several reasons for thinking, however, that this is not the key hermeneutic for interpreting the notion of "stages" and "progression" in catechesis. This is not to deny the obvious point that Church teaching documents on catechesis pay detailed attention to the specific needs of particular age groups.[34] Nor is it to deny that any pedagogy, which is to inspire catechesis, must take account of theories of human development. The point is rather that an understanding of what is meant by God's pedagogy being one of gradual preparation, in stages, is to be sought mainly elsewhere than in an appreciation of parallels to the natural development of the person and his cognitive, affective, and human development.

---

33 For an overview of Aristotle's educational philosophy see R.S. Brumbaugh and N.M. Lawrence, *Philosophers on Education: Six Essays on the Foundations of Western Thought* (Boston: Houghton Mifflin Co., 1963), ch. 2. Aristotle almost certainly composed a treatise specifically on education, περι παιδειας, so that the account of education we now have in his works is incomplete, but is found in his works on politics and ethics. For the existence of the lost treatise, see Diogenes Laertius, *Lives of Eminent Philosophers*, vol. 1, Loeb Classical Library, trans. R.D. Hicks (Cambridge: Harvard University Press, 1925), bk 5, 22.

34 So, see GCD 77–97; CT 35–43; *Catechism*, no. 24; GDC 171–188.

There are two reasons for wanting to think in a different way about the meaning of "progressive" within the Church's presentation of the pedagogy of God. *The first is the clear referencing to an understanding of stages in history.* The progressiveness of the pedagogy, then, is not so much to do with the natural growth and development of the individual person from infancy until adulthood as with *God's gradual unfolding of His economy of salvation within history.* It is the activity of God with which we are primarily concerned. If this is what is meant by "progressive" and "in stages," then it will certainly impact upon the work of catechesis, which will be "inspired" by this. Nonetheless, this is not the primary reference point for our understanding of what the phrase means. The impact on catechesis may be mainly, we might think, through the ordering and the content of the curriculum. The curriculum might use this gradual revelation of God as a key to the order of its presentation of topics. In addition, a right understanding of topics will be enabled through a presentation of them that makes reference to, and is structured upon, a narrative approach.

The second reason for thinking that the progressive nature of God's pedagogy is something other than simply a paralleling of the natural growth of the person is that the *"progressive" character of catechesis is an intrinsic feature of each catechetical period*, whether of childhood, adolescence, or adulthood. The progressions is not so much one of movement according to the development of the human person according to his or her age, as of movement according to the intrinsic "logic" and development of God's Revelation and to the corresponding gradual stages of understanding that accompany this.

STAGES, HISTORY AND THE "NARRATIO"

The most obvious reference point we are given when asked to focus upon the progressive, staged, nature of the pedagogy of God, is that of God's activity in history. God gradually and progressively reveals Himself, over historical time.[35]

On this view, history can be conceptualized as a series of "stages" according to the activity of God at particular times, as certain events or groups of events form boundary points for our understanding.

Saint Augustine, for example, held that a Christian understanding of salvation history could be divided into "six ages,"[36] with the appearing of Christ marking

35 A helpful, general discussion of the *narratio* in the catechesis of the early Church, focusing especially on the work of Saint Irenaeus, is provided by A. Minto, "How the Divine Pedagogy Teaches," *The Sower*, vol. 25, no. 4, 6–8 and vol. 26, no. 1, 8–11.
36 Saint Augustine, *De Catechizandis Rudibus*, 22, 39.

the beginning of the sixth and final "stage" or "age." The stages, taken together, make up the *narratio*, the overall story of sacred history that reveals God's pedagogy. The catechist's *narratio* is "full," or complete, when it covers the whole sweep of creation, from the beginning until the present time, and taking into account the future fulfillment to which the creation is directed. It does not need to include all details, of course, but the overall summary should be coherent and allow one to draw out of this summary pertinent features for a particular focus.[37] Helping others to understand that there is a fundamental unity to the whole of God's progressive Revelation can be best ensured, Augustine believed, through an attention to the *telos*, since this provides the key to the purpose of creation, which is the love of God:

> Take this love, therefore, as the end that is set before you, to which
> you are to refer all that you say, and, whatever you narrate, narrate
> it in such a manner that he to whom you are discoursing on hearing
> may believe, on believing may hope, on hoping may love.[38]

The *Catechism* tends to use a simple, threefold model when it presents any doctrine or feature within a *narratio* structure: of "the time of the promises," "the Old Testament" or "the Old Covenant"; "the fullness of time"; and "the time of the Church," or "the Last Days."[39] The *General Directory for Catechesis*, likewise, speaks of "the three phases in the narration of the history of salvation": the Old Testament, the life of Jesus, and the history of the Church (GDC 130). It describes the main sections as:

> the great stages of the Old Testament by which he [God] prepared
> the journey of the Gospel; the life of Jesus, Son of God, born of the
> virgin Mary who by his actions and teaching brought Revelation to
> completion; the history of the Church which transmits Revelation.
> (GDC 108)

This overall threefold point of reference is fundamental to the *narratio*, corresponding to what Saint Ambrose calls "the shadow of the Law, the image in the Gospel, the truth in the heavenly realities."[40] The center of history is, of course, the coming

---

37 Saint Augustine, *De Catechizandis Rudibus*, 3, 5–6.

38 Saint Augustine, *De Catechizandis Rudibus*, 4, 7–8. One can see the influence from Augustine in the overall instruction for the orientation for catechetical explanations which is set forth in the *Roman Catechism* (Preface 10) and is repeated in the *Catechism*, no. 25.

39 See, for example, the treatment of the Holy Spirit (*Catechism*, nos. 702–741).

40 Saint Ambrose, *Enarr. 25 in Ps.* 38, PL 14, 1051 C.

of God in time, the good news of Christ Himself and of His teaching and redemptive work; this is the point where time reaches its fullness. Before this lies the time of the prefigurement, of expectation, all of which is to be understood through an appreciation of historical typology in terms of persons, objects, and events.[41] Then the whole of the *narratio* has a fulfillment in the future to which it looks forward: the *eschaton*. This development of the stages, corresponding to God's gradual Revelation of Himself and of His plan, is why the *Directory* describes them as "progressive."[42]

In the twentieth century, this narrative approach has especially influenced the salvation history school of catechetics through the work of Jungmann and Hofinger.[43] It has also been influential through the work of the Catechesis of the Good Shepherd movement, inspired by Sophia Cavelletti, and rooted in the work of Maria Montessori.[44]

The narrative approach has not been without its critics. Groome, for example, laments an apparent lack of integration between doctrine and experience in this pedagogy, arguing that Augustine uses the didactic narrative approach, in *De Catechezandis Rudibus*, "to instruct people in the story of salvation history with no apparent attention to the lived experience of the students as a dimension of knowing."[45] He accepts that this approach might be appropriate for those being newly-instructed in the Faith since the presentation of the *narratio* might have as its intention that these new converts "enter into the relational experience of the Christian community where another and deeper kind of knowing would take place."[46] However, he does not consider this a sufficient methodology to ensure

---

41 The reading of Scripture using typology is only possible because it is based upon this typology of historical realities.

42 In her manual for catechists explaining how to teach salvation history as the pedagogy of God, Sophia Cavalletti explains, "Salvation history progresses in stages. The preceding stage prepares for the one that follows; each stage contains in itself the stage that preceded it." (*History's Golden Thread: The History of Salvation* [Chicago: Catechesis of the Good Shepherd Publications, 1999], 15. The title of her work is drawn from Augustine's *De Catechizandis Rudibus*, 6.6, where he speaks of the "golden thread" of the unity of God's plan which the catechist is to reveal in and through the coherence of the events in history.

43 Representative works setting out their approach would be J. Hofinger, *The Art of Teaching Christian Doctrine: The Good News and its Proclamation* (Notre Dame: University of Notre Dame Press, 1957), and J. Jungmann, *The Good News and its Proclamation* (New York: Sadlier, 1961).

44 Sophia Cavalletti's main work for catechists, detailing a salvation history approach is *History's Golden Thread: The History of Salvation*. Cavelletti places less emphasis on the third moment; there is comparatively little attention paid to the history of the Church and on God's continuing activity leading to the present. In general, while Cavalletti engages strongly with the Church's interpretation of Scripture, it might be argued that her work suffers from a certain neglect of Tradition (cf. the general note in the *Directory* that this is a common difficulty in much catechetical work [GDC 30].)

45 T. Groome, *Christian Religious Education*, 159–160. Gabriel Moran concurs with this view, arguing that however imaginative the reconstruction of the past history might be, "a description of past events is—especially for a child—a set of propositional truths. ... The experience that Moses had of God may have been personal, concrete, and existential; but Moses is dead." (*Catechesis of Revelation* [New York: Herder and Herder, 1966], 46).

46 Groome, *Christian Religious Education*, 160.

the necessary attention to "lived experience" for any ongoing catechetical process. Groome's concern that experience be well-integrated is certainly consistent with the view of the *General Directory for Catechesis*, which works with a model of the unification of the person, including their experience, for which he is seeking; the pedagogy of God asks that the educator assist in bridging the gap between people's faith and their lives, bringing the whole into integration.[47] However, two points are worth making in response here to his criticism of the narrative approach, as a means of further clarifying the role of historical narration within the pedagogy of God.

First of all, it is to be remembered that the narration of salvation history is, as Groome implies, only one part of a broader model in patristic catechesis, of a progressive, staged process. Within the "initiatory," or "catechumenal"[48] model of catechesis, of which this narration forms a part, the handing over of the Creed and of the *Our Father* follow; and, after this, the period of mystagogical catechesis and on-going formation, which are concerned to assist catechumens to "interiorize ... and to savor the experience of configuration to Christ and of communion with him" (GDC 129).

Secondly, however, there is a fundamental intention, through this narration, to "provide a new history, different from that which the world teaches us, and which we used to think was our history."[49] The narrowness of each individual's experience is to be inserted into a wider patrimony, into the ecclesial experience of receiving God's Revelation "gradually" over time. The goal, as we have seen, is *to participate in the experience of sonship shared by the Body of Christ united to the Head, the divine Son*. For this, the learning of a history of pedagogy, which one can identify as one's own, is a crucial element. The *narratio* is announced by the catechist so that each person, with his own unique "life story," may find his identity within the context of this overarching history.

The telling of the *narratio*, therefore, is intended to assist in the formation of the person as a member of a people, a Body, a Church. It lies at the service of communion, supporting the communion of God's people with each other, and of the one People of God with the Blessed Trinity. This element of the pedagogy is intended to move catechumens beyond any private learning of the Faith into an understanding that they belong to a community with a history. The *General Directory for Catechesis* emphasizes that catechesis "nourishes the bond of unity and brings

---

47 Cf. GDC 153.

48 See GDC 59, 65–68.

49 C. Schönborn, "Address on 10th Anniversary of the Publication of the Catechism" (Oct. 2002), *The Sower*, vol. 25, no. 2 (2003), 9.

about an awareness of belonging to a great community which cannot be limited by space or time" (GDC 106). The *narratio* helps each person to relocate himself into this history and its memories. It also helps each person to move beyond what Michael Roth has described as the "psychologization of memory," which with the "doubts about the possibilities for objective history" has, he argues, "combined to create an attitude that lets each person have his or her history." Roth describes this as a form of "social amnesia" which depends on a "superficial relativism in which one has no investment in the past that one might share with another."[50]

Conversion involves the discovery of a new identity and a new goal. As we have seen, it is centered upon the discovery that one has been adopted and is now a child of the Father. The Church has always understood an inseparable aspect of this process of adoption as being the discovery that one also has a family. The sending of the Holy Spirit so that believers will not remain orphans includes the drawing of each adopted person into a new group of brothers and sisters.[51] Part of the waking up to one's true self that is at the heart of the catechetical process involves a waking to find that one has an identity in communion with others; one belongs to a common world. "The world of the waking is one and shared, but the sleeping turn aside each into his private world."[52] Roger Simon speaks of the "transactional space" of public memory, where one's personal memories may engage with that of others, and of collective stories and memories. This is then the place of decision-making.[53] The fundamental question is: whose memories are to be my own? We find points of connection enabling us to be "claimed in relation to the experiences of others."[54]

Telling the *narratio* offers the Church's public "memory" of the great deeds of the Lord to the catechumen, thus providing the possibility of a kinship between the memories of the catechumen and those of the Church. The "space'" which Simon describes as "transactional" we might call "covenantal." It is through the telling of the great deeds of the Lord, the *Directory* insists, that the Church is able to place herself into a state of *expectatio*, of waiting in hope for the Lord's coming, a coming that is fulfilled at the end of time and that also is able to "fill" each moment of time

---

50 M.S. Roth, *Memory, Trauma and the Construction of History* (New York: Columbia University Press, 1995), 15.

51 Jn. 14:18, Mt. 19:29.

52 Heraclitus, Fr. 89, cited in R. Polito, *The Sceptical Road: Aenesidemus' Appropriation of Heraclitus* (Leiden, Netherlands: Brill Philosophia Antiqua, 2004), 187.

53 We might compare this with the way in which the *Catechism* describes the heart as "the place of encounter," which is also the "place of decision" where I choose life or death (*Catechism*, no. 2563).

54 R.I. Simon, "The Touch of the Past: The Pedagogical Significance of a Transactional Sphere of Public Memory," in *Revolutionary Pedagogies*, ed. P.P. Trifonas (New York: Routledge Falmer Press, 2000), 63.

until that end.[55] In this time of *expectatio* one faces what Simon calls "boundary work," that of discerning whose memories one will allow to become personal for me, so that I identify with them as memories of my own. One then moves from the position of being an observer simply, a listener, hearing a historical retelling as an account of others with whom I am not involved, to a different place. One moves from the "spectatorial" to the "summoned."[56]

I sense in myself the call to respond. In its section dedicated to the role of memory in catechesis, the *Directory* reminds us that this is described in the Tradition as the *redditio*, the "response of the subject during the catechetical journey and subsequently in life" (GDC 155). Elsewhere, this is spoken of as the response of the obedience of faith, or even more simply as the *Fiat*.[57] One makes the decision to allow oneself to be "summoned" and henceforward be found in a covenant relationship with the divine Pedagogue, as a member of His people.

Summarizing this section, then: we can see that there is a fundamental reference-point being given in the historical stages of God's gradual revelation of Himself to man, and that this fact is to "inspire" the work of catechesis.

STAGES ON THE ROAD TO WISDOM

There is, in addition, a more general way in which the Church is asking catechists to be inspired by an understanding of the progressive nature of God's pedagogy, taking place in stages, for good catechesis is undertaken in steps.[58] To some extent, this point picks up the earlier theme of a progressive catechesis accompanying the natural stages of development in a person's life, but it is not necessarily tied to the actual development of the person, from child to adult; rather, it is seen as a necessary way of characterizing all catechetical work. "The Church, while ever containing in herself the fullness of the means of salvation, always operates 'by slow stages' (*Ad Gentes* 6)" (GDC 47).

We might initially see this as the simple notion that there needs to be a *systematic ordering in catechetical work*. Within the whole process of evangelization, catechesis is viewed by the Church, as we have seen, as a particular "moment" (see GDC 63) with its own character: "authentic catechesis is always an orderly

---

55 GDC 107. See also *Catechism*, no. 2816.

56 See Simon: "The Touch of the Past," 66–68. This movement is what the Church describes as "effective" catechesis: thus, "catechetical pedagogy will be effective to the extent that the Christian community becomes a point of concrete reference for the faith journey of individuals." (GDC 158).

57 See *Catechism*, nos. 144, 2617.

58 Cf. *RCIA* 6–7.

and systematic initiation into the revelation that God has given of himself in Jesus Christ."[59] The significant terms for our purpose here are "orderly" and "systematic."

This systematic ordering, or progression, should be understood in two ways, as related to *the subject content* on the one hand and to *those receiving the catechesis* on the other. There is therefore a twofold reference point for this systematic transmission of the Faith, a double attentiveness, which is described in the *General Directory for Catechesis* as "fidelity to God and to the person."[60]

The Content

In the case of the subject matter, what is asked for is an appropriate organization of studies to bring out the hierarchy of truths clearly and the relationships of various doctrines to each other. The ordering of the presentation of doctrines needs to be such that it aids understanding through a progressive unfolding of the dependence of various doctrines upon each other. The *General Directory for Catechesis*, therefore, specifies those doctrines that must serve as the organizing principles for any curriculum concerned with the transmission of the Faith,[61] as well as, following the *Catechism*, a conceptual framework of the different dimensions of the Christian life, which can also serve to organize the curriculum effectively and holistically.[62]

The orderliness of the presentation of content also serves the learner, as well as providing the necessary coherence among the topics being taught. Properly understood, in other words, fidelity to God entails a fidelity to the person as well. An orderly presentation enables the mind to see the objective order in reality and to find coherence and satisfaction in this. A study of the order of the universe enables the soul to become ordered.[63] "All things cohere in an order, and this is the form by which the universe is like God."[64] Thus, for example, Augustine's *De ordine*, in setting out the organization of the curriculum for the Christian *paideia*, begins from

---

59 *CT* 22; *GDC* 66.

60 *GDC* 145. See also *CT* 55: "the law of fidelity to God and of fidelity to man in a single, loving attitude." This is a particular instance of a more general educational principle, that in all learning one must adopt a method of study that is suitable to the nature of the subject matter on the one hand and to the nature of the person studying the subject on the other. See Aristotle, *Nicomachean Ethics* I, I, 1094b, 11–14.

61 *GDC* 97, 123.

62 See *GDC* 122. The Introduction to the *Compendium of the Catechism of the Catholic Church* identifies these dimensions by means of four "laws" or "rules" governing the Christian life: the *lex credendi*, the *lex celebrendi*, the *lex vivendi*, and the *lex orandi*.

63 *De Ordine Libri II* I, 2, 3, in "Divine Providence and the Problem of Evil," *Writings of St. Augustine*, vol. 1, trans. R.P. Russell (New York: Cima Publishing Co., 1948). See further on Augustine's structuring of the curriculum in Kevane, *Augustine the Educator*, 170–179.

64 Dante, *Paradiso* I, 103–5.

the concept of the order and causation revealed in the universe, so that the mind can grasp firmly the notion of God as creator and His providence.[65]

This need for a systematic setting out of doctrines in a certain order also revealed for the Fathers an underlying metaphysics and epistemology which involved the movement from something held as a unity in intellectual apprehension—whether this be in the mind of God or in the mind of the catechist—and then necessarily extended through time in a certain order. Saint Augustine:

> You recall that one and the same Word of God extends throughout Scripture, that it is one and the same Utterance that resounds in the mouths of all the sacred writers, since he who was in the beginning God with God has no need of separate syllables; for he is not subject to time.[66]

God is not in time and so holds all truth as a single Word. This is reflected, in time, in the multitude of words, syllables, phrases and sentences that we find in the Scriptures. However, rightly understood, they are all part of the "same Utterance," the same single divine Word that is beyond time. In his catechetical work, *De Catechizandis Rudibus*, Augustine writes of the teacher, similarly, who is aware that he cannot express everything that is held immediately in his mind:

> Intellectual apprehension diffuses itself through the mind with something like a rapid flash, whereas the utterance is slow, and occupies time, and is of a vastly different nature, so that, while this latter is moving on, the intellectual apprehension has already withdrawn itself within its secret abodes.[67]

Although utterance is slow and cannot seem to do justice to the vision of what is illuminated in the mind Augustine does not despise language: it is precisely the "condescension" of the teacher that is needed, inspired by love, to patiently make available to those being taught what is present in the teacher's mind. The catechist models himself on God's pedagogy when he unfolds in language that which is in the mind. Moreover, he does it with sensitivity to the different kinds of learners in

---

65 *De Ordine Libri II* II, 2, 7.
66 *En in Ps.* 103:4, 1: *PL* 37, 1378; cf. Ps. 104; Jn. 1:1.
67 *De Catechizandis Rudibus*, 2.3.

front of him, and the various educational backgrounds they may have.[68] Different language and a different tone is needed, depending upon who it is you are teaching.[69]

We can compare this catechetical process of teaching the Faith to what composers such as Beethoven have said about composition: that they "hear" in their mind the whole of a piece of music, and that subsequently there is the process of ordering it and writing it out, sequencing the themes and their development to make the most satisfying musical logic of what they hold in their mind.[70] This presents us with an interesting analogy to the process of the communication of Revelation, especially given the comparison made by John Paul II between the composition of the *Catechism* and the composition of a symphony.[71] Artistic inspiration in other fields than music can also, of course, flow from, or contain, visions, or conceptions, of such organic wholes. The conclusion of Dante Alighieri's *Divine Comedy* would be one well-known example. At the close of the third part of the poem, Dante offers a glimpse of paradise as a vision of God and of all creatures in Him:

> In that abyss I saw how Love held bound
> Into one volume all the leaves whose flight
> Is scattered through the universe around;
> How substance, accident, and mode unite
> Fused, so to speak, together, in such wise
> That this I tell of is one single light.[72]

---

68 For example, when you are instructing those whom you suspect already know what you are about to teach them, Augustine advises, go over what you think is probably familiar to them, merely by way of telling them that you think that this is what they already know, so that they do not "hear it from you as from a teacher." And if they are not familiar they can, in fact, be learning it from you. (*De Catechizandis Rudibus*, 8.12).

69 Augustine even encourages the deacon Deogratius, for whom he has written this work on catechetical pedagogy, to empathize with the learner so that he is able to "learn again," with a new freshness and insight "through" those whom he is teaching (*De Catechizandis Rudibus*, 12.17).

70 On Beethoven and his methods of composition, and especially his grasp of the whole of a piece of music in one apprehension, see J.W. Sullivan, *Beethoven: His Spiritual Development* (London: Unwin Books, 1959), 42–44 and M.M. Scott, *Beethoven*, ed. J. Westrup (London: J.M. Dent & Sons Ltd., 1974), 120–126.

71 "This response [of the Episcopate of the Catholic Church] elicits in me a deep feeling of joy, because the harmony of so many voices expresses what could be called the 'symphony' of the faith." (Apostolic Constitution *Fidei Depositum* [October 12, 1998]). John Paul's own thinking in this area forms part of the *ressourcement* of the transcendental of beauty in relation to the Faith. A significant theological work in this area is H.U. von Balthasar's *Truth is Symphonic* (San Francisco: Ignatius Press, 1987), especially 7–18. The *General Directory for Catechesis* expands this symphonic motif to describe the relationship between the *Catechism of the Catholic Church* and local catechisms which are published with the authority of bishops of particular churches. Then the "chorus of voices of the universal Church" (*RM* 54) is also heard in the local churches (*GDC* 136). The achieving of harmony here, between the symphony "inherent" in the *Catechism* and then "manifested" in local catechisms is one which can take place only after "adequate assimilation" of the *Catechism of the Catholic Church*, which can take "a long period of time" so that the "theological, catechetical and linguistic" work is accomplished (see *GDC* 135, note 55). Clearly, the *General Directory for Catechesis* wants "time" for the renewed vision of catechesis present in the *Catechism* and in the *Directory* to be properly seen and appreciated, in order to avoid over-hasty productions of local catechisms, which would then lack the organic vision of a catechesis inspired by the pedagogy of God.

72 *Paradiso*, XXXIII, 85–90.

From this vision, held in "one single light," there follows the process of setting it forth in time, in parts and in sequence.

The Person

We have seen, then, a number of ways in which catechetical processes are to be "staged" and "progressive" for the sake of an authentic communication of content, following the pedagogy of God. We can turn now to the question of the learner and how catechesis must also be progressive and in stages for his sake.

In the case of an ordering that is suited to those receiving catechesis, what needs to be born in mind here is an appropriate presentation moving from what is most accessible for the learner and gradually building to what is more difficult. So, for example, when studying Scripture, Augustine counsels beginning with the more familiar texts and with those whose meaning is reasonably clear, "for the more one learns about these things the more capable of understanding he becomes."[73] Building from what is securely known makes one more capable of taking the next step.

This movement of systematic and gradual building is certainly one that needs to be undertaken in the area of intellectual formation, so that steps of understanding are progressively put in place. This developmental approach, moreover, goes wider than simply the intellectual formation of the person; it needs to embrace the whole of the person.[74] The stages are ordered for the sake of the person as a whole: they take cognizance of the different dimensions of the person, so that they are attuned to an adequate anthropology that understands and encompasses all aspects: will, intellect, affections and passions, judgments and spirit. The stages also take account of the relational nature of the person: catechesis is "rooted in inter-personal relations" (GDC 143), and in wider friendships, associations and communities, especially the family and the parish.[75]

---

73 *De Doctrina Christiana* II, IX, 12. The danger of moving too quickly, he points out, is that if we meet a point that appears obscure to us "we feel as though we are wiser than it is." We react to the lack of immediate comprehension by dismissing wisdom and leaving our own original understanding in place. Thus, we never progress in learning. In this situation we need to ask for the gift of piety so that "we should rather think and believe that which is written to be better and more true than anything which we could think of by ourselves, even when it is obscure." (*De Doctrina Christiana* II, VII, 9). Augustine is writing here of the Scriptures, of course; he is not proposing that we think anything obscure more true than our own thoughts. What is written elsewhere may simply be obscure because it is confused or mistaken.

74 We can recall here the wider context of the conversion of the whole person, and that catechesis itself is placed as a "moment," of systematic initiation, into a progressive movement which the Church terms "evangelization" and which features the three key stages of initial proclamation of the Gospel; catechesis; and on-going formation (see GDC 60–72).

75 Groome rightly says that the pedagogy of God "seems appropriate to such holistic intent." (T. Groome, "Total Catechesis/Religious Education: A Vision for Now and Always," in T. Groome and H.D. Dorrell, *Hopes and Horizons*, 26).

The notion of stages of progressive enlightenment was used as a major structuring principle for the early Fathers (GDC 89). So, for example, Clement of Alexandria's *Paedagogus* is one of three works—*The Exhortation to the Heathen, Paedagogus,* and *Stromata* ('miscellanies')—which are best conceived as a trilogy, and which themselves indicate "progressive stages" in the journey of Christian growth. The common theme and center of the three works is that of the Word, the Son, and the three can be placed in chronological order, following the passage of the person in his journey from paganism to a fully mature Christian discipleship. *The Exhortation to the Heathen* is an apologetic work, aiming to reveal the essential bankruptcy of pagan religion so as to provide a general appeal to conversion. At the same time, it shows a commitment to the idea that there are "seeds of the Word" present in all religions and religious practices. The journey can take its starting point from these "seeds."

Paedagogus follows this, treating of the process of conversion itself and the training and formation of the person who has been attracted to the Word and now wishes to place himself under the Word's tutorship. The basic theme of the *Paedagogus* is the formation of the whole person so that he can take on the discipline of Christ. It functions as a guide for the new convert to the Christian faith, placing him securely under Christ the Pedagogue. It comprises three books. The first focuses on Christ the true Pedagogue, His person, aims, methods and means; His character, faithfulness, graciousness and goodness. It also examines why Christ's goodness is compatible with His apparent severity and His system of punishments. The second and third books then present detailed guidelines for living according to Christ so that the Pedagogue and His principles might shape the whole of one's life. The topics Clement covers here include walking, sleeping, laughter, and the general care of the body.

The work of Christ the Pedagogue is related to questions of anthropology in the opening section of the work.[76] Here, Clement argues that the Pedagogue is concerned differently with human *habits*, human *actions*, and human *passions*, and that these correspond to three different modes of address to us used by the Pedagogue— the exhortatory, the prescriptive, and the persuasive. In order to establish us in good habits, the Pedagogue seeks to rouse us to faith through an exhortatory form of address, to lead us to embrace certain dispositions. Then, in order to provide a set of structuring principles for our actions, the Pedagogue provides us with commandments, stabilizing our discipleship and placing it within secure boundaries. Finally,

---

76 Paedagogus I, 1.

to provide us with an ongoing healing of our passions, the Pedagogue employs the art of persuasion in order to convince us to embrace the life of Christ in its fullness.

Finally, *Stromata* examines a range of questions broadly in the area of developing true Christian wisdom and is aimed against Gnostic variants that would tempt new converts into a spiritual elitism, derived from a false notion of spiritual illumination, into a way of life reliant upon a false intellectualism and characterized by a separation between the intellectual and the broader human and spiritual dimensions of the Christian way. True Christian wisdom, Clement argues here, consists in following and in sharing in the life of the Word who was made flesh and who shared in humanity, so that the things of the flesh are not unspiritual or to be despised on account of their fleshliness. The stages of conversion and of catechetical development are, therefore, seen by Clement as stages of growing enlightenment on the path to wisdom.

We find another example of the image of a progressive journey towards true Wisdom in Augustine's *De Doctrina Christiana*. He describes the path to be followed in one place as a gradual movement in understanding, as we progress through the different forms in the hierarchy of being: from bodily to living forms, thence to sentient form, and then to intelligent form. Then in the final movement in understanding, we make the intellectual journey from mutable to immutable Wisdom.[77] Thus we reach at last the end of our journey in the knowledge of the nature of God as infinite Wisdom.

This movement is conceived as a journey of cleansing, undertaken in stages, towards the truth that is God Himself. And Augustine does not consider that the journey can be taken by the intellect in isolation from the whole person; it is the whole man who undertakes the journey towards Wisdom, and he does so through the cultivation of good habits of living:

> Let us consider this cleansing to be as a journey or voyage home. But we do not come to Him who is everywhere present by moving from place to place, but by good endeavor and habits.[78]

Again, he says, "we are on a road which is not a road from place to place but a road of the affections, which was blocked, as if by a thorny hedge, by the malice of our past sin."[79]

---

77 *De Doctrina Christiana* I, VIII, 8.

78 *De Doctrina Christiana* I, X, 10.

79 *De Doctrina Christiana* I, XVII, 16.

Augustine is clarifying that it is not, of course, a literal, physical journey of which he is speaking. And he is also making it clear that he is not a Platonist who believes in letting go either of the affections or of the flesh in this journey towards Wisdom; he seeks rather for their transformation. Those who "war on their bodies as though they were natural enemies" are perverse, he says, for no one hates himself. It is rather that we long for incorruptible bodies and purified affections that desire the highest happiness and good.[80]

Finally, this is not a journey towards Wisdom which man can attempt on his own. Because of the Fall, the pedagogy of God involves Wisdom Himself making Himself "congruous"[81] with our infirmity, appearing in the flesh to weak and fleshly eyes, and applying his "humility as a cure"[82] so that all of our affections and loves "should be directed into that channel into which the whole current of love flows."[83] He joins Himself to the stages of our life, so that we might join ourselves to His.[84]

The Catechumenal Model

Finally, let us examine how this vision for a progressive and gradual communication of Revelation, taking place in stages, found a point of incarnation in a specific catechetical framework and pattern, in what the *Directory* describes as the "catechumenal model" (GDC 129).[85] This model will also enable us to draw attention to a further feature identified in the pedagogy of God, the fact that it uses both "words and deeds."

The *General Directory for Catechesis* identifies, as the model for catechetical activity, the baptismal catechumenate, a model drawn from the patristic period (cf. GDC 90). The baptismal catechumenate is a catechesis for adults who are seeking baptism into the Church. This was the most usual context for catechesis during the patristic time.[86]

---

80 *De Doctrina Christiana* I, XXIV, 24.

81 *De Doctrina Christiana* I, XI, 11.

82 *De Doctrina Christiana* I, XIV, 13.

83 *De Doctrina Christiana* I, XXII, 21.

84 See *Catechism*, no. 518, 521.

85 Vatican II had called for the restoration of the catechumenate. It is most fully expressed in the document on missionary activity, *AG* 14. See also *SC* 66 and *CD* 14.

86 For the single best account of the catechumenate during the patristic period, see E.J. Yarnold, *The Awe-Inspiring Rites of Initiation* (Oxford: Oxford University Press, 1976). Clearly, the way in which the adult baptismal catechumenate should function as a paradigm for all catechesis needs to be flexible depending upon the concrete cultural and social situations in the particular churches. That this catechumenal model is held up as the paradigm, nonetheless, is precisely because it incarnates in a concrete form the "original pedagogy of the faith" which is to inspire all catechetical activity.

This catechumenal model is held up to our attention because it draws together the dimensions of catechetical, pastoral, and liturgical activity into a harmonious whole and, through this, unites the dimensions of the Christian life, the four "pillars" of the Christian faith: doctrine, liturgy, life, and prayer.[87] Thus, the catechumenal model ensures a holistic initiation and development of the person. The catechesis begins with the *narratio* of salvation history, explaining the pedagogical activity of God in the life of His people over time, and it then proceeds to a catechesis on the Creed and the *Our Father*, together with the moral implications of these. Finally, after the "handing over," the transmission, of the Creed and the *Our Father*, it moves onto a sacramental and liturgical catechesis, enabling the interiorizing of the sacraments and an understanding of how the pedagogy of God in the life of grace grounds the whole of life.

In this model of catechesis, which offers a systematic presentation of the mystery of Christ, catechetical activity is understood to be that which follows and supports the work of the divine Pedagogue in the gradual and on-going conversion of the person. "Faith, moved by divine grace and cultivated by the action of the Church, undergoes a process of maturation. Catechesis, which is at the service of this growth, is also a gradual activity."[88] Catechesis, we remember, is given to enable people to be in communion with Christ, so that He can lead them to the Father, as children of the Father, in the Holy Spirit. Catechesis serves and accompanies the work of the divine Pedagogue in this process of opening the person to the possibilities of communion and assists them in understanding "the relationship that the person has with God so that he can make it his own and allow himself to be guided by God" (GDC 139).

The *Directory* speaks of the unity of "deeds and words" in the pedagogy of God,[89] and it is also here that we can see the way in which the baptismal catechumenate functions as a paradigm for all catechetical activity. The uniting of deeds and words refers, of course, primarily to the works and words of God in history, mutually interpreting and explaining each other, through patterns of action and explanation, prophecy and fulfillment. The two come together in the pedagogy of God at the fullness of time, when the Word becomes flesh. It is from this unity of

---

87 These are the structuring principles of both the *Roman Catechism* and the *Catechism of the Catholic Church*.

88 GDC 88. Cf. John Paul on this, describing the "specific character of catechesis": it "has the twofold objective of maturing the initial faith and of educating the true disciple of Christ by means of a deeper and more systematic knowledge of the person and the message of our Lord Jesus Christ" (CT 19). Catechesis serves the maturing of faith in particular through the intellectual formation of the person.

89 *Catechism*, no. 53; cf. GDC 38.

Word and flesh that the sacramental life of the Church flows, illustrating for us the importance of ensuring a liturgical catechesis, where word and deed are held together.[90] The liturgical dimension to the catechumenal model consists in a series of rites that punctuate the "stages" of development[91] through which the person passes in the ongoing work of conversion, providing grace for the next stage of catechesis-supported growth.

The unity of words and deeds is also expressed in the way in which catechetical activity is united to the pastoral activity of the Church, through a holistic care for the person. This principle has its roots in the Church's understanding of Christology—that in Christ, "his words, his parables and his arguments are never separated from his life and his very being" (CT 9). The communication of Revelation requires that "saying" and "doing" are held together. John Paul refers us to the Gospels for a better understanding of this:

> "Jesus began to do and teach" (Acts 1:1)—with these two verbs, placed at the beginning of the book of Acts, Saint Luke links and at the same time distinguishes two poles in Christ's mission. (CT 7)

Jesus' unique authority was recognized both in His teaching and in His pastoral activity.[92] This holistic linking of catechesis to both the liturgical and the pastoral dimensions of the Church's work, incarnating the pedagogy of God working in both words and deeds, assists the person in supporting a truly unified formation.

On a personal level, that of the catechist, the pedagogy of God asks that the catechist be also a "witness," so that teaching and life, words and deeds, flow together in his own person. Put negatively, the catechist's life must not be an obstacle to those on the "journey of faith" (GDC 156); put positively, the Church insists that it is precisely the life of the catechist that is the "soul" of his work.[93] Aware that this ongoing integration of faith and life is the great drama of his own life, since the divine Pedagogue must lead him in an "uninterrupted" conversion[94] for this to take place,

---

90 See *Catechism*, no. 1074. See also *Catechism*, nos. 1084, 1153–1155. On the uniting of catechesis to liturgy see P. de Cointet et al., *The Catechism of the Catholic Church and the Craft of Catechesis*, 113–127.

91 The stages of development are designated as the "pre-catechumenate," the "catechumenate," the period of "purification and enlightenment," and the period of "mystagogy" (see GDC 88, together with the relevant sections of the RCIA for the details of the periods). The threefold account of the stages has also been described, according to its appearance in the apostolic and immediate post-apostolic period, as "kerygma," "catechesis," and "didascalia": see A. Rétif, "Qu'est-ce que le Kérygme?," *Nouvelle Revue Théologique* LXXI (1949), 910–922.

92 See, for example, Mt. 7:29, 9:8.

93 "The charism given to him by the Spirit, a solid spirituality and transparent witness of life, constitutes the soul of every method" (GDC 156).

94 See *Catechism*, no. 1428.

the catechist also seeks to assist those whom he teaches to be aware of this ongoing work of God who restores us and "makes our hearts return to him" (*Catechism*, no. 1432). This involves assisting others in the "reading" of their own lives as a pedagogy in which God "reaches man with his grace and saves him" (*GDC* 152c).

Let us sum up our findings from this overview of the aim and processes of the pedagogy of God which, as we have seen, clearly lays down certain key markers with regard to what we could describe as a "pedagogy of integration" and of a "pedagogy of communion," focusing on the formation of the whole person for the sake of communion. This formation is achieved gradually, and by stages, by God Himself, working in the lives of His creatures, and through the pedagogy of the Church in her pastoral, liturgical, and catechetical dimensions. It encompasses the different dimensions of the person, who is in this way invited to, and enabled for, a new childlikeness, the "maturity of a free son," able to enter into a fullness of communion with others and most fundamentally with the Blessed Trinity.

PART 2

The Pedagogy of God
and the Four Parts of the Catechism

5

Divine Pedagogy and Doctrinal Formation of Catechists

Bishop Richard J. Malone, STL, ThD

It is truly a privilege and, more importantly, a great blessing to have been invited to share in this Amicitia Catechistica as a participant in this Conference on "The Pedagogy of God in Catechesis and Catechist Formation."

In preparation for our conference, I have in recent weeks been reading materials generated over the past few years through the collaboration of Notre Dame De Vie, Maryvale Institute, and Franciscan University. I am grateful for the deepening of my own appreciation of the divine pedagogy as source and model of all catechesis. Thanks to your work together, this central theme of the Magisterium, hitherto underdeveloped, is becoming less of a "hidden jewel," and is being embraced for the constitutive element of catechesis that it is.

Before I offer my brief reflections on the pedagogy of God and the doctrinal formation of catechists, I will indicate to you the lenses through which I view this subject. For many years, I was involved in several of the ministries that this catechetical family represents: parish priest, university chaplain, seminary and college professor of theology and catechetics, archdiocesan catechetical director. The latter was my ministry when in 2000 I was appointed Auxiliary Bishop of Boston. I serve now as Bishop of the Diocese of Portland in Maine, in the northeastern United States—New England, as we call it.

My background in catechetical ministry is pastoral, academic, and administrative. The primary lens through which I now view and approach catechesis is as chief catechist and shepherd of my diocesan church, a role more pastoral and administrative than academic. I mention this to prepare you for the likelihood that you will find my remarks more practical in nature, and perhaps lacking in erudition and scholarly sophistication. Theologian to the Papal Household, I am not. It is enough to be theologian of my own household, a task of an entirely different order!

CATECHIST FORMATION IN GENERAL
IN LIGHT OF THE PEDAGOGY OF GOD

Before I comment on the special topic of doctrinal formation of catechists, just a word on catechist formation in general, speaking of course in the context of catechetical developments in the United States.

Excellent work is being accomplished for the renewal of catechetics in the United States, by Franciscan University, which has taken a prophetic leadership role and, I must humbly say, by the United States Conference of Catholic Bishops. I regret to report, however, that in my judgment, the wisdom and inspiration of the divine pedagogy as source and model of catechesis has not yet become the prevailing vision. Many, if not most of the faithful, generous disciples who are doing the work of catechesis have not yet been steeped in—or even exposed to—the rich broth of the pedagogy of the Faith. There is often thus a deficit, a staleness, in their approach to catechesis, a defect that frustrates—but surely does not thwart—the initiatives of the divine Pedagogue. We must do better, much better.

A recent example may help to elucidate my assertion that we in the U.S. have, in the work of renewing catechesis, many "miles to go" before we sleep, to quote American poet Robert Frost.

I currently serve as chairman of the United States Bishops' Committee on Evangelization and Catechesis. This committee, under the leadership of its previous chairman, Archbishop Donald Wuerl of Washington, DC, labored for several years to publish a resource intended to strengthen the catechesis of adolescents in both Catholic secondary schools and parish youth ministry and catechetical programs. The genesis of our work was a report given several years ago by the United States Conference of Catholic Bishops' sub-committee charged with reviewing catechetical texts for conformity with the *Catechism of the Catholic Church*. I reviewed a number of texts myself. The majority of secondary level texts—for adolescents—were sadly deficient. That report sounded the alarm that triggered a major commitment on the part of the U.S. bishops to improve the situation of biblical and doctrinal catechesis for our teenagers.

In 2007, our committee produced and published, with the unanimous vote of the Episcopal Conference, the resource document *Doctrinal Elements of a Curriculum Framework for the Development of Catechetical Materials for Young People of High School Age*—quite a mouthful! This document is totally based on the *Catechism of the Catholic Church* and is Christocentric from beginning to end.

Most importantly, it is intended not only for the effective communication of "information" about the Faith, but for the evangelizing catechesis that, in response to and in cooperation with the Holy Spirit, would help form hearts and wills, as well as minds, in Christ Jesus and His Gospel. I quote from the introduction:

> The Christological centrality of this framework is designed to form the content of instruction as well as to be a vehicle for growth in one's relationship with the Lord so that each may come to know him and live according to the truth He has given to us. In this way, disciples not only participate more deeply in the life of the Church but are also able better to reach eternal life with God in heaven. (Introduction, para. 1)

The document's primary audiences are catechetical publishers and those responsible for overseeing catechetical instruction, curriculum development, and assessment within dioceses. Obviously, this resource—a promising one that will assist the pedagogy of the Faith with teens—is a tool only, an instrument.

Now to the reason I mention this new document to you. Almost immediately upon its publication, a veteran, popular and much published American Jesuit, with many decades of experience teaching the Faith in Catholic secondary schools and colleges, and a frequent conference keynoter, objected in strident terms to our document. Basically, he judged it to be theologically sound, but pedagogically/catechetically weak, quite hopeless, in fact. Our committee was given the draft of his article, which was to be published with some revision in the autumn of 2009 in the American Jesuit weekly magazine *America*. The original proposed title reveals the author's basic problem, which is the bifurcation of content and method that an authentic doctrinal catechesis rooted in the divine pedagogy-inspired catechesis of the Faith would identify and correct. Here is the proposed title: "The Bishops and High School Catechetics: Indoctrination (Brainwashing) vs. Persuasion (Conversion)."[1] You see immediately the ominous sign: The word "versus" says it all, caricaturing doctrinal catechesis as "indoctrination"—bad enough—and then as "brainwashing."

---

1   The article, by William O'Malley, S.J., was published as, "Faulty Guidance: A New Framework for High School Catechesis Fails to Convince," *America*, vol. 201, no. 6 (Sept 14, 2009). A response to this article was made by Father Alfred McBride, O.Praem. in "Sturdy Framework," *America*, vol. 201, no. 7 (Sept 28, 2009).

I think a few minutes of discussion right now would unearth several better words for "conversion" than "persuasion"—although persuasion is surely a valid educational dynamic, properly understood and correctly engaged. Our commentator-critic seems to be at some distance from the vision of catechesis inspired by the *General Directory for Catechesis* and so fruitfully developed by your collaboration, where one finds no tolerance for false dichotomies between content and method, personal and propositional.

PEDAGOGY OF GOD IN THE
DOCTRINAL FORMATION OF CATECHISTS

I will approach this theme by making some points, none of them unique insights, about what I believe to be the basic and essential building blocks for a proper formation for catechists in light of the divine pedagogy that inspires and shapes our ministry.

l. We Are Created for Communion with God

My doctoral work is in catechetics, my STL in systematic theology, my master's in Old Testament. I regret not a minute of my studies. I admit, though, that I occasionally think that if I had to begin graduate studies again, I would do more work in Patristics. Irenaeus is a favorite of mine. Consider his remarkable statement, which I will paraphrase rather than quote: "God created us so as to have something on whom to confer His love." It's all about love, all about communion. As I often say to young people to make this point, God who is love created us so as to have a beloved! And so, I tell them, "we are by God's grace 'wired' for God, for relationship with Him, Father, Son, and Holy Spirit."

What a consolation, an exhilaration, a reason for hope and joy in our ministry when we read at the very beginning of the *Catechism* these stunning words: "The desire for God is written in the human heart, because man is created by God and for God; and never ceases to draw man to himself" (*Catechism*, no. 27).

The *Catechism* goes on to say that the invitation to converse with God is addressed to us as soon as we come into being. Karl Rahner, in a popular rendering of his notion of the "supernatural existential," would say that we are, by God's creative design, made "hearers of the Word." We are created with a kind of spiritual "sonar system."

The challenge that we and our catechists face is also noted in the *Catechism*: "This 'intimate and vital bond of man to God' (GS 19.1) can be forgotten, and overlooked, or even explicitly rejected by man" (*Catechism*, no. 29). Even then, though, the divine pedagogy reminds and reassures us that grace is always present, at least as an offer. The "Hound of Heaven" never rests.[2]

As we can see from Jesus' dialogue with the Samaritan woman at the well, told in John chapter 4, the catechetical opportunity is often, perhaps most of the time, a matter of awakening people to their thirst for God, for Christ, for the truth of the Gospel and the Church's rich doctrinal tradition. And never may we forget the working of grace in men's and women's, boys' and girls' hearts, attuning them to the voice of the Good Shepherd as He calls them to follow Him.

2. Theology of Revelation and Its Transmission

Doctrinal formation for catechists like catechesis itself must be deeply rooted in the Church's doctrine of divine Revelation. The key here, of course, is *Dei Verbum*, Vatican II's Dogmatic Constitution on Divine Revelation, and its articulation of Revelation as both God's gracious self-communication to us in love inviting us to communion with Him, and as the divine Pedagogue's gradual communication in word and deed of His plan for our salvation—what we need to know in order to grow in holiness, to be saved, that plan fully revealed in the Incarnation, the Paschal Mystery, and the sending of the Holy Spirit who opens minds and hearts to the divine Word.

It is essential that catechists be formed in an authentic understanding that there is one common *source* of Revelation, and that it is expressed in the two distinct *modes* of Scripture and Tradition.

Catechesis must be steeped in the truth that "sacred Scripture is the word of God inasmuch as it is consigned to writing under the inspiration of the divine Spirit," and that "sacred tradition hands on in its full purity God's word, which was entrusted to the apostles by Christ the Lord and the Holy Spirit." The successors of the apostles, the bishops, "may in proclaiming it preserve this word of God faithfully, explain it, and make it more widely known" (*DV* 9).

Related to and flowing from this truth is the fact that the *depositum fidei* given to the Church by the divine Pedagogue, that doctrine that attracts our minds and hearts in their longing for truth, beauty, and goodness, is entrusted to the whole

---

2 For this image of the divine Pedagogue as a "Hound of Heaven," see the famous poem of that name by Francis Thompson in *The Hound of Heaven and Other Poems*, with an introduction by G.K. Chesterton, (Wellesley MA: Branden Books, 1978).

Church, even if in a particular way to the Church's Magisterium, for safeguarding, interpreting, proclaiming, and living.

There can be no authentic doctrinal catechetical formation apart from these fundamental affirmations. In practical terms, these foundational elements, set by *Dei Verbum* and expressing the age-old *sensus fidei* of the Church, form the proper context and reliable basis on which catechists, responding to the inner promptings of the Holy Spirit, are drawn gradually deeper into the mysteries of faith, indeed, the very mystery of God. These basic elements also help them come to embrace their role as chosen participants in the dialogue with God, which the great Christian story—Scripture and Tradition—announces, and to which all are invited, and into which Christians by virtue of Baptism are received.

The authors of *The Catechism of the Catholic Church and the Craft of Catechesis* call for a learning and teaching of the Faith as a "living whole ... a call derived from the intrinsic nature of the Faith itself." They refer to Alasdair MacIntyre's assessment in his masterful work, *After Virtue*, of the fragmentation in ethical theory that robs that theory of its unity. "What we possess ... are fragments of a conceptual scheme, parts of which now lack those contexts from which their significance derived."[3] MacIntyre warns, "it is our lack of consciousness of this which constitutes part of our predicament."[4]

The authors of *The Craft of Catechesis* draw a parallel with the "comparable loss (that) has occurred in catechetics," noting that "the loss in much catechetical work of an 'overall framework' and 'overarching picture' of the world, has been particularly destructive."[5] This is true of Scripture. It is true of the Creed.

In an essay entitled "On Taking the Creed Seriously," Luke Timothy Johnson, not without critics on some of his opinions, makes a strong argument. "The creed constructs a vision of the world as created and saved by God, guides the reading of the scriptures that reveal such a vision, and provides the basis for practices consistent with that vision."[6] Take seriously the creed, he demands. And he is right.

Too many of the good people who want generously to respond to the call to catechetical ministry lack a holistic, organic knowledge of the Faith, of even the

---

3   Pierre de Cointet, Barbara Morgan, and Petroc Willey, *The Catechism of the Catholic Church and the Craft of Catechesis*, (San Francisco: Ignatius Press, 2008), 2.

4   Alasdair MacIntyre, *After Virtue* (London: Duckworth, 1985), 263.

5   MacIntyre, *After Virtue*, 3.

6   Luke Timothy Johnson, "On Taking the Creed Seriously," *Handing on the Faith: The Church's Mission and Challenge*, ed. Robert P. Imbelli (New York: Crossroad, 2006), 72.

basics of the great narrative of God's saving dialogue with humankind as it is pro-claimed in Scripture and Tradition, celebrated in sacrament, witnessed in gospel living, and nourished by prayer. Consider this essay that appeared a couple of years ago in the *New York Times Sunday Magazine*, in which Michael Handler, at the time an undergraduate at Yale University, characterizes his generation as a "post-everything generation."

> A true post-modern generation, we refuse to weave together an over-arching narrative to our own political consciousness, to present a cast of inspirational or revolutionary characters on our public stage, or to define a specific philosophy. We are a story seemingly without direc-tion or theme, structure or meaning.[7]

Our conviction, on the contrary, is that indeed there is an "overarching narrative," and we don't weave it ourselves—we are invited to enter it by the divine Pedagogue and so, to make it our own. There is indeed a "cast of inspirational or revolutionary characters"—we meet them in Scripture, the canonized saints, and the holy men and women of our own time—and we do have a "specific philosophy," handmaid, of course, to a specific theology rooted in Revelation that surely gives "direction, theme, structure and meaning to our lives." And we create none of it! It is God's work, God who opens our ears and our hearts to receive it.

3. The "Symphony" of the Faith: Organic and Personal

The *Catechism of the Catholic Church*, declared John Paul II in his Apostolic Exhortation *Fidei Depositum*, is offered to the Church for the renewal of catechesis "at the living sources of faith" … "a very important contribution to that work of renewing the whole life of the Church, as desired and begun by the second Vatican Council."[8]

In our work of reviewing catechetical texts, the U.S. Bishops received an interim report in June of 1997 from Archbishop Daniel Buechlein, then chairman of the committee responsible for the review. He identified a number of serious defi-ciencies found consistently in catechetical texts. I offer just a few examples:

- an impoverished presentation of grace and of the divine initiative—im-plied Pelagianism.

---

7 *New York Times Magazine* (September 30, 2007).
8 Pope John Paul II, *Fidei Depositum*, I.

- incomplete, even absent, eschatology, with many texts saying little or nothing about the "last things."
- a tendency to present the sacraments more as mere human celebrations than as the work of the Holy Spirit, making things "happen" in our encounter with the Risen Christ.
- a Christological imbalance, with too strong an emphasis on the humanity of Christ (Jesus as "my friend," "my brother," which, of course, He is), with a weak presentation of His divinity.

The United States Conference of Catholic Bishops' review of catechetical texts for conformity with the *Catechism* has triggered a true renewal of the texts used in the United States. They are much better than they were. The continuing challenge is that many catechists themselves grew to adulthood at a time when the catechesis they received was hardly deserving of the name, and when the texts used were defective, even harmful to the Faith. At the same time the methodologies, to which they were too often subjected, were shallow and deformative of faith.

An authentic, systematic, organic treatment of the entire symphony of faith, built upon the four pillars of the *Catechism*, is a *sine qua non* element in the doctrinal formation of catechists. "*Nemo dat quod bon habet.*" The symphony of faith breaks down if any "movement," "phrase," or even a "single note" is altered or deleted. As Pope Paul VI wrote in *Evangelii Nuntiandi*, the Roman Pontiff together with the world's episcopate is responsible for "preserving unaltered the content of the Catholic faith which the Lord entrusted to the apostles ... it must remain the content of the Catholic faith just exactly as the ecclesial Magisterium has received it and transmits it" (*EN* 65).

At the same time, and just as importantly, the catechist and those they would catechize, must learn to internalize the wisdom of the *Catechism* when it describes the Church's dogmas as "lights along the path of faith," thus highlighting the "organic connection between our spiritual life and the dogmas" (*Catechism*, no. 89). This point is treated compellingly in the chapter by Willey et al. entitled "A Personal Pedagogy: Teaching the Living Realities of the Faith."

> We are called, then, to know the truths of the faith, and to know them as truths belonging to the Truth, who is a person. Knowledge of Jesus as the Truth sets us free (John 8:32), and knowledge of doctrine as personal sets catechesis free.[9]

---

9 Pierre de Cointet et al., *The Catechism of the Catholic Church and the Craft of Catechesis*, 45.

For doctrinal formation of catechists to be truly faithful to the pedagogy of the Faith, they must learn gradually to "connect the dots," we might say, between the propositions of the Church's doctrine and their own lives as they live them in friendship with Christ.

I was describing the theme of our conference and of this presentation to a friend who is a professor of homiletics and director of spiritual formation at a seminary in the States. As he listened to my explanation of the pedagogy of God as it defines and inspires catechesis, he observed that the divine pedagogy is also a defining and inspirational principle for the work of homiletics and spiritual direction. Both, he noted, are about helping others to become open, receptive, and responsive to the Spirit who dwells in our hearts. It is a matter of cooperation with the Holy Spirit in establishing the conditions for receptivity to an encounter with Jesus Christ. In the words of Benedict XVI in *Deus Caritas Est*, "being Christian is not the result of an ethical choice or a lofty idea, but the encounter with an event, a person, which gives life a new horizon and decisive direction."[10]

In light of this encounter with the Lord, which the catechist assists humbly as one standing on holy ground, the teaching of Scripture and Tradition must be presented so as to invite what Cardinal Newman called "real assent," assent that touches the person, rather than "notional assent," which can be simply assent to an abstraction. I believe, though, that Newman would agree that even notional assent could constitute a grace–born step toward faith.

There is much more to be said in depth and in breadth about the doctrinal formation of catechists in light of the pedagogy of God. I will conclude with a reference to the post-synodal apostolic exhortation of John Paul II, *Pastores Dabo Vobis*. While the Pope's exhortation concerns the 1990 Synod on the formation of priests in the circumstances of the present day, I would argue that the four areas identified as essential to priestly formation can by extension be applied to catechist formation, doctrinal and otherwise.

These four pillars are, of course, human, spiritual, intellectual, and pastoral formation. Note a few of the assertions made about the formation of priests and see if they might not also apply to those not ordained who are called to the ministry of catechesis. In each case, replace the reference to "priest" with "catechist."

---

10 Benedict XVI, *Deus Caritas Est*, (Washington, D.C.: USCCB Publishing, 2006), para. 3.

HUMAN FORMATION

"[I]t is important that the priest should mold his human personality in such a way that it becomes a bridge and not an obstacle for others in their meeting with Jesus Christ." ... "Of special importance is the capacity to relate to others ... this demands that the priest not be arrogant, or quarrelsome, but affable, hospitable, sincere in his words and heart, prudent and discreet, generous and ready to serve."[11]

SPIRITUAL FORMATION

"First there is the value and demand of 'living intimately united' to Jesus Christ. Our union with the Lord Jesus, which has its roots in baptism and is nourished with the Eucharist, has to express itself and be radically renewed each day."[12] ... "Christians expect to find in the priest not only a man who welcomes them, who listens to them gladly and shows a real interest in them, but also and above all a man who will help them turn to God, to rise up to him."[13]

INTELLECTUAL FORMATION

"In reflecting maturely upon the faith, theology moves in two directions. The first is that of the study of the word of God: the word set down in holy writ, celebrated and lived in the living tradition of the Church, and authoritatively interpreted by the Church's magisterium. ... The second direction is that of the human person, who converses with God: the person who is called 'to believe,' 'to live,' 'to communicate,' to others the Christian faith."[14]

PASTORAL FORMATION

"Pastoral study and action direct one to an inner source, which the work of formation will take care to guard and make good use of: this is the ever-deeper communion with the pastoral charity of Jesus."[15]

The bottom line: We are created for communion with God, Father, Son, and Holy Spirit. God graces us with invitation and welcome, shows us the way and gives us the means to go there. The divine Pedagogue is powerfully, lovingly at work. We are His co-operators in that work.

---

11 *PDV* 43.
12 *PDV* 46.
13 *PDV* 67.
14 *PDV* 54.
15 *PDV* 57.

CONCLUSION

I conclude with a story. When I was a very young priest, I came to know a very old priest who lived in a residence for the elderly. I would visit him every week and came to enjoy my conversations with him.

One day, I asked him, "What is it that you fear most as you grow older?" He thought for a moment, and then said, "What I fear most is that I would ever lose my ability to see." Completely misunderstanding his meaning, I said, "I have an excellent ophthalmologist. I will get you an appointment with him and take you to his office." The old priest just gently laughed and said, "No, no, my eyes are fine. What I fear most is that I would ever lose my ability to see as God would have me see—to see the world, other people, myself, even God Himself, as God would have me see."

Let's pray for one another, and for our catechists, that we may have what Tertullian called "grace-healed eyes," eyes of the heart formed in love and truth that will allow us to see as God—our divine Pedagogue—would have us see. Then, with His grace, we may fully appreciate the mystery of our own discipleship, and confidently carry out our ministry as co-operators with the Holy Spirit in the holy work of making disciples for Jesus Christ.

6

Divine Pedagogy in Christian Initiation

Rev. Manuel del Campo Guilarte

At the beginning of this exposition on the pedagogy of God in Christian initiation, allow me briefly to sketch some basic points on the nature of Christian initiation. As we know, it concerns the insertion of a candidate into the mystery of Christ, dead and risen, and into the Church, by means of faith and the sacraments. The Catechism of the Catholic Church refers to Christian initiation as the "sharing in the divine nature" which is realized by means of the three sacraments of initiation (see Catechism, nos. 1212 and 1275). This insertion into the mystery of Christ is united to a catechetical itinerary, since, as the General Directory for Catechesis affirms, "catechesis is a fundamental element of Christian initiation and is closely connected with the sacraments of initiation" (GDC 66).

Indeed, in Christian initiation a person, helped by divine grace, responds freely and generously to the Word of God, to the gift of God; he follows a way of liberation from sin, experiences the joyful reality of the encounter with Christ, and grows in the Faith until he comes to sit at the table of the Eucharist. Through this itinerary of initiation, the Church accomplishes its maternal function of giving life to the children of God.

Now, Christian initiation signals, and to a certain point it defines, the model or paradigm of present-day catechesis. It does so in such a way that choosing, as the pastors of the Church did, to promote and consolidate the renovation of the pastoral care of Christian initiation in the Church of today, means by the same token making a decision for a specific model of catechesis: a catechesis with a catechumenal character, at the service of Christian initiation. The task of making new Christians is hereby brought to the fore and Christian initiation becomes the main pastoral objective.

This means that catechesis is focused not so much on the task of educating in the Faith that one already professes (even when it is fragile and elemental), as on arousing faith; a catechesis which is directed not so much towards the maintenance of the Faith and of a Christian life, but directed first to the task of making new Christians. For this reason, it is a catechesis that attends to the birth of faith and to the laying down of the foundations of the spiritual life in the Christian. This is the catechesis of Christian initiation. As we know, a catechesis of this nature is given in the *General Directory for Catechesis* when the Church proposed making a new and determined effort in present-day catechesis (GDC 65–69).

For the pedagogy of God in Christian initiation there are various areas or levels that must be considered and differentiated. We can note the three descriptive levels.

The *first level* is that of **general principles and criteria**, which are based firmly on the action of God in history. These principles provide the great pedagogical axis with their roots plunged in the pedagogy of God, that is, in the original and effective pedagogy of God during the history of salvation and in God's benevolent actions towards mankind. It is, in fact, a question of discovering and developing the theological foundations of catechetical pedagogy that, as such, must inspire and configure the whole of the pedagogy of faith. This is the first level or area of reference and it constitutes, as its historical and essential core, the fundamental doctrinal basis of catechetical pedagogy. The *General Directory for Catechesis* refers to this first level in the first chapter of part 3 where, as we have seen, the basic principles are presented which inspire and demand a wider and purer systematic development.

The *second level* to be considered is that of **the pedagogical lines of action** to promote and articulate the pedagogical processes of the catechesis of Christian initiation. These are the pedagogical elements of the itinerary of faith in Christian initiation. They are the constitutive and operative components that should be considered in the planning of *concrete programs* for Christian initiation. By this I mean a development from the initial core (level 1) with a view to concrete action, but in an explicitly pedagogical manner. By this, the practical dimension becomes more visible, since it incorporates the concrete reality of those to whom we wish to: a) transmit the Faith of the Church and b) accompany on their way to their encounter with Christ.

The *third level* of this "corpus" of the pedagogy of faith in Christian initiation refers, in my mind, to **the action of catechesis** and contains the process of shaping concrete procedures and specific educational actions using catechetical media and materials, didactic methodologies proper to the communication of the Faith, and the putting into action of the very act of catechizing.

These three levels or areas of reference which constitute the pedagogical body of the catechesis of Christian initiation must maintain between themselves a relationship which is both intimate and necessary, even when discussion of them must be isolated for methodological reasons.

The thoughts that I now propose pertain to the **second level** and refer to it explicitly. Naturally, I do not pretend to exhaust all its contents. I shall only consider one of the dimensions that, in my mind, is of great importance; the itineraries of faith in Christian initiation. This is a question, which has great importance in my country, and must be given some clarification, since the correct order of the processes of initiation depends on the way this is seen and understood. I shall also try to offer suggestions for the elaboration and development of the educational programming of the itineraries of Christian initiation. This, then, is the precise objective of my contribution here.

I want to warn you that the statements and proposals that I present here take their foundations and inspiration from the content of the first level that I refer to above. That is, in the general principles and criteria that should sustain all the developments and processes of the pedagogy of faith.

AN ITINERARY OF FAITH IN CHRISTIAN INITIATION

What is the itinerary of faith in Christian initiation, and what does it consist of? What do we mean by "itinerary of faith" in Christian initiation?

As we know, Christian initiation, which is an event of grace and constitutive of the proper identity of the Christian through his insertion into the mystery of Christ, has been understood by the Church from its very beginning as a "process" or "journey" of faith through which one becomes a Christian, a process which presupposes a progressive advance on the journey of faith. The *Catechism of the Catholic Church* refers to Christian initiation in this way:

> From the time of the apostles, becoming a Christian has been accomplished by a journey and initiation in several stages. The journey can be covered rapidly or slowly, but certain essential elements will

always have to be present: proclamation of the Word, acceptance of the Gospel entailing conversion, profession of faith, Baptism itself, the outpouring of the Holy Spirit, and admission to Eucharistic communion. (*Catechism*, no. 1229)

That is, the *Catechism* speaks clearly of a journey of faith, focused on proclamation of the Word and on the listening and welcoming of it by someone, which leads that person to conversion to, and profession of, the Faith, and to the reception of the gift of salvation through the sacraments. In other words, the perspective of progression along the journey of faith is accentuated. This same idea was taken by the Spanish bishops in their Instruction on *Christian Initiation: Reflections and Orientations*, speaking of the dynamic character of initiation as an itinerary of faith. In another, later text, *Pastoral Orientations for the Catechumenate*, the bishops were even more explicit: "Christian initiation will be done gradually by means of a liturgical, catechetical and spiritual itinerary, as a way of conversion which develops within the Christian community, making stages through which one progresses towards the faith" (no. 12).

In this sense, one must define the process, or itinerary, of Christian initiation as a way of progressive participation in the mystery of salvation, developing knowledge of the mystery of God and a progressive advance, with the grace of God and the help of the Church in the following of Christ.

The model for the journey is the history of salvation, the history of the presence and love of God, and of the faith response on the part of mankind; a historical framework in which the event of the Revelation of God and the dialogue of salvation take place; a history, finally, which is shown to be the itinerary of faith of a *whole people*, and which would culminate in the Covenant, in the paschal event of Jesus Christ.

Today, as always, God continues to act through words, events, and the intervention of grace, in the personal history of men and women, in order to lead them to participate in the Paschal Mystery of Christ and in their incorporation into His people, which is the Church.

In the light of the history of salvation we can understand the nature of Christian initiation as a progressive movement, through the action of the Holy Spirit, towards an encounter with Christ and transformation into Him, as a process of a maturating and perfecting in the Faith. This reality should inspire and direct any pastoral program of Christian initiation, its objectives and lines of action.

In the same way, it should define the itineraries or concrete processes of Christian initiation programs, which are to be put in place at the service of this event that is Christian initiation.

ITINERARIES OF CHRISTIAN INITIATION

Let us take one more step. The itinerary of faith, an event of grace and freedom, which is the soul of Christian initiation, must be considered, on the one hand, as a personal reality that follows the cadence and rhythm of each person. In this sense we may say that each itinerary of faith is, in a certain way, unique and personal inasmuch as it expresses the personal relationship between God and a particular human being.

But on the other hand, the itinerary of faith can and must be driven, ordered, and organized in a catechetical manner, precisely in order to be at the service of this dialogue of salvation between God and man. That is, we must drive the progression in the Faith pedagogically, both in accompanying the person and in the orientation of the itinerary of faith of those being initiated, which constitutes Christian initiation.

This way of understanding the "itinerary" of faith becomes a helpful catechetical tool; a pedagogical proposal for accompaniment and guidance; a structure of orientation that drives the progressive search for, the welcome of, and encounter with the Lord on the way to Easter.

At any rate, we must not identify or confuse what is a helpful catechetical and pedagogical tool, which always retains its relative and adaptable character, with the essential and basic reality that the itinerary of faith mentioned above brings about, and which is the constitutive element of the process of Christian initiation. This itinerary of faith is substantive and always necessary in Christian initiation; the other is only a tool at its service, as a concrete and possible process that may be pastorally convenient according to the specific circumstances and situations of those who are being initiated. In practice many use the same expression (itinerary of faith) for each of those two aspects; we must remember that each keeps its distinct nature and identity and for this reason must be differentiated.

The itinerary (or itineraries) of Christian initiation, when we see it as a helpful tool, is at the service of the dialogue of salvation between God and each concrete person; it is configured as a possible way for discovery of, and maturation in, the Faith, with the help of a catechist and of the Christian community; it is ordered to driving forward and enabling an encounter with Christ and insertion in His mystery of salvation and in the Church by means of faith and the sacraments.

PASTORAL FUNCTIONS IN CHRISTIAN INITIATION

We enter now upon the description of the itineraries of Christian initiation, and consider first some of their dimensions, which are pastoral functions that the Church cannot do without in Christian initiation.

We do this by considering again those dimensions referred to above, and which are proper to the itinerary of faith as much as to the itineraries of Christian initiation or the catechetical processes at the service of Christian initiation. The first thing to remember is that initiation is achieved *gradually*. The second is that it is achieved through an effective progression, which is all at once *catechetical, liturgical, and spiritual*.

We refer first of all to the gradual movement of initiation. Among other documents, the *Rite of Christian Initiation for Adults* (1–40), the *General Directory for Catechesis* (88–89), and the Spanish Bishops' document *Christian Initiation: Reflections and Orientations* (24–31) show this gradual process, marked as we know by stages, times, and levels. Thus we speak of a pre-catechumenal time given over to missionary proclamation; of a time of catechesis as such; of a time of purification and illumination; of the celebration of the sacraments of Christian initiation as a central moment and reality of the process of initiation; of the time of deepening of the mysteries that have been received, or "mystagogy." We must take into account that this dynamic process, as well as defining the times and stages, demands a specific type or model of catechesis: the catechesis of initiation and no other. We must realize that even today there are areas in catechesis where the catechesis of Christian initiation encounters serious difficulties and resistance, or is simply unknown or ignored as specific field.

But as well as this perspective which is marked by gradualness and a process of on-going maturation and growth in faith, we must refer, as I mentioned above, to the three dimensions and ecclesial functions that configure the itineraries of Christian initiation: catechesis, liturgy, and spiritual and ascetic exercises; or in other words, the catechetical, liturgical, and the spiritual itinerary. These three aspects, articulated organically and inseparably, complement each other. Through them, considered as a whole, the Christian personality of the person who is being initiated will be configured and strengthened.

The Spanish bishops, in their instruction on *Christian Initiation*, refer to these three dimensions as "ecclesial functions" and "pastoral functions" which are intimately related to each other. "Catechesis and liturgy," they affirm, "constitute visible dimensions of the same reality, which is to introduce people into the mystery of Christ and of the Church" (*CI* 39). For this reason, they advise that "we must not lose sight of their intimate complementarity and mutual support" (*CI* 40; cf. *Catechism*, no. 1072).

The person who is being initiated will need a spiritual impulse in order to be able to recognize the gift of God and to live the new life in the Spirit. Since this recognition and welcoming of the gift of God and living of the new life of grace is the heart of Christian initiation, it requires the attention and work of the spirit, of the interior life of the person who is being initiated.

Catechesis: From the Proclamation of the Word to the Profession of Faith

Catechesis is the first of the ecclesial dimensions and functions to be taken into account in the itineraries of Christian initiation. Through catechesis, which is an act of the living tradition, the Church transmits to the catechized the experience that she herself has of the Gospel, her faith, so that they may make it theirs and profess it. For this reason, authentic catechesis is always an ordered and systematic initiation into the Revelation that God made to mankind in Jesus Christ, a Revelation which is kept in the deep memory of the Church and in the Sacred Scriptures and is constantly being communicated, by means of a living *tradition* which is active from generation to generation (cf. *GDC* 66). It includes initiation into the knowledge of the Christian mystery, into the liturgy of the Church and into prayer, and the apprenticeship of the whole of the Christian life, which allows a true following of Jesus Christ and introduces the person to the ecclesial community (cf. *GDC* 67).

Finally, catechesis puts in place the foundations of the spiritual edifice of the Christian, feeds the roots of the life of faith, and enables it to receive the solid food obtained in the ordinary life of the community (cf. *GDC* 67).

The Liturgy: Towards Communion with the Mystery of Christ

The risen Christ Himself, whom catechesis announces, works the salvation of man by means of the liturgy. As *Sacrosanctum Concilium* affirms the liturgy "involves the presentation of man's sanctification under the guise of signs perceptible by the senses and its accomplishment in ways appropriate to each of these signs" (*SC* 7).

The sacraments, which are the work of Christ the Priest and of His Body—the Church—are sacred actions *par excellence* "surpassing all others. No other action of the Church can equal its efficacy by the same title and to the same degree" (*SC* 7). The sacraments of Baptism, Confirmation, and the Eucharist are the fount and summit of Christian initiation (cf. *SC* 10 and *CI* 45).

The celebration of the sacraments of initiation, together with other liturgical celebrations, manifests the bonds that are progressively being formed between those who are being catechized and Christ, at the same time it communicates the salvation that springs from the paschal mystery. For this reason, the spiritual fruit of all the itinerary of salvation, and even the very meaning of the Christian life itself, will depend in large measure on our care and attention in relation to these liturgical celebrations, so that they may be, together with the action of catechesis, true events of the saving encounter with Jesus Christ for those who are being initiated.

In this sense, we must continue to insist on the necessity of coordinating the efforts of theologians and experts in liturgy and in catechesis, in order to develop and propose adequately the explanation of the sense and meaning of liturgical celebrations, as well as their place in the process of initiation and above all, the living reality of their celebration.

The Spiritual Itinerary: The Third Pillar of Christian Initiation

The itinerary of Christian initiation involves a spiritual process of laying down foundations and growing in faith, which must be attended to in each person. Concretely, this means that the spiritual journey through which the person who is being initiated advances includes some important milestones that must be considered in the task of accompanying and guiding him, such as

- initiation in the discovery of the presence and the intervention of God in the realities of life;
- preparing the spirit of the person to learn to recognize and welcome the action of the Holy Spirit, who is the inner Teacher;
- beginning a life of prayer; practicing a Christian ascesis and the adequate use of the goods of this world as an exercise of fighting against evil;
- learning to renounce the various suggestions of idolatry which the cultural and social world of today presents;
- exercising oneself in the service of our brethren; and
- strengthening a firm decision of following the Lord, as a new horizon of life.

It is obvious that, to achieve all of this and to discover the deep meaning contained in the words, interventions and facts of the whole process of faith in Christian initiation, the person who is being initiated will need the testimony of faith, the orientation and the guidance of the catechist and of the Christian community where he is welcomed.

In brief: these three itineraries (catechetical, liturgical, and spiritual), which are irreducibly joined and all act each on the other, must be the object of special consideration and care on the part of those responsible for the pastoral care of Christian initiation. Concretely, they should be taken into account as a whole in the processes of pedagogical programming and development of the catechesis of Christian initiation. The success of any concrete itinerary of faith in Christian initiation depends in great measure on their adequate articulation and careful programming.

VARIABLES IN THE ITINERARIES OF CHRISTIAN INITIATION

Let us now take another step forward, a more specific and operative step, giving us access to the more concrete and also more relative aspects of the itineraries of Christian initiation. I refer to the *variables* in Christian initiation.

In speaking of variables, I refer to those factors that become part of the concrete outline and articulation of the itineraries of Christian initiation; that is, those elements that must be taken into account in a specific catechetical program. I propose some variables here. I should point out that this is an open list, and it may be important to incorporate others.

The Recipients

Throughout the itinerary, we must consider with realism and truth those who are being initiated and who take part in the process that is being undertaken. These people should be considered in the concrete reality of their age and life situation; their mental, affective, and relational capacity; their religious situation and level of faith; their socio-cultural context; their family and work circumstances; and so on; and thus, considering each of those persons individually.

The Objectives

In any growth process, we must establish the orientation and, consequently, the objectives of the process. These objectives must be clear, reachable, and subject to evaluation in reference to the process as a whole, as much as to its successive moments or stages. The concrete specification of the objectives represents in any program a factor of major importance inasmuch as, at this stage, it demands a high degree of definition and precision, since sometimes they will have a more missionary and apologetic character, at other times the dimension of reflection will be accentuated, at times, that of spirituality and interiorization, at others, that of experience or celebration, and so on.

The Contents

We speak here of the order and of the organization of the Christian message; concretely, of the adequate distribution and sequence of the message of faith, of the contents of faith. We must overcome the risk of leaving everything that has to do with the exposition of the Faith in a fog of global and generic formulations. Rather, it is necessary to establish with precision a thematic journey that will propose the truth of the Faith in a sequential and ordered way. That is to say that, since we are dealing here with the programming of the contents of the Faith, we must take into account the pedagogical principles of progression and proportionality, but also those of systematic and organic learning, those of assimilative capacity, of meaning and of adaptation, as well as those of unity and integrity.

Furthermore, in programming the contents of the Faith, we find the possibility of establishing various lines of work: we may follow, for example, the thematic journey which presents the liturgical year and allows us to point out the continuity between the events of the history of salvation and the sacramental signs, between the profession of faith and the participation in the "mysteries." Another journey may be as follows: the apostolic kerygma, which will be developed progressively and in succession in a process of growth and explanation as the person advances, proceeding as in a spiral movement, until it completes, at the end of the process, an integral and united presentation of the Christian message. Another possible way in placing the message concretely within a program could follow the classical itinerary (the symbol of faith, the sacraments, the commandments, prayer) in order to develop it successively and gradually, even while incorporating to it the modifications that may be deemed necessary in their order and to deepen them, according to the concrete circumstances and conditions of those for whom it is meant.

At any rate, we must warn that this presentation of the truth of the Faith has, in its catechetical and pedagogical treatment, its own proper demands which, as we know, are explained quite clearly and extensively in the second part of the *General Directory for Catechesis*, where "the norms and criteria for the presentation of the gospel message in Catechesis" (GDC 97–118) are proposed.

Pedagogical Criteria

It seems also appropriate to offer some references to the pedagogical and methodological approaches that the communication of the Faith demands, according to the age, situation, life, and cultural conditions of those for whom it is meant.

This must also be defined with precision, offering concrete methodological and didactic help for a better development of the process of maturation. At any rate, it must be made evident that the methods and procedures should have the pedagogy of faith and, more deeply still, the pedagogy of God, as their principle of inspiration and their guide.

Liturgical and Sacramental Celebrations

We mean here the definition, firstly, and the adequate programming, afterwards, of the distinct liturgical actions, which integrate Christian initiation. I refer to the rites, celebrations of the Word, scrutinies, handings over, and so on; and above all, to the celebration of the three sacraments of initiation. Whatever the program, we must not forget that the sacraments are the fountain and the summit of Christian initiation and communicate the salvation that springs from the Paschal Mystery. This sacramental centrality must be reflected in the programming of the itineraries in such a way that the celebration of the sacraments is first considered, and then interiorized by those who are being initiated in its entirety, in its salvific meaning, in its value and its substantial reality, and not only in its ritual dimension.

In its turn, the place of celebrations should be specified, as well as their opportune moment, their meaning, and their characteristics. On the other hand, we take into account that we find ourselves in the presence of basic demands that, because of their importance, must be attended to above all, such as the preservation of the unity of the three sacraments and the order of their celebration.

Time and Gradual Development

Time is at the service of the gradual development of the Faith. Indeed, the gradual process of advancement in the Faith, requires that we attend to this variable by establishing with precision the times and stages of the process, that is, the months or years during which this itinerary of initiation, as well as its stages, are expected to last. These stages don't necessarily have to be the same in all itineraries, neither in their identity nor in their duration. As we know, we have a general model to refer to in the *Rite of Christian Initiation for Adults* and in the *General Directory for Catechesis,* which is ratified by other documents of the world's episcopate, for example, the Spanish bishops in their document *Christian Initiation: Reflections and Orientations*.

Now this framework/itinerary can and should be adapted when the circumstances and the situations of those to whom it is directed demands it. Not all itineraries should be identical. Thus, for example, an itinerary of Christian initiation designed for baptized children from six to ten or twelve years of age, can include three stages: a first stage focused on the awakening of the Faith, an interest for the Christian life, the initial knowledge of the Christian mystery leading to an initial adhesion to God; a second stage of discovery and knowledge of Christ in His Word, in the sacraments, in the Gospel life; and a third stage (with a mystagogical character) of consolidation of the Faith through the deepening of the "mysteries" that have been celebrated.

Places and Environments

Another of the variables which are to be taken into account in any program is that of the places and environments where the Church exercises her maternal function in Christian initiation. These are mainly *the parish*, as proper and main environment; *the family*, as institution of origin; *the lay associations and movements, and the Catholic school*, as spaces and subsidiary and complementary means. In my country, we are conscious of the importance of the peculiar contribution of the *teaching of the Catholic religion*, which is given both in public and in private schools. Each of these places and environments where Christian initiation is imparted has both a specific and a complementary character (cf. CI 32). "Although in all those places the Church, the subject of Christian initiation, is present, the parish has this condition of being the ultimate 'localization' of the Church and representing the visible Church which is established throughout the world" (CI 32).

The Catechists

Within the community of the Church, which is the subject and the place of initiation and in whose bosom the new children of God will be brought to life, the catechist is the delegate of this community and, as such, acts in its name. His availability and preparation, his responsibilities and tasks, his individual traits as witness, master, and guide in the Faith, must be considered and put into operation throughout the process of initiation. Because of the need to work within the variables we have been describing, we must insist on the strong Christian and ecclesial identity of the catechist, and on his adequate formation and competence. We must insist also on the cordial welcome and close reception, recognition, and support by the Christian community and especially by those who bear the primary responsibility for the pastoral program of Christian initiation.

Catechisms and Catechetical Materials

It is also necessary that the program should present clearly and precisely the concrete references to catechisms and other catechetical materials. It is not sufficient to make generic reference to these texts.

Correlation with the Education System

There is another variable that, in my country, is considered an important factor to take into account. It is a question of bringing out the points of correlation with the general education system. Given the importance that the education system has in the configuration and the formation of the personality of children and pre-teens, it seems suitable to pay specific attention to this aspect of things, especially as we are talking here of itineraries of initiation where those to whom they are addressed also follow classes on the subject of the Catholic religion at school.

This is, on the one hand, an excellent field for the application *in situ* of the principles of inculturation of the Faith and of the evangelization of culture, as well as an opportunity to respond to the great challenge made nowadays to every believer, given the relationship that our culture establishes between faith and reason, and faith and culture.

Given all of this, and focusing finally on the concrete work of the elaboration of a program for an itinerary of Christian initiation, I offer the following as a possibility for its articulation.

Create a chart, with a horizontal and a vertical axis. The vertical or synchronic axis would include the variables and the factors that I have just explained, while the horizontal or diachronic axis (the succession or development through time) would indicate the stages of the itinerary, signaling thus the evolving or historical dimension of the catechetical process.

CONCLUSION

So, let us conclude these reflections. Any effort or attention that can be given to the development of the itineraries of Christian initiation as pastoral guides and instruments of orientation represent a step forward at the service of the itinerary of faith which is Christian initiation. It is, without a doubt, a necessary and praiseworthy task.

Offering concrete programs of catechetical processes or itineraries which would be pastorally possible in a given situation represents an effort to incorporate little by little the model of catechetical pedagogy, which is proposed in the *General Directory for Catechesis*.

Nevertheless, we should underline that the so-called itineraries of Christian initiation are not an end in themselves, but a means to an end, and for that reason they are relative. Neither the reality of the Faith, nor the action of the Holy Spirit, the interior Master, nor the free response of a person to the Lord, can be enclosed in human categories. We are called only to direct and facilitate the process of faith and its consolidation in those who are being initiated. We are called to do this, and we wish to respond generously as witnesses and servants of the Word and of the Faith of the Church.

Translated by Anne Harriss

7

Divine Pedagogy and Moral Formation in Catechesis

Rev. Wojciech Giertych OP

Let us examine divine pedagogy in relation to moral formation in catechesis. Pedagogy is defined as the science, or rather the art, of being a teacher. It refers to educational strategies and the style of instruction in teaching. The Greek root of the term "pedagogy" refers to children and so we immediately think of the art of teaching children. In correspondence with this term, however, another term "andragogy" has been coined, referring to learning strategies focused on adults. How are adults engaged in the process of learning? The teaching of adults requires different methods than the teaching of children.

This leads us to a fundamental pastoral question: should catechesis be primarily focused on children or should it not rather be focused on adults? An excessive focus on the catechesis of children, particularly in Catholic countries has, as some people clearly see, led to a situation where parents think that the transmission of faith is the task of the priest, the religious sister, or lay catechist, and not necessarily of the parents who focus on making money and other interests. Ultimately such an understanding is disastrous. In Christian antiquity catechesis was primarily focused on adult catechumens as they were preparing for the sacraments of initiation. In completely de-Christianized countries, such as contemporary Russia, if catechesis is to bring any fruit, it has to focus primarily on young adults, on people who are in their early twenties and who are making fundamental decisions about their lives. If they learn how to live their lives in unison with the divine mystery that is accompanying them, they will then take care of the religious formation of their children.

The question we are considering here concerns "divine" pedagogy. How does *God* conduct the process of education leading to a moral formation? Should we try to decipher God's pedagogy, or rather God's andragogy? Is God treating us as adults or as children? Does God want us to behave like adults or like children? What can we learn from the way God has been treating us that will help us in moral catechesis, both when it is addressed to children and to adults?

Happily, the term *paidagogos* appears in Scripture in reference to God's dealing with us. We read in the *Epistle to the Galatians*, the following:

> Now before faith came, we were confined under the law, kept under restraint until faith should be revealed. So that the law was our custodian (*paidagogos*) until Christ came, that we might be justified by faith. But now that faith has come, we are no longer under a custodian; for in Christ Jesus you are all sons of God, through faith. (Gal. 3:23–27)

Saint Paul was reacting to the infiltration into his missionary territory of emissaries sent by the church in Antioch, who were insisting that the neophyte Galatians were to be trained in the requirements, both moral and cultic, of the old Jewish Law. Saint Paul had preached the Gospel to the Galatians, who were a Celtic people living in central Anatolia. They had never been formed in the traditions of the Old Testament, and Paul led them straight from their paganism into the fullness of faith in Christ. The emissaries from Antioch that followed Saint Paul were Christians of Jewish descent, who insisted that Christians of pagan origin had to be initiated first according to the Jewish Law. Saint Paul's Epistle was addressed more to these emissaries than to the Galatians themselves. The question concerned not only the many cultic prescriptions that we find in the Old Testament, but also the moral law of the Old Testament itself, as it is expressed primarily in the Decalogue. In his response Saint Paul described that Law as the *paidagogos*, a term that apparently meant *not* the teacher, but the slave that led the child to school and back home.

Can we therefore conclude that the old moral Law was like a babysitter that was important and necessary in the initial stage of formation of humanity, but that it only led to the moment when the highest relationship to God, as God's adopted sons through faith in Christ Jesus, is recognized? Does divine pedagogy require an initial stage of formation according to an external moral law before leading to a life based on faith, or is it possible to begin directly with the fullness of the Gospel? Or maybe God has various approaches for various people and some people may skip certain stages?

As we reflect on the ways in which God has dealt with humanity, we think of the history of salvation. Whatever God had revealed in the initial stage to which the Genesis story refers, it seems that history began with the economy of the natural law. God did not reveal Himself and His moral teaching all at once. Then through Abraham and Moses God entered into a relationship with one, small, chosen people, revealing to them in stages the high moral standard of His guidance, allowing in great patience that the rest of humanity for centuries, or even millennia, was unable to accept a higher moral ideal. But even the Old Testament is full of brutal wars, mass exterminations, slavery, and polygamy, seemingly with divine approval. The divine education of God's own people was a slow process.

The very special forty-year period in the wilderness was a time of profound formation of the people of God that remained as a memory of God's pedagogical guidance. During this difficult period, the people of God enjoyed their liberation from Egyptian slavery but they did not immediately proceed to the chosen land. In the face of the limitations of life in the desert, they grew to become one people, discovering at the same time their own infidelities and weaknesses, their own lack of trust in God, and finally learning that God was present to them in the midst of their wandering, struggles, hunger, and thirst. It is within this pilgrimage of faith in the desert that the Covenant between the chosen people and God was made and it found its expression in the Law that God revealed to them on Sinai as a sign and seal of their special relationship with Him.

This desert experience was a long period of formation, engineered by God, that covered not only the habituation to the requirements of the moral law and to public social expressions of religiosity in which due reverence was rendered to God, but it was also a period of divine formation of the interiority of the people as they lived out their relationship with God. The memory of this privileged period rings out throughout the Old Testament as a point of reference and return—to a purity of relationship with Him, as it had been pedagogically taught by God Himself in the desert.

Is the historical process, covering not only the desert experience but also the entire history of salvation, from a natural perspective, through a long period of life according to the rules imposed by a revealing God and leading finally towards the fullness of life in Christ, a metaphor of the spiritual and moral journey of each individual?

CATHOLIC MORAL THEOLOGY
MARKED AMONG OTHERS BY AQUINAS

Catholic moral theology has been deeply marked by the vision of Saint Thomas Aquinas, who in his *Summa Theologiae* presents a well-crafted treatise on the moral law. Aquinas preceded his reflection with a general definition of law that is applicable both to the moral law and to various human laws. He began with a reflection on the eternal law that basically is a philosophical construct, located uniquely in the mind of God, as the wise foundation of the objective moral order that is expressed in various manifestations of the moral law.

Aquinas' reflection then moved on to the natural law that is an echo of the eternal law, as perceived by men. By analyzing the innate urge of the practical reason to do good and to avoid evil and applying this intuition to the various metaphysical inclinations—in common with all beings focused on the preservation of their being, in common with all animals focused on the transmission of life and the education of offspring, and in common with all men focused on the search for truth and living in society—the human mind is capable of deducing the basic precepts of the natural law. On their basis, civic societies formulate their human laws.

The search for a fundamental moral orientation that the human mind is capable of undertaking alone is subject, however, to limitations arising from the intellectual capacities of individuals and from distortions caused by disordered passions. The human mind has a dignity as it reaches out to the truth, but that search is prone to error. The Revelation of the moral law in the Old Testament offered humanity, therefore, a God-given support and correction. The Decalogue basically does not supply new moral precepts that are not accessible through a natural law reflection. Divine Revelation, however, supplements these judgments with a divine authority. It strengthens the rational intuition offering certitude, where doubts may appear, and the old Law offers also an eschatological dimension as it leads towards the future Christ.

At the end of his treatise on the moral law, Aquinas gave us a short treatise on the new law that precedes his lengthy discourse about grace. This new law, described also as the law of the Spirit, the law of Christ, the law of liberty, and the law of charity is the law of the Gospel. Aquinas does not describe it as an evangelical law, which would suggest that it consists in the moral exhortations that are only a fragment of the Gospels. The new law is the law of the Gospel, and the term "Gospel" here refers to the entire event: the Incarnation, life, passion, death, and Resurrection of Jesus, His ascension into heaven, and the descent of the Holy Spirit. The new law of the Gospel is, therefore, the summing up of the entire orientation offered to humanity in the new dispensation. It is also, therefore, more than an external teaching.

That which is central and most powerful in the new law is the grace of the Holy Spirit, given through faith in Christ. Indwelling the souls of Christians, the Holy Spirit moves them from within, animating not only their minds but also their wills and hearts. Secondarily, the new law contains also a written element, consisting in the text of the Gospels, and the Sermon on the Mount in particular, and it includes also all the teaching that is offered in the Church, both by official prelates and by parents, educators, and catechists. This teaching, presented orally and in writing, in union with a faith in the accompanying presence of the Holy Spirit, has the double finality of disposing towards the grace of the Holy Spirit and of ordering the use of that grace in various human situations. This teaching in the Church concerns that which is to be believed and that which is to be done. In the agenda are both the administration of the sacraments, through which grace is objectively given, and the application of received grace within moral action. Moral formation in the Church, therefore, consists primarily in such a direction of human action so that the grace of the Holy Spirit may flower within it.

The reception of the teaching of Aquinas in modern centuries, or rather the lack of reception of it caused by distortions originating in fourteenth century nominalism, involved the marginalization of the perspective of the New Law of the Gospel. The presentation of the various types of moral law by Aquinas that is in accord with the sequence of the history of salvation, was combined with the nominalist understanding of divine potency as being in rivalry with the human will. This led simultaneously to *rationalism* and *voluntarism* in moral theology. Instead of presenting the fecundity of grace within human agency, using all the powers of the human mind, the will and the passions without denying their inherent value, moral reflection focused almost uniquely on moral obligation—this was at times presented as being a pure expression of the divine will, at other times presented as having an inherent and therefore demonstrable reasonableness—and on the obedient or disobedient will as it was obliged to fulfill the externally imposed moral obligations. This meant that the prime accent in moral formation consisted in the presentation of the moral norms, and their rational and theological justification together with an expectation of their execution. In this limited vision the reasonableness of the moral norms was presented as deduced philosophically from the natural law, and these conclusions were then supplemented with the divine authority of the Decalogue that confirms the intuitions of the natural law.

Such a presentation seemed to be in conformity with the history of salvation, that is, with divine pedagogy, because it focused on the natural law that corresponds with man's natural capacity for the formulation and understanding of moral dilemmas, and with the Decalogue that has been revealed by God. The perspective of the new law of the Gospel, of the Sermon on the Mount, and of the flowering of the grace of the Holy Spirit was not excluded, but it was promoted to the final stage, the realm of extraordinary mystic graces.

This vision of moral theology applied the process of the history of salvation to the life of individuals, ascribing the stages of the universal divine pedagogy to the stages of moral development, meaning that the highest perspective was reserved for the chosen few at the last stage of development. This vision corresponded well with the catechetical need of the moral formation of children. Children need first to learn the rules of behavior, they need to habituate customs, so it seemed that the commandments of the Decalogue—appropriately transcribed from the Biblical future indicative to the imperative—offered in moral formation the best pedagogical tool, better than the Sermon on the Mount in which Jesus Himself comments on the Decalogue in an entirely new perspective. An eventual spiritual thirst was not denied, but it was sent to a more distant and seemingly optional stage.

CRITIQUE OF THIS VISION

This vision of morality, deeply rooted in Catholic pastoral practice, has justly met with criticism. The insistence that the presentation of the norms is central in moral formation meant that moralists tried to work out their rational justification, suggesting that once people are convinced about the validity of the norms they will follow them. This, of course, is not true. One may clearly understand the importance and significance of the moral norms and yet fail to follow them. Even those moralists who referred to Aquinas, noting that he made scant reference to the commandments and built his particular morals on the virtues, theological and moral, often understood these virtues not so much as internal psychic dispositions flowing out of grace that enable the facile, speedy, pleasurable, and creative living out of the perceived values, but rather as descriptions of moral obligations. This shift in the understanding of the nature of a virtue confirmed the predominance of obligation in morality, and also ultimately caused a marginalization of interest in the virtues, making obedience, de facto, the main virtue. The natural law reflection was pulled out of its theological context and presented as a purely rationalist discourse, having supposedly in itself its internal coherence—*etsi Deus non daretur.*

The recent statement of the International Theological Commission criticizes the modern rationalist model of the natural law because it suggested an essentialist, immutable, and a-historic understanding of human nature. It bracketed out the concrete situation of the person within the history of salvation, marked by sin and by grace. It claimed that it is possible to deduce *a priori* the precepts of the natural law from the definition of human nature. And it attempted to conduct this process of deduction as extensively as possible thereby covering almost the totality of human acts. It is this vision that has generated the serious contemporary crisis in morals.[1] Furthermore, the commencement with a presentation of the inherent rationality of the moral discourse meant that the reference to the revealed Decalogue seemed to function either as a divine confirmation of the rationality of the ethicist's discourse or as an ultimate religious argument brought in only when the rational discourse was found to be unconvincing.

The predomination of the rational, ultimately philosophical discourse in morals was not set against a theological vision. Grace was understood to be necessary, but it seemed that first there needs to be a natural presentation of moral challenges and even a description of the abomination of contemporary evils, followed by a presentation of the moral norms with their rationally obligatory character. Grace appeared at most as an addendum offered to those who experienced their moral weakness and needed a divine support, whereas the greater part of the moral material was presented in a Pelagian spirit. The primacy of human experience and rational reflection entered even the issue of faith, which in a semi-Pelagian way was suggested to be born at the end of a rational apologetic discourse. It is, of course, possible to reflect philosophically on moral challenges, and on human hungers, including the natural desire for the vision of God, which is an extension of natural intellectual curiosity. There is, however, no natural desire for the supernatural. The life of grace, including the grace of faith, is a free divine gift to be received as such in all its fascinating and surprising splendor.

ATTENTIVE READING OF AQUINAS
IN THE LIGHT OF SAINT PAUL

While it is true that Aquinas presents the various laws in a sequence that corresponds to the history of salvation (eternal, natural, human, old and new laws), it is not correct to deduce from this that the final, new law of the Gospel can be transferred to the limits of eschatology and that the pedagogy of moral formation is to

---

1 *Alla ricerca di un'etica universale: nuovo sguardo sulla legge naturale* (Vatican: LEV, 2009), no. 32–33.

always begin with a purely rational natural law reflection. In fact, what is presented at the end is most important for Aquinas. The short treatise on the new law that insists that the grace of the Holy Spirit is the most powerful element of that law is the apex of Aquinas' vision of morals. The entire moral teaching that he offers is a part of theology, and theology is the study of God, not as a philosophical idea, but the living mysterious God, who enters into a relationship with men. Moral theology is a discourse about grace and an attempt to spell out in detail the fecundity of grace within the human psyche in the face of various vocations and moral challenges.

What distinguishes moral theology from dogmatic theology is a different mode of being of God. The theological discourse that is imparted in moral catechesis is a description of the presence of God by grace within man, as God elicits within human activity the divine image. The Christian, applying the grace of the Holy Spirit to his various activities, is changed from within in such a way that the graced person becomes a living icon of God. Following the intuition of Saint John Damascene, the great defender of icons against the iconoclasts, Aquinas perceives the image of God in the Christian who uses his own intellect and his capacity for personal free choice and who responds from within on the basis of a personal stance to the true good that he or she perceives. For this reason the description of the richness of divine grace, working through the graced but mature individual, is viewed through the panorama of virtues. The precepts of the commandments are not denied, but they are presented as an external aid, important in the genesis of personal moral responsibility, but the moral discourse is not centered upon them. It is centered on grace that is annunciated in all its capacity to generate goodness. The pedagogical influence of the moral formator is to assist in the genesis of personal virtues that have the grace of God as their basic source and foundation.

In reflecting about moral pedagogy, if one wishes to be true to the theological vision of Aquinas, the sequence therefore that spontaneously springs to mind needs to be reversed. The first and primary accent needs to fall on the new law of the Gospel, the law of the grace of the Holy Spirit, and moral challenges need to be viewed within a context of a personal relationship with the indwelling Spirit. The prime biblical moral text that nudges us from without towards a continuous response to the Holy Spirit is not the Decalogue, but the Sermon on the Mount. A rational, natural law, ethical reflection is of course still possible, because faith does not denigrate the reason, but that reflection needs to be located within a preceding, fundamental relationship with the living God in faith.

Such a reversal of the angle of approach is in accord with the experience and teaching of Saint Paul. As a biblical scholar has noted, Saint Paul first discovered the solution and then he perceived the problem.[2] Normally we first see a problem and then search for a solution. Saint Paul first met Christ on the road to Damascus and then in the light of that experience he began to understand better the depth of human misery that needs a Savior. The experience of encountering Christ allowed him to see with greater clarity the limitations of the two great moral theories that he knew: the Jewish and the Greek. The Jews emphasized their covenant with God, to which they responded by their detailed fidelity to the prescriptions of the Law. They tried to be just, believing that this fidelity granted them justice. Even though they did occasionally fall, they continued to place their trust in the divine promises and then returned to their covenant and the fulfillment of the requirements of the Law. The Greek moral ethos was built on the intellectual and moral virtues, carefully analyzed by the philosophers and presented as a model to be imitated.

The opening of Saint Paul's eyes by Jesus showed him how inefficacious were both of these approaches. The Jews, sure of their election, in their concentration on their own fidelity to the letter of the Law fell into hypocrisy and pride. They gloried in the Law that they did not follow. "If you call yourself a Jew, if you really trust in the law and are proud of your God, if you know God's will through the Law and can tell what is right ... then why not teach yourself as well as the others?" (cf. Rom. 2:17–22). Whereas the pagans, "the more they called themselves philosophers, the more stupid they grew, until they exchanged the glory of the immortal God for a worthless imitation. ... That is why God has abandoned them to their degrading passions. ... Since they refused to see it was rational to acknowledge God, God has left them to their own irrational ideas and to their monstrous behavior" (cf. Rom. 1:22–23, 26, 28). Both those who had the divinely revealed moral Law and those who possessed a rational knowledge of moral principles fell into sin. Their moral knowledge was insufficient and furthermore, left them locked in pride.

Saint Paul rejected the salutary function of the Law, not because he arrived at the conclusion that it was weak and inefficacious, but because he was initiated into the life of God that manifested its saving power on the cross of Christ. This provoked a radical change in all his previous convictions. "Because of Christ, I have come to consider all these advantages that I had as disadvantages" (cf. Phil. 3:7). The main advantage in which Saint Paul hitherto had pride was precisely the old Law,

---

2 E.P. Sanders, quoted by R. Penna, *Paul the Apostle. Wisdom and Folly of the Cross*, vol. 2 (Collegeville: The Liturgical Press, 1996), 126–129.

which in his youth he had studied and to which he had tried to be faithful. Had he
not met Christ, he would have never criticized the Law. But now, as he wrote:

> "For I through the law died to the law, that I might live to God. I have
> been crucified with Christ; it is no longer I who live, but Christ who
> lives in me; and the life I now live in the flesh I live by faith in the Son
> of God, who loved me and gave himself for me." (Gal. 2:19–20)

Even though "the law is holy, and that commandment is holy and just and good"
(Rom. 7:12), which Saint Paul never denied, it lost its previous meaning because
"God sent forth his Son, born of a woman, born under the law, to redeem those who
were under the law, so that we might receive adoption as sons" (Gal. 4:5). Our access to God is attained not by fidelity to the Law, but by faith directed to the person
of Christ, who has become "our wisdom, our righteousness and sanctification and
redemption" (1 Cor. 1:30). The descriptions of the moral degeneration of the pagans
(cf. Rom. 1:18–32) and of the painful incapacity of the Jews of living up to the stan-
dards of the Law (cf. Rom. 2:1–29; 7:7–25) given by Saint Paul did not stem from a
socio-religious analysis of his contemporaries nor from an earnest self-analysis of his
own pain, but from a profound faith in Christ. The encounter with Christ so illuminated Saint Paul that it showed him his own limitations and weaknesses. Above all,
he was moved by the greatness of Christ, which is a value in itself.

Jesus did not come to fix what needed repair in society, nor did He come to
fill in what was missing in the hitherto known Law. Jesus enters into lives directly,
unasked and unexpected, and He grants more than can ever be expected. Faith
therefore is the reaching out towards Christ, who has made Himself available and
has enabled that reaching out towards Him, a reaching out that is not only theoretical, but is a real basing of oneself upon Him, precisely within the context of those
matters that concern us most: the desire for happiness, honesty, weaknesses, morality. Faith is the transfer of the basic burden of sanctification from our own shoulders
to those of Christ, on the basis of His invitation in the conviction that He grants
us His Spirit. In the center of moral life there is, therefore, not a pedagogically
offered external teaching, nor a model that is to be studied and imitated, but the
living person of Jesus Christ, who enters human lives and who is the source of divine
grace that changes from within all human endeavors and moral responses. Moral
pedagogy is not therefore a process in which a knowledge is acquired, nor is it an ap-

prenticeship in which an art is mastered. Basically it is an initiation into the mystery of the living God, a mystery, the fullness of which can never be fully grasped.

We could claim that in the life of Saint Paul there was the same sequence that we have in the history of salvation. Paul was born as a little pagan, he was circumcised and formed in the traditions of the old Jewish Law, and then he was discovered by Christ and brought into the plenitude of a life based in faith on Christ. His insistence, however, upon the force of Christ's grace and its centrality in the life of the Christian manifests clearly that God does not always follow the same pedagogical strategy with all people. Some are led directly to that which is central. This is the focus of Saint Paul's writing to the Galatians. By referring to Abraham, who had not known the Law, which was given centuries later through Moses, Saint Paul dethroned that Law from the excessively high position that it was given in the Jewish moral horizon. "Those who rely on faith receive the same blessing as Abraham, the man of faith. On the other hand, those who rely on the keeping of the law are under a curse" (cf. Gal. 3:9–10). The old moral Law and the Decalogue in particular, has a value, as it points out the erroneous moral avenues and clarifies the understanding of what is sin but, in itself, it leaves the individual with his weakness. The old Law needs to be interpreted within the context of the friendship with God that has been made supremely possible through Christ.

> Is the law then against the promises of God? Certainly not; for if a law had been given which could make alive, then righteousness would indeed be by the law. But the scripture consigned all things to sin, that what was promised to faith in Jesus Christ might be given to those who believe. (Gal. 3:21–22)

It follows therefore that a Christian moral pedagogy should focus always on the highest level, that of the union with Christ in faith. It is true that we do not meet Jesus in the same way that Jesus met Saint Paul on the way to Damascus, but in the sacrament of Baptism, we are already immersed in the life of the Blessed Trinity. This means that the encounter in faith with the living God is already possible on the basis of the received baptismal graces. A truly Christian moral pedagogy needs to stress primarily the perspectives that are made open due to the divine filiation that has its origin in Baptism. The external educative value of a natural law reflection and of the Decalogue is not to be denied, in particular in childhood, but these rational and revealed external precepts need to be located within something much deeper that is a spiritual relationship centered on Christ through faith. The Christian is not so much engaged in the fulfilling of an externally imposed code, nor of correcting himself according to some sublime model, nor of working out a project for arranging the world that would be better than other projects, but in the expanding of the space of the workings of divine grace, as he or she lives out life in faith and charity. In this, the Christian can always count on the fecundity of grace, because the prime vocation of the Christian is to be a child of God, and a child is not paralyzed by its faults nor is it worried about the entire world. A child can live in trust, in the certitude that divine support will not be lacking, when and where it is needed and where it is asked for in a pure heart.

IN THE CENTER: LIFE IN THE SPIRIT

The life of a Christian consists primarily in gratitude for the gift of grace and the living out of one's life in a permanent counting upon divine support. The Christian pedagogy, therefore, needs to initiate into the mystery of being in the loving hands of God. This mysterious divine support is not a response of God to our pleading. The project that God has for us precedes our existence. We read in Saint Paul that "before the world was made, God … chose us in Christ … to live through love in his presence, determining that we should become his adopted sons" (cf. Eph. 1:4–5). "We are God's work of art, created in Christ Jesus to live the good life as from the beginning he had meant us to live it" (cf. Eph. 2:10). This means that the divine pedagogy began with the initial divine project that preceded the creation of the world, preceded the sin of Adam, and preceded our own existence and sinfulness. In God's plan we are to enter into a relationship with God as adopted children, through our adopted brother Jesus Christ. The childlike relationship with God entails a fundamental trust in God's mercy and goodness, without of course denying the truth about the evil of sin. That truth about sin is not dissolved into insignificance, because God has treated sinfulness seriously, liberating us from it through the redemptive work of Christ, but it is not paralyzing. Before God, therefore, we need to be like children, living out a persistent belief in the availability of divine grace. In the face of our human responsibilities, however, we are not to be infantile, but mature and responsible. An error that needs to be corrected in moral formation appears when the two are reversed: when one believes that before God we have to be adult, proving to God our own merits and rights, and when in the face of real life responsibilities we are immature and irresponsible. Living out a life in childlike trust in God requires maturity in the face of human challenges, because the indwelling

Holy Spirit is demanding. The more one responds in faith to the suggestions of the Holy Spirit, the more one has to be generous.

A profound explanation of what it means to be led by the Holy Spirit is given by Saint Paul in the eighth chapter of the *Epistle to the Romans*. It is here that Saint Paul declares: "For all who are led by the Spirit of God are sons of God" (Rom. 8:14). A childlike trust in the support of the divine Father entails docility towards the Holy Spirit. Responsiveness to His inspirations allows one to live in the familiar atmosphere of the Blessed Trinity. It is not so much important what we do in life. What is more important is whether we relate to the living God within what we do in life. Just as Jesus listened to the voice of His eternal Father, so the Christian needs to listen in prayer to divine suggestions so as to respond to them creatively. This requires serious moments of prayer in which the daily life is correlated with the Word of God. It requires an unwavering conviction that the Holy Spirit is wise, that He knows what He is doing and where He is leading us. In the pilgrimage of life there are moments when the divine guidance seems to be hidden in darkness or appears to be surprising, when it involves the cross; but it is precisely these moments that require a deeper faith in the accompanying presence of God. The Holy Spirit does not send His lights constantly. Most of the time the lights that are given through the Church and through the station of life are sufficient. But occasionally one needs to stop for a moment to ensure that the divine track is there, even though these moments entail darkness. Fidelity towards the Holy Spirit does not lead to greater lights, but to a deeper faith, which is experienced within darkness. The divine pedagogy takes place within these moments of darkness. The desert experience of the people of God, wandering through insecurity, hunger, and thirst is a model of that divine leading which needs to accept that the divine light ahead of us is sometimes just a little flicker. A conscious perseverance in faith and charity is demanding as it requires a constant gift of self, given in the face of darkness accepted in faith, but in this there is the profiting from the mysterious divine grace that is given. This may all take place in internal peace because ultimately "we know that in everything God works with those who love him" (Rom. 8:28).

A moral formation in line with the divine pedagogy is ultimately not just a moral formation but a spiritual formation initiating into the divine mystery as it unfolds in life, in constant trust that the loving God is present and that a relationship with Him may be truly maintained through faith. The habituation to invite God into all human activities requires a certain formation so that the person will introduce the disclosed divine mystery not only into a theoretical declaration of belief in the existence of God, but also into thinking, into practical decision making, and into the affective life. The long process of catechesis worked out in antiquity for catechumens was centered not just on the cognition and memorization of the salutary truths, but also on the initiation into the divine mystery in practical life. As the Christian learns to trust in the gift of divine grace, he or she begins to view all moral problems through the supreme prism of infused charity. That charity generates permanent dispositions enabling an easy, speedy, pleasurable, and creative choice of the true good as it is perceived by the individual, including in the action all the dynamism of the affective life that becomes habituated to respond to the light of reason and even more to respond to the inner movement of the Holy Spirit. The infused moral virtues, stimulated by the gifts of the Holy Spirit are tied by "faith that makes its power felt by love" (cf. Gal. 5:6). This inner change of view that has infused charity as its foundation allows one almost instinctively to exclude egoism from human sexuality; it allows one to enjoy personal generosity in human relationships; it allows one to view ethical problems, be they social or bioethical from the angle of generosity in truth. The spelling out of the moral consequences of living out a permanent relationship with God requires some pedagogical guidance, as this is built around the inner fundamental axis of the theological virtues.

THE CONTENTS AND LOCATION OF CATECHETICAL PEDAGOGY

In my childhood it seemed that in the Church there were three distinct realities. Prayer was deemed to be most important and liturgical prayer was understood to be an encounter with a mystery that is objectively happening. Catechesis consisted primarily in the memorization of vocal prayers and of dogmatic and moral formulae, the meaning of which the child did not immediately understand. This was not interpreted as inappropriate because through these formulae the child had access to the truth, the meaning and importance of which the child would discover later in life. Moral formation was given in the family, in the Catholic school, or in the parish, or some social group like a scout troop. This was given by somebody close, who corrected the behavior on the way, and invited to creative generosity. I have the impression that in many parts of the world these three realities have now become confused. The liturgy has become a communal celebration with some catechetical teaching or even worse, entertainment, charming towards values and concerns. Catechesis has ceased to require the memorization of dry, but precise and true formulae, and moral correction seems to have been dropped. In the place of an encounter with the living God in prayer and in the place of learning true expressions of the Faith, there are "happenings." It is true that some people are moved by "happenings," and some are more touched by parables and stories than by precise formulae. Jesus Himself used such methods, but He did not refrain from using precise and mysterious language, even when it would be rejected. After the "happening" of the miraculous multiplication of the loaves and the fishes, Jesus pronounced a long discourse in which He made seemingly impossible statements such as: "He who eats my flesh and drinks my blood lives in me and I in him" (cf. Jn. 6:56), and when the confused crowds started to walk away, Jesus even chided the apostles on saying: "What about you, do you want to go away too?" (cf. Jn. 6:66). Jesus was not afraid of saying what could not be understood. In later centuries the Church has tried to grasp the sense of Jesus' words with the help of the dogmatic formula "transubstantiation," but the mystery still remains.

Catechesis needs to take place within a life of prayer, based upon the graces of Baptism. It needs also to develop those graces through a deepened encounter with God. Secondarily, it needs to offer a clear set of concepts that spell out the ramifications and implications of the Faith, even though these statements appear mysterious. In this, it is the intelligibility of the truths that is to be sought for rather than their reasonableness. The truths of faith are not to be scanned according to criteria coming from an independent reason or from ideologies, fashions, and ideas about relevancy. They are to be accepted as true and mysterious, and their intelligibility, which corresponds with the need of the intellect for clear and cohesive concepts, needs to be brought out. The recognition of the intelligibility of the revealed truths generates a certain fascination with the taste of the mysterious truth. The perception of the mutual cohesiveness of the mysteries and their correspondence with the natural structures of being, grants something solid on which one can then build and hold onto. "We hold these truths" means not only that we hold onto them in scary moments of difficulty and insecurity. It means that we hold these truths permanently through the intellectual virtues that furnish the mind with principles. It is on the basis of truths that are held that conscious and responsible decisions can be made. When the mind will be furnished with formulae that grasp the mysteries of faith in their truth, these mysteries will then inhabit the mind, influencing decision-making and the handling of the emotions. And, finally, the helpful and observing comment of a friendly person close at hand will be of great use.

Catechesis therefore is to be addressed primarily within faith, to those who are *ad intra* rather than to those who are outside the Church, *ad extra*. The catechist needs to have the courage to initiate people into truths that surpass the intellectual and even moral capacities of the catechist himself. Sometimes there may be the temptation to back out of the truth, because the catechist may be accused by the observant pupil of not always practicing what he preaches. The response, however, lies not in the backing out of truth and the lowering of the teaching to the level of the sinfulness of the catechist, but in the humble acceptance that the catechist preaches not himself, but Christ, on the basis of the truths that have been revealed, even though the catechist, like every other Christian, is still on the way. In this the catechist himself manifests his belief that he himself has been graced, and that the grace of God precedes everything that he says and does. It is only when catechesis is conducted within a lively faith in the active presence of the Holy Spirit Himself, both within the catechist and within the catechized, that catechesis truly profits from the grace of preaching.

8

Divine Pedagogy in Prayer

Rev. Louis Menvielle

I. JESUS, MASTER OF PRAYER

Catechists Need to Be Rooted in Christ

As we know and we often hear nowadays, *Catechesi Tradendae* and all the subsequent documents of the Magisterium on catechesis affirm that "the definitive aim" of the latter is "to put people not only in contact but in communion, in intimacy with, Jesus Christ: only he can lead us to the love of the Father in the Spirit and make us share in the life of the Holy Trinity" (CT 5). This definition only makes more precise the one the Council gives in *Christus Dominus* 14, repeated in Canon Law "the aim [of catechetical teaching] is to give to men the living faith, explicit and active."[1] Consequently, the *General Directory for Catechesis* presents this definition: The Church, and hence the catechist, "transmits to catechumens and those to be catechized, her living experience of the Gospel, her faith, so that they may appropriate it and profess it" (GDC 66).

To transmit her faith, "her living experience of the Gospel," is to transmit a personal reality, lived in such a way that the person receiving it can live in it himself. The *Directory* gives this definition of the catechist's vocation:

> The Lord Jesus invites men and women, in a special way, to follow him, teacher and formator of disciples. This personal call of Jesus Christ and its relationship to him are the true moving forces of catechetical activity. (GDC 231)

---

1 CIC 773.

The *Directory* makes explicit the relationship with Christ: it is a "loving knowledge" from which "springs the desire ... to lead others to the 'yes' of faith in Jesus Christ" (GDC 231). This loving knowledge permits "communication of the living Mystery of God" (CT 7). This expression gives us the "doctrine" which Christ teaches as coming from His Father.

One cannot put someone "in communion, in intimacy with Jesus Christ" if one is not in such intimacy oneself. One cannot transmit the loving knowledge of the "living Mystery of God" if one does not possess it oneself. That is why the *Directory* insists on personal formation of catechists, not only on an intellectual or pedagogical plane with a view to carrying out teaching given in a tailored manner, but first of all on the spiritual plane of conversion to Christ and His Gospel:

> Formation seeks to enable catechists to transmit the Gospel to those who desire to entrust themselves to Jesus Christ. ... The christocentric purpose of catechesis, which emphasizes the communion of the convert with Jesus Christ, permeates all aspects of the formation of catechists. (GDC 235)

"The preparation and formation of catechists in the deep riches of the faith" is thus a "primary task" of catechetical pastoral care (GDC 33). Their formation is qualified as "true" if it "above all, nourishes the *spirituality* of the catechist" (GDC 239). In these conditions, catechesis can "deepen man's encounter with God" so as to prepare appropriate witnesses to make "known the true face of God and his loving plan of salvation for man, as it has been revealed in Jesus Christ" (GDC 23).

KNOWING THE PEDAGOGY OF GOD THROUGH EXPERIENCE

Prayer allows catechists not only to have a view conforming to their life but also to use a pedagogy that they draw from God Himself because they have personal experience of the manner in which God leads His children on the path of faith and holiness.

Spirituality, an encounter with God, a living and profound faith, the pedagogy of God, all these priorities put prayer at the center of the formation of catechists, and most particularly contemplative prayer; as the *Catechism* says "Contemplative prayer is also the pre-eminently *intense time* of prayer" (*Catechism*, no. 2714). Our aim is to highlight how the *Catechism* recognizes in God the pedagogy of prayer.

JESUS, OUR GREAT PEDAGOGUE

Each part of the *Catechism* has an introductory illustration. The fourth part, dedicated to Christian prayer, opens on a miniature of the Monastery of Dionysius, on Mount Athos. We see the Lord Jesus turned in prayer towards the Father. The commentary explains that "his disciples watch him from a respectful distance. Saint Peter, the head of the apostles, turns toward the others and points to him who is the Master and the Way of Christian prayer" and the text ends with this request by the apostles: "Lord, teach us to pray" (Lk. 11:1). The second section, on the Our Father, also begins with this request (*Catechism*, no. 2759). The *Catechism* tells us that "The sacred humanity of Jesus is the way by which the Holy Spirit teaches us to pray to God our Father" (*Catechism*, no. 2664). Turn, therefore, to Jesus and ask Him to be your great Pedagogue. He is Revelation itself. What He is, what He says, what He has done, constitutes the Way, the Truth, the Life. Jesus is "the one way of prayer" (*Catechism*, no. 2707) and to understand how Jesus is the Pedagogue of prayer, let us pause for a moment on the concept of divine pedagogy.

The Pedagogy of God

WHERE DOES THE EXPRESSION COME FROM?

The recent Magisterium refers the origin of this expression to Pius XI in his encyclical *Mit Brennender Sorge*, written in 1937.[2] The formula was taken up again by *Dei Verbum*, and then by the *Catechism of the Catholic Church*[3] and the *General Directory for Catechesis*.[4] When it uses this expression "pedagogy of God," the *Catechism* (*Catechism*, no. 122) relates explicitly to *Dei Verbum* 15 which itself refers to the encyclical of Pius XI in which the Pope remembers that "the books of the Old Testament bear witness to the whole divine pedagogy of God's saving love," of which the "principal *raison d'être*" was to "prepare the world for the coming of Christ our Savior."

The *Directory* (GDC 38) makes the link between *Dei Verbum* 15 and *Dei Verbum* 2. God uses pedagogy because He "acts in a way that men can come to the knowledge of his plan of salvation." It is an action completely imprinted with an "abundance of ... love" (*DV* 2). To signify this in its turn, the *Directory* (GDC 137) cannot but refer to Hosea:

---

2 "[O]ne perceives the striking perspective of the divine tutorship [pedagogy] of salvation, as it warns, admonishes, strikes, raises and beautifies its elect. Nothing but ignorance and pride could blind one to the treasures hoarded in the Old Testament." *Mit Brennender Sorge*, 15.

3 See *Catechism*, nos. 53, 122, 684, 708, 1145, 1950, 1964.

4 See *GDC* 8, 38, 100, 111, 129, 131, 132, 137–147, 148, 152, 243.

Yet it was I who taught Ephraim to walk, I took them up in my arms; but they did not know that I healed them. I led them with cords of compassion, with the bands of love, and I became to them as one who eases the yoke on their jaws, and I bent down to them and fed them. (Hos. 11:3–4)

EVENTS AND WORDS IN THE OLD TESTAMENT …
ABOUT THE WORD MADE FLESH

What pedagogy does God use? He reveals Himself "by means of the events of salvation history and the inspired words which accompany and explain them" (GDC 38; cf. DV 2).

First of all, there are the events and the words reported by the Old Testament, which prepare the ground for the Revelation of the New Testament. Events and words are inseparable:

> … deeds and words having inner unity: the deeds wrought by God in the history of salvation manifest and confirm the teaching and realities signified by the words, while the words proclaim the deeds and clarify the mystery contained in them. (DV 2)

That is to say, pedagogy underpins temporality. There had to be centuries and centuries of progressive discovery, through fidelity and infidelities, joys and sorrows, so that the people of God would be ready to welcome the whole Revelation accomplished in Jesus Christ and to enter, thus, into "the fullness of time" (cf. Gal. 4:4). One sees here the importance of the concepts of spiritual growth and time for integration.

Everything, therefore, is about preparing to receive Jesus who is Revelation itself insofar as He is the Word, that is, the very act of knowing in God, "the image of the invisible God" (Col. 1:15), "the radiance of glory of God and the very stamp of his nature" (Catechism, no. 241; cf. Heb. 1:3), who is made flesh. As the only Son, He alone is able (cf. Mt. 11:27) to enable us to know the God whom no one has ever seen (cf. Jn. 1:18). And Jesus continues the divine pedagogy already begun in the Old Testament, using acts and words to announce the mystery, which was hidden (cf. Eph. 3:5–12):

> He who has seen me has seen the Father; how can you say: "Show us the Father"? … The words that I say to you I do not speak on my own

authority; but the Father who dwells in me does his works. ... Believe me for the sake of the works themselves. (Jn. 14:9–11).

If Jesus chose the Twelve so that they would be with Him before sending them out to preach (cf. Mk. 3:14), it is because He wished to take care of their formation, exercising a true teaching throughout His life, stimulating them with appropriate questions, and finally sending them the Spirit of the Father to introduce them into the complete truth (cf. GDC 137). The *Directory* sees a complete pedagogy of Jesus in this passage from Mark:

> And when he was alone, those who were about him with the twelve asked him concerning the parables. And he said to them, "To you has been given the secret of the kingdom of God. ... But privately to his own disciples he explained everything." (Mk. 4:10–11, 34)

Hence the words,

> The whole of Christ's life was a continual teaching: His silences, His miracles, His gestures, His prayer, His love for people, His special affection for the little and the poor, His acceptance of the total sacrifice on the cross for the redemption of the world, and His resurrection are the actualization of His word and the fulfillment of revelation. (CT 9)

The great biblical text on the pedagogy of God is in the *Letter to the Hebrews* 1:1–2. The *General Directory for Catechesis* refers to this saying: "God revealed himself progressively to man, through the prophets and through salvific events, until he brought to completion his self-revelation by sending his own Son" (GDC 40).

With the pedagogy of the Faith taking as its model the pedagogy of God, the *Catechism* has chosen to explain each mystery of the Faith by presenting, first, that which God has revealed about it in the Old Testament; then in the New Testament; and thirdly what the Church has grasped about it across the centuries.

APPROACHING JESUS "AS FROM THE BURNING BUSH"

As God has said everything in His Son and His pedagogy consists in revealing Himself through acts and words, we must approach Jesus "as in the burning bush" (cf. *Catechism*, no. 2598) to see Him alive and to listen to Him.

In fact we can allow ourselves to meet Him like the disciples on the road to Emmaus or like the Samaritan woman. The *Catechism* assures us that He "comes to meet every human being. It is he who first seeks us" (*Catechism*, no. 2560).

As it is the beloved Son who knows how to speak to His Father, we contemplate Him in prayer (cf. *Catechism*, no. 2598). The *Catechism* points out to us that, "When Jesus prays he is already teaching us to pray" (*Catechism*, no. 2607), with this remark: "In seeing the Master at prayer the disciple of Christ also wants to pray" (*Catechism*, no. 2601). The disciples did well when they saw Him pray and asked Him: "Lord, teach us to pray" (Lk. 11:1). We will listen then to how the "Master of prayer" (*Catechism*, no. 2601) "teaches us to pray, in order to know how he hears our prayer" (*Catechism*, no. 2598). Our prayer is *Christian* insofar as it is of Christ and is in communion with Christ. "Its dimensions are those of Christ's love" (*Catechism*, no. 2565).

The Prayer of Jesus

In the light of the Spirit of Truth, the Christian community has contemplated the mystery of the prayer of Jesus and has understood that He is, as Son, in permanent relationship with His Father. While Mark (1:21–39) seems to describe to us a typical day in the life of Jesus, he does not fail to report to us, like Luke (cf. 3:21ff), that Jesus withdrew to pray. We read in Mark: "in the morning, a great while before day, he rose and went out to a lonely place, and there he prayed" (Mk. 1: 35). It is to this text that the *Catechism* refers first of all when it describes Jesus as a man of prayer (cf. *Catechism*, no. 2602).

RELATIONSHIP OF SONSHIP, OFFERING, AND BLESSING

Jesus is more than a man of prayer: He *is* prayer. Isn't this what the *Letter to the Hebrews* is saying, when it presents the attitude of God's only Son on coming into the world: "Lo, I have come to do thy will, O God" (Heb. 10:7)? In this way the prayer of Jesus was at the same time the expression of His filial relationship and of His self-offering. It is worth pausing to consider this attitude of filial self-offering, which seems to define the whole life of Jesus, because it reveals something about the dialogue between the Father and the Son, a dialogue that can be called "blessing."

As the divine pedagogy has aroused the enthusiasm of the great figures of the Old Testament who appear to us as the types of Christ, let us look at Noah: his offering after the flood is blessed by God who seals an alliance with his creatures (Gen. 8:20–9:17). The *Catechism* comments: "Noah's offering is pleasing to God, who blesses him and through him all creation, because his heart was upright and undivided" (*Catechism*, no. 2569).

This "event"—in the sense of *Dei Verbum* 2—tells us something of the offering of Jesus since His entrance into the world, and of the paternal benediction, which it arouses. The letter to the Ephesians (1:3) explains to us that, in Christ, God has blessed us with all sorts of spiritual blessings, and this blessing of God sparks off in turn our own blessing. This is the fundamental movement of the Our Father, whose first word "Father" is by itself a hymn to the glory of God who has blessed us because He has revealed His name to us. And He has given us "the gift of believing in it" together with the very "indwelling of His Presence in us" (*Catechism*, no. 2781). The very first word that Jesus gives us in the Our Father consists, therefore, in what the *Catechism* calls a "blessing of adoration" where we address the Father in an "ever new sense of wonder" (*Catechism*, no. 2781). And our blessing, as in a circular and incessant movement, releases new divine blessings: "God's gift and man's acceptance of it are united in dialogue with each other" (*Catechism*, no. 2626). This is so fundamental that the *Catechism* repeats in the "In Brief" section that which it has affirmed in the main body of the treatment: "Because God blesses, the human heart can in return bless him who is the source of every blessing" (*Catechism*, no. 2645). Thus, the filial offering of Jesus, from the first instant of His existence, is a response to the Father's blessing which begets Him eternally and gives Him humanity in the womb of the Virgin; and His filial offering arouses in its turn a new blessing from the Father which extends to all humanity.

THE CHILD'S HUMILITY

We know the great blessing of Jesus in response to the gift of the Father, as one of the explicit prayers that the evangelists preserved from the time of Christ's public ministry, which the *Catechism* calls "the exultant blessing of the Father" (*Catechism*, no. 2701). It is recorded in Saint Luke's Gospel that Jesus is filled with joy under the action of the Holy Spirit and confesses the Father by thanking Him and acknowledging Him as "Lord, of heaven and earth." Jesus then thanks Him for revealing "to babes" what has been hidden "from the wise and understanding" (Lk. 10:21).

This blessing from Jesus provides us with great teaching on the necessity of humility before God. Anyone who approaches Jesus "gentle and lowly in heart" (Mt. 11:29) discovers that "humility is the foundation of prayer" (*Catechism*, no. 2559). We ourselves pray—like the psalmist—with a "humble and contrite heart" and we are well aware that when we can humbly recognize that "we do not know how to pray as we ought" (Rom. 8:26) only then are we ready to receive prayer as a gift like "a beggar before God"[5] (*Catechism*, no. 2559), just as Christ, God and Son, receives everything from His Father. Humility and trust make us become like little children. Jesus makes us understand: only these little ones can bless the Father because it is the little ones who fill the Father with joy. This makes us understand who the children in the Kingdom are: they are those little ones whom the Father fills with joy, precisely because of this littleness; they are those who receive everything, in the image of the Son. Like Him, they are "gentle and humble of heart."

We can discover something about the humility of Jesus and of His prayer in another typological figure: that of Moses, who was "a very meek man, more than all men, that were on the face of the earth" (Num. 12:3).

ENTERING INTO INTIMACY WITH GOD AND KNOWING HIS PLAN

With Moses, we discover that God brings the humble into a true contemplative relationship, and that He reveals His mystery to them so that they can unveil it to others. In the *Book of Numbers* we read these words of the Lord: "[Moses] is entrusted with all my house. With him I speak face to face, clearly" (cf. Num. 12:7–8). Before that it is said that "Moses was very meek, more so than anyone else on the face of the earth" (Num. 12:3). The *Catechism* makes a link of cause and effect when it says that God spoke to Moses face to face *because* Moses was so meek (cf. *Catechism*, no. 2576). Jesus, we know, is the new Moses, and, with its sense of the pedagogy of God who drives history towards the fullness of Christ, the *Catechism* looks at the mystery of Jesus while presenting typically, contemplative prayer by citing the *Book of Exodus* 33:11: "Thus the Lord used to speak to Moses face to face, as a man speaks to his friend." These words resonate in us with the words of Jesus: "the Father who sent me has himself given me what to say and what to speak. ... I declare to the world what I have heard from him" (Jn. 12:49, 8:26). Jesus is the only Son, turned to the Father, to whom the Father shows everything He has done (cf. Jn. 1:18, 5:20). And Jesus makes us know the Father by revealing what He has taught Him (cf. Jn. 1:18, 8:28).

After Moses, the second great figure of the Old Testament is Elijah. Elijah is a figure of Christ, in particular when he climbs the Mountain of God and, like Moses, hides in a cleft of the rock. It is then that "the mysterious presence of God" (*Catechism*, no. 2583) passes by. Jesus often prayed alone and in the silence of the mountain, preferably at night (cf. *Catechism*, no. 2602).

---

5   Saint Augustine, *Sermo* 56, 6, 9: *PL* 38, 381.

Prayer in Christ and a Relationship to the Father

JESUS AND HIS FATHER

What does Jesus essentially do in prayer? We can say with assurance that, in this immersion, Jesus revels in the mystery of His Father. From the age of twelve, He lives in the temple because He must be "about his Father's business" (cf. Lk. 2:49). In citing these words of Jesus, the *Catechism* comments: "Here the newness of prayer in the fullness of time begins to be revealed: his *filial prayer*, which the Father awaits from his children, is finally going to be lived out by the only Son in his humanity, with and for men" (*Catechism*, no. 2599). It is thus in *"contemplating* and hearing the Son, the master of prayer, the children learn to pray to the Father" (*Catechism*, no. 2601, emphasis in the original). Matthew reported these words of Jesus: "No one knows the Father except the Son and any one to whom the Son chooses to reveal him" (Mt. 11:27). In praying to the Father and revealing Him to us, Jesus makes us "enter into his mystery as he is" (*Catechism*, no. 2779) and thus He purifies from ambiguity all that our image of God the Father might contain.

The *Catechism* (nos. 2599–2601) thus looks at the whole life of Jesus to grasp how it is a filial relationship. The sacerdotal prayer is a key time where Jesus "reveals and gives to us the 'knowledge,' inseparably one, of the Father and the Son, which is the very mystery of the life of prayer" (*Catechism*, no. 2751). In addressing the Father in front of His disciples, Jesus is at the same time the person praying and the master teacher of prayer.

The *Catechism* then pauses at the passion and death on the cross where, having pronounced several times the name *Abba* or Father, Jesus gives out a "loud cry" (Mk. 15:37) and dies, or "gave up the spirit," as Saint John says (Jn. 19:30). What does that cry represent?

> All the troubles, for all time, of humanity enslaved by sin and death, all the petitions and intercessions of salvation history are summed up in this cry of the incarnate Word. Here the Father accepts them and, beyond all hope, answers them by raising his Son. (*Catechism*, no. 2606)

THE SPIRIT OF JESUS AND THE GIFT OF THE FATHER
WHICH MAKES US HIS CHILDREN

We are "given" to the Son as His inheritance because, through His death and Resurrection, we receive the Holy Spirit, which makes us children of God. In the Spirit, Jesus reveals and makes us pronounce the name of the Father, "Our Father," and He draws us into His own filial relationship, of which His passion has shown us "boundless depth" (*Catechism*, no. 2605). He gives us in the Gospel of Saint John the foundation of our own filial relationship: "I do not say to you that I shall pray the Father for you; for the Father himself loves you" (Jn. 16:26–27).

Thus, watching Jesus pray, we discover Him in His mystery as Son, on whom rests the Holy Spirit, and who addresses His Father, presenting all His brothers to Him, each and every one of us. In Him and through the Spirit, we can open our whole being to the Father who gives Himself, and say, in a contemplation that is at the same time praise, blessing, and offering, the words Jesus taught us: "Our Father."

"Like a wise teacher he [Jesus] takes hold of us where we are and leads us progressively toward the Father" (*Catechism*, no. 2607) to have with Him that vital and personal relationship that is prayer.

II. THE PRAYER OF FAITH

The "Tradition" of Prayer

By what means does the Spirit teach us prayer and its rules? First and foremost, He does this through witnesses.

Jesus is the great Pedagogue of prayer, in the sense that "there is no other way of Christian prayer than Christ" (*Catechism*, no. 2664 and 2674). But beside Him, Mary is wholly transparent to God. She shows us the way, which is Christ, and the way that is prayer in Christ, under the action of the Holy Spirit. In this sense, she forms part of the pedagogy of God for our consideration.

And that pedagogy is pursued in the Church by means of ordained ministers, of religious, of catechesis, of prayer groups, of spiritual direction (cf. *Catechism*, no. 2686–2690), especially of the Christian family, which is the first place to be formed in prayer. It suffices to recall how Jesus will have learned formulas of prayer from His mother, who we know pondered things in her heart and meditated upon "he who is mighty," who "has done great things" (Lk. 1:49). In this light, we understand that for young children in particular, the witness of daily family prayer is the way the Holy Spirit patiently awakens the Church's living memory for His little ones (cf. *Catechism*, no. 2685).

Throughout the history of the Church, the Holy Spirit has not ceased to arouse a horde of witnesses. The *Catechism* alerts us to this beautiful thought of Saint Basil:

> The Spirit is truly the dwelling of the saints and the saints are for the Spirit a place where he dwells as in his own home, since they offer themselves as a dwelling place for God and are called his temple. [6]

The saints have experienced relationship with God. They are also our guides in prayer, providing richly diverse schools of Christian spirituality, called by the *Catechism* "refractions of the one pure and light of the Holy Spirit" (*Catechism*, no. 2684). Learning how to pray needs living transmission by a "believing and praying Church" (*DV* 8), through which the Holy Spirit teaches the children of God how to pray.

Thus, we ask of Scripture and of Tradition, at the same time, what is prayer and how does God exercise His pedagogy in it?

Prayer is First of All a Call from God

"What is prayer," asks the *Catechism* at the start of the fourth part. "'If you knew the gift of God!' The wonder of prayer," the *Catechism* replies, "is revealed beside the well [referencing the Samaritan woman] where we come seeking water." Prayer is first and foremost an initiative of "Christ [who] comes to meet every human being. It is he who first seeks us" (*Catechism*, no. 2560). Genesis reports something to us in God's cry to Adam who is hiding in fear: "Where are you?" (Gen. 3:9). Here, we are completely in the pedagogy of God. As with Adam, God who is true and faithful, "tirelessly calls each person to that mysterious encounter known as prayer" (*Catechism*, no. 2567). Even if we are unfaithful, God remains faithful (cf. 2 Tim. 2:13). Even in prayer, "God's initiative of love always comes first" (*Catechism*, no. 2567). It is He who starts the dialogue with us because "God thirsts that we may thirst for him" (*Catechism*, no. 2560).

We all have a thirst for God, in one way or another, conscious or unconscious, because this is an essential quest of man. Man after the fall retains his desire "for the One who calls him into existence" (*Catechism*, no. 2566). The catechist is a

---

6 Saint Basil, *De Spiritu Sancto*, 26, 62.

sort of Bernadette of Lourdes who helps to separate someone from all that which, in the human heart, prevents the Source of life from gushing out.

As the pedagogy of God is expressed in the Old Testament through words and deeds that mutually illuminate each other, let us keep to the method of the *Catechism* which looks at the revelation of God in history and consider how the Lord comes to meet His people to teach them that prayer is the "encounter of God's thirst with ours" (*Catechism*, no. 2560), in a "vital and personal relationship with the living and true God" (*Catechism*, no. 2558).

The *Catechism* thinks of Moses when it highlights the initiative of God in prayer: "God calls Moses from the midst of the burning bush" (cf. Ex. 3:1–10) and through this event, not only Moses but all Jews and Christians alike have benefited from God's pedagogy in this event (*Catechism*, no. 205), where despite all Moses' excuses God confides Himself in confiding His name. A live, personal relationship between God and Moses is established. From then on we read that Moses often conversed with God, listening to Him, and entreating Him. We know that they spoke like one friend to another (cf. Ex. 33:11).

Prayer Is a Response of Faith

But before Moses, there was Abraham, archetype of the one who responds perfectly to the call of God and who responds docilely to what God wants to teach him. To Abraham applies exactly what the Magisterium calls "pedagogy of God," because the events and words which the *Book of Genesis* reports to us on the subject of Abraham are illuminated by other words, those of the *Letter to the Hebrews*, which returns to the faith of Abraham. We also have the commentary in the *Letter to the Romans*: "Abraham believed God, and it was reckoned to him as righteousness" (Rom. 4:3; cf. Gen. 15:6).

This free submission of Abraham to the Word of God is called by the *Catechism*, "*the obedience of faith*," a phrase from Saint Paul (Rom. 1:5).[7] This concerns us because prayer, contemplative prayer, is the privileged moment of that obedience of faith. It involves not only hearing the Word of God but also "the unconditional acceptance of a servant, and the loving commitment of a child" (*Catechism*, no. 2716).

Abraham believed and his faith grew when he saw the power of God at work in his life. This is the general way in which God's pedagogy can be seen. Acting with power throughout history, God teaches us to believe in Him, in His Word and His action. We see Him, long after the time of Abraham, at the moment of

---

7 Cf. *Catechism*, nos. 143–149; 494; 1125; 1204; 2087; 2716.

the consecration of the temple by Solomon (cf. 1 Kings 8:10–61) where Solomon's prayer recalls God's promise and Covenant and the active presence of His name among His People.

The psalms are called in the *Catechism* a "mirror of God's marvelous deeds in the history of his people" (*Catechism*, no. 2588), to such a degree that in this book above all, the Word of God becomes the daily prayer of the whole Church. The *Catechism* speaks of the *Book of the Psalms* as "the masterwork of prayer in the Old Testament" (no. 2596). God also reveals Himself in each of our lives. His pedagogy leads us little by little to put all our faith and all our trust in Him.

God educates people in faith, either directly or through collaborators such as the prophets. To grasp something of their prayer, we must look at Elijah, "the father of the prophets." The *Catechism* uses a phrase from a psalm to describe him: "such is the generation of those who seek him, who seek the Face of the God of Jacob" (Ps. 24:6; cf. *Catechism*, no. 2582). Knowledge of God and of His will, which the prophets drew on in their own meeting with God, makes them educators of the faith of the people. In this sense, the prophets are models for catechists.

If Scripture, particularly the *Letter to the Hebrews*, praises so much the people of faith amongst Israel's ancestors, it is because faith is the required passageway for an encounter with God. "By faith Enoch was taken up so that he should not see death. ... Without faith it is impossible to please [God]" (Heb. 11:5–6). To strongly insist on the necessity of faith in prayer, the *Catechism* tells us in the manner of Saint John of the Cross: "One enters into prayer ... by the narrow gate of *faith*" (*Catechism*, no. 2656).

CERTAINTY ABOUT THE FECUNDITY OF THE FAITH

To say that faith is necessary to please God and take part in the status of His sons, is to affirm the fecundity of faith. Because he was "strong in his faith" (Rom. 4:20), Abraham became the "father of all who believe" (Rom. 4:11, 18; cf. Gen. 15:5).

Thus prepared by the Revelation of the first Covenant, we can receive the teaching and education of Jesus Himself, who is the great Pedagogue of faith. He is "the pioneer and perfecter of our faith" (cf. Heb. 12:2). He demands faith of those who approach Him and He hears their prayer whether it is expressed in words by the leper (cf. Mk. 1:40–41), Jairus (cf. Mk. 5:36), the Canaanite woman (cf. Mk. 7:29), the good thief (cf. Lk. 23:39–43), or in silence by those carrying the paralytic (cf. Mk. 2:5), the woman with the haemorrhage who touched His garment (cf. Mk. 5:28), the tears and ointment of the sinful woman (cf. Lk. 7:37–38). Jesus always responds to a prayer offered in faith: "Your faith has made you well; go in peace" (Mk. 5:34; Lk. 8:47).

Jesus also teaches us to have the audacity of faith or "filial boldness" (Eph. 3:12). "Whatever you ask in prayer, believe that you receive it, and you will" (Mk. 11:24). Such is the power of prayer and faith! This is why Jesus is saddened when He encounters a lack of faith or the "little faith" (cf. Mt. 8:26) of His disciples. This, too, is why "he is struck with admiration at the great faith of the Roman centurion and the Canaanite woman (cf. Mt. 8:10; 15:28)" (*Catechism*, no. 2610).

To grasp something of the fruitfulness of faith in prayer, we must return to the definition of faith that the *Catechism* gives us: It is inseparably "a personal adherence of man to God" and "a *free assent to the whole truth that God has revealed*" (*Catechism*, no. 150, emphasis in the original). Faith is trust in the divine Person and intellectual adherence to what that Person has revealed. This signifies that, in the act of faith, all our being adheres to God in considering Him in His mystery as the Word of God, and the Magisterium presents it to us through the revealed formulas. These formulas cannot be ignored because they express the mystery, and we pass through them to join ourselves to Him. We don't stop at the formulas which can satisfy our intelligence, but the dogmatic formula allows us to "touch" the reality which it sets out, that is to say, God Himself. The *Catechism* takes up explicitly the teaching of Saint Thomas and implicitly that of Saint John of the Cross, who said, "faith communicates and gives to us God himself."[8]

Using quotation marks to say that faith "touches" God, it seems that the *Catechism* takes up a teaching dear to Fr. Marie-Eugène.[9] The fruitfulness of faith comes from faith being only a response to the thirst of Jesus who wants us to drink of His Spirit (cf. *Catechism*, no. 2560). "If any one thirst, let him come to me and drink. He who believes in me, as Scripture has said, 'Out of his heart shall flow rivers of living water'" (Jn. 7:37–38). In faith, the sick woman touched Christ from whom flowed a saving force; he who believes in Jesus drinks the living water of the Spirit which Jesus pours: such are the biblical foundations of certainty of the fecundity of faith; he who makes an act of faith in prayer "touches" God, and God communicates Himself to him. Thus, in prayer, I fix God with my gaze of faith and I adhere with all my being to the mystery of God, who only awaits from me that orientation of faith to give Himself to me.

---

8 Saint John of the Cross, *Spiritual Canticle* B, v 12.

9 Cf. P. Marie-Eugene O.C.D., *I Want to See God* and *I Am a Daughter of the Church: A Practical Synthesis of Carmelite Spirituality*, Combined Edition (Allen, TX: Christian Classics, 1986), *I Want to See God*: 78.

Fr. Marie-Eugène summarizes this teaching, which belongs to the universal treasure of the Church:

> Just as one cannot plunge one's hand in water without getting wet, or in the fire without getting burned, in the same way one cannot have contact with God through faith without drawing something from His infinite richness. The poor sick woman who tried to get to Jesus across the thick crowd, in the streets of Capernaum, was saying to herself: "If I can just touch the fringes of His garment, I will be healed." She finally reaches Him and extracts, through contact that makes the Master tremble, the desired healing. All contact with God through faith has the same efficacy. … It draws from God an increase in supernatural life, an enrichment of charity." [10]

Whoever wants to draw near to God needs faith because he must first "believe that He exists" and also that He "rewards those who seek him" (Heb. 11:6). This verse expresses well the necessity and the fecundity of faith. Yes, "faith is *certain*. It is more certain than all human knowledge, because it is founded on the very word of God who cannot lie" (*Catechism*, no. 157, emphasis in the original). Another verse of the *Letter to the Hebrews* describes faith in its certainty and fecundity, "Now faith is the assurance of things hoped for, the conviction of things not seen" (Heb. 11:1).

THE OBSCURITY OF FAITH, SOURCE OF STRUGGLE

Through the figure of Abraham and so many others in the history of salvation, Jesus teaches us that there is also an obscure aspect to faith: Abraham left "not knowing where he was to go" (Heb. 11:8). Faith is very much a personal adherence of man to God even when "revealed truths can seem obscure to human reason and experience" (*Catechism*, no. 157). They are even habitually so because Saint Paul reminds us that "we walk by faith, not by sight" (2 Cor. 5:7), and we know God as if "in a mirror, dimly" (1 Cor. 13:12).

This helps us realize the importance of the definition: "Faith is a filial adherence to God beyond what we feel and understand" (*Catechism*, no. 2609). There is an apprenticeship to be done. The *Catechism* (cf. no. 53) takes from Saint Irenaeus the notion of needing to take time for "becoming accustomed" to perceive God. This is very relevant here; we must make a *habit* of fixing our gaze on the mystery of God, even when feeling nothing, seeing nothing, tasting nothing. Although there

---

10 P. Marie-Eugene, *I Want to See God* and *I Am a Daughter of the Church: I Want to See God* : 59.

is obscurity, there is also certainty that I am in contact with Him, because through baptism I received the virtue of faith, which has that capacity.

Prayer "in faith" is the beginning of a real encounter, which takes place in obscurity. "Enlightened by him in whom it believes, faith is often lived in darkness" (*Catechism*, no. 164). Such is the paradox of faith: it is at the same time luminous and "obscure" (cf. *Catechism*, no. 157). It's the teaching of Saint John of the Cross, which Fr. Marie-Eugène summarized in this cornerstone formula: "faith [and thus contemplative prayer] is a face-to-face in the darkness."[11]

That is to say that the prayer of faith does not come from itself. We can believe this from the definition of the prayer of faith given by different saints, for example, in the words of Saint Thérèse of the Child Jesus: "For me, *prayer* is a leap of the heart, a simple gaze thrown at the heavens, it is a cry of recognition and love in ordeal as in joy."[12] Prayer is this, in effect, in its loving simplicity and its permanence, but the prayer of faith is also a struggle, and Saint Thérèse had a sad experience with her ordeal of faith. We know that God can put our faith to the test, but, in His bounty, He invites us to gaze on witnesses of the Faith (cf. Heb. 12:1) to support us in this struggle. The pedagogy of God consists in presenting to us concrete models of the response, which He awaits from us.

Here also, Abraham is the great witness of faith. The *Catechism* reminds us of Abraham's prayer as, "a veiled complaint reminding God of His promises which seem unfulfilled" (cf. Genesis 15:2–3, *Catechism*, no. 2570). Here again, we see in prayer a test of faith. Abraham is put to the test again with the demand to sacrifice Isaac and he would have to believe, the *Letter to the Hebrews* tells us, that God "was able to raise men even from the dead" (Heb. 11:19). And "Abraham's faith does not weaken" (*Catechism*, no. 2572). This is what is at stake in prayer, and it is to help us strengthen our faith, keeping faithfully awake in prayer in an interior gaze constantly turned towards the Lord.

Another figure, that of Jacob, shows us how this struggle can last for a long time, a whole night; but the struggle finishes with a blessing from the Lord (cf. Gen. 32:24–29). In itself, the obscurity of faith—and hence of prayer—is normal, because faith is not through sight. But it is also presented to us as a pedagogy, a means of purification, which the Lord uses, making us persevere in wakeful waiting or even in demanding the impossible of us so that we have trust only in Him.

---

11 Cahier C, 19, cited in Louis Menvielle, *Thérèse Docteur racontée par Fr. Marie-Eugène*, vol. I, *Histoire d'un thérésien* (Venasque, 1998), 57.

12 Saint Thérèse of the Child Jesus, *Manuscrits autobiographiques*, C 25r.

DISTRACTIONS

The obscurity of faith implies almost of necessity that we experience distraction. This is a habitual difficulty. On this subject, one can find many comparisons between the *Catechism* and *I Want to see God* by Fr. Marie-Eugène.[13] The *Catechism* warns us not to hunt down distractions, as this would be precisely "to fall into their trap" (*Catechism*, no. 2729). We will only wear ourselves out with this kind of struggle. The most effective solution is "to return to the heart," that is to say, to contemplation in faith to find again the mysterious presence of the Lord. A vigilant heart waits for the Bridegroom who "comes in the middle of the night; the light that must not be extinguished is that of faith: 'Come,' my heart says, 'seek his face' (Ps. 27:8)" (*Catechism*, no. 2730).

Distraction also has a pedagogical function: it "reveals to us what we are attached to" (*Catechism*, no. 2729). The distraction reveals the battle: which master do we want to serve? (cf. Mt. 6:24). So that distractions do not make us become lukewarm we must nourish ourselves with Scripture; we must beg Our Lord to increase our faith; we must depend on the virtues of charity and hope; we must place our trust in the Faith of the Church.

This shows us that prayer is inseparable from the gift of self. "Prayer and the gift of self are but one" (*Catechism*, no. 2605). Mary is a perfect example of this indispensable union of faith and self-giving (cf. *Catechism*, no. 2622). Mary, with Abraham, is a principal "witness of faith." She is even the "most perfect embodiment" of the obedience of faith (*Catechism*, no. 144).

DURATION AND PERSEVERANCE IN PRAYER

The problem of distraction leads us to the question of the duration of prayer. Saint Paul insists on continual prayer: "Pray constantly" (1 Thess. 5:17). "Always and for everything [give] thanks in the name of Our Lord Jesus Christ to God the Father" (Eph. 5:20). "Pray at all times in the Spirit, with all prayer and supplication. To that end keep alert with all perseverance making supplication for all the saints" (Eph. 6:18).

We have already remarked that Jesus wasn't only a Man of prayer; He *was* prayer. And Jesus is still prayer, since risen again and at the Father's right hand, "he always lives to make intercession" (Heb. 7:25).

However, the *Catechism* is realistic in acknowledging that no one can "pray at all times." Realistically one needs to give some specific lengths of time to intense

---

13 See P. Marie-Eugene, *I Want to See God* and *I Am a Daughter of the Church: I want to see God* 213.

conscious attention to prayer. This is effectively what Jesus did, who prayed—apparently habitually—(e.g. in the morning before daybreak, cf. Mk. 1:35; in the evening, cf. Mt. 14:23; or at night on the mountain, cf. Lk. 6:12). The *Catechism* also makes clear, "prayer cannot be reduced to the spontaneous outpouring of interior impulse" (*Catechism*, no. 2650). It is important to set aside specific time dedicated to the Lord and freely will to pray with *humility, trust, and persevering love* (cf. *Catechism*, no. 2742). Without this there is no continual prayer, no approaching "praying at all times." That is why the *Catechism* affirms that the deliberate choice of a length of time set aside for prayer is what truly reveals "the secrets of the heart" (*Catechism*, no. 2710).

The formation of catechists will pass, thus, through the apprenticeship of that fidelity to contemplative prayer where faith is strengthened, penetrates the depths of God, and, mysteriously, draws in its richness from the treasures of light and love that reflects back on others. Our conviction must be that contemplative prayer, often experienced in darkness, is actually "a communion of love bearing Life for the multitude" (*Catechism*, no. 2719).

"So," Jesus asks each of us, "could you not watch with me one hour?" (Mt. 26:40)

III. THE ACTION OF THE SPIRIT

From the preceding lectures, one could believe that all Christians should do to pray is do as Jesus did and exercise their virtue of faith. They would thus be the only protagonists of prayer. Prayer would consist only in the human act of addressing oneself to God. Many people believe that prayer is only a human act and they get discouraged when they do not depend on the Holy Spirit to help them persevere. God Himself acts in prayer.

When we do not know that prayer comes from the Holy Spirit, we become discouraged because we believe ourselves to be alone and "we do not know how to pray as we ought" (Rom. 8:26); and we become discouraged eventually because we do not understand what is happening in prayer while the Holy Spirit intervenes in it "with sighs too deep for words" (Rom. 8:26).

The Presence of the Spirit in Us

"The Holy Spirit ... is the *interior Master* of Christian prayer" (*Catechism*, no. 2672, emphasis added). It is therefore important to be conscious of His presence in us and to know how He intervenes in our prayer.

His presence in us is affirmed by Jesus Himself. Jesus' promise is recounted in John's Gospel. "And I will pray the Father, and he will give you another counselor, to be with you for ever, … you know him, for he dwells with you, and will be in you" (Jn. 14:17). And since the mission of the Holy Spirit consists, in particular, in reminding us of all that Jesus said and in leading us to the complete truth, He also reminds us of Christ's teaching on prayer and He leads us to it. Jesus tells us about the Holy Spirit "will teach you all things, and bring to your remembrance all that I have said to you" (Jn. 14:26).

A first consequence of this truth is that it would be pointless for us to begin to pray if we did not commence by invoking the Holy Spirit, like the apostles who, "in the upper room, where they were staying … with one accord devoted themselves to prayer" (Acts 1:13–14), and waited upon "the Spirit of the Promise" (*Catechism*, no. 2623). This is why the *Catechism* gives two traditional formulas of the prayer "Come, Holy Spirit," which it invites us to begin with as we pray (cf. *Catechism*, no. 2671).

The Spirit Who Makes Us Cry: Abba, Father!

So what does the Spirit do in our prayer? He always intervenes, in one manner or another, since "no one can say 'Jesus is Lord' except by the Holy Spirit" (1 Cor. 12:3). This signifies that it is impossible for us to place ourselves in the supernatural plane without the action of the Spirit. Faith, hope, and charity are *theological* virtues, that is, virtues which "relate directly to God" and dispose us to live in a relationship with the Holy Trinity.

It is necessary to go further. We know that Jesus is the perfect Son of the Father and that He draws us into His filial relationship. He makes us divine in identifying us with Himself and thus authorizes us to say, with Him and in Him: Abba, Father! He realizes this in us by giving us His Spirit. It is the act of receiving the Holy Spirit itself which identifies us with Jesus, in making sons of us. Just as, in the eternity of the Trinity, the Father is Father because He gives all that He is to His Son, in the same way God gives us in the Holy Spirit participation in His divine nature (cf. *Catechism* no. 1988). The act of giving us what He is Himself makes of us His sons, in the image of the unique Son to whom He has given everything. That is why the *Catechism* affirms that "the proof and possibility of our filial prayer is that the Father 'sent the Spirit of his Son into our hearts, crying: "Abba, Father!"' [Gal. 4:6]" (cf. *Catechism*, no. 2766).

The *Catechism* insists on this great reality so that we do not get satisfaction from particular gifts which our prayer obtains for us from God. Beyond these particular gifts, there is the Giver Himself (cf. *Catechism*, no. 2740), the Father, and filial prayer consists in placing oneself confidently under His fatherhood to receive, not only such and such a gift, but the perfect Gift and fullness that is His Spirit (cf. *Catechism*, no. 2741).

The Spirit make us divine in making sons of us (cf. *Catechism*, no. 2673). The two missions of the Son and the Spirit cannot be separated: one gives us His Spirit, the other unites us with Christ. One always sends us back to the other to introduce us into the filial relationship. It is truly a "joint mission" (*Catechism*, no. 689).

The "Joint" Pedagogy of the Son and the Spirit in the Our Father

To grasp something of the pedagogy of God in prayer, one must look at how this "joint mission" of the Son and the Spirit causes a common pedagogy to be carried out in the perfect prayer of the *Our Father*.

The whole section of the *Catechism* dedicated to the *Our Father* shows how this prayer is the typical example of the pedagogy of Jesus, and this is precisely why it is called the *Lord's Prayer*, because it was taught and given to us by the Lord Jesus. He prays in front of His disciples to give them the desire to pray like Him. When they ask Him to teach them to pray, Jesus shows Himself as simultaneously the Master and the Model of prayer (cf. *Catechism*, no. 2765) when He teaches them this prayer to "Our Father" which corresponds exactly to our filial relationship and our needs. The text of the *Our Father* is itself pedagogical. The *Catechism* cites Saint Thomas Aquinas who explains that, in this prayer, "we ask, not only for all the things we can rightly desire, but also in the sequence that they should be desired. This prayer not only teaches us to ask for things, but also in what order we should desire them."[14]

The *Our Father* is also the prayer where the pedagogy of the Holy Spirit is exercised because Jesus does not leave us merely a formula to repeat mechanically. At the same time He gives us His Spirit through whom our filial prayer becomes "spirit and life." It is about the Spirit of the Son crying in our hearts "Abba, Father!" (Gal. 4:6), the very cry of Jesus. Only the Spirit by whom we live can make "our own" the same mind that was in Christ Jesus (cf. Gal. 5:25; Phil. 2:1, 5). We are impelled by the Spirit, and by the Father, who "knows what is the mind of the Spirit" (Rom. 8:27). The mind of the Spirit is the "sighs too deep for words" (Rom. 8:26), the call

14 Saint Thomas Aquinas, *ST*, 2a, 2ae, 83, 9.

of the parched earth which longs for streams of living water. It is the "Maranatha," the cry of the Spirit and the Bride: "Come, Lord Jesus" (Rev. 22:20).[15] We do not say the *Our Father* alone but in the Spirit with Christ.

The "Sighs too Deep for Words" of the Spirit

We must return to the "sighs too deep for words" of the Spirit and the two formulas of Saint Paul who made this expression explicit: "the Spirit helps us in our weakness; for we do not know how to pray as we ought" (Rom. 8:26) and "it is the Spirit himself bearing witness with our spirit that we are children of God" (Rom. 8:16).

How should we understand these affirmations? We can be certain that the Lord leads each of us by diverse paths and in ways that please Him (cf. *Catechism*, no. 2699). The *Catechism* holds up, above all, one person as a guide among those who, throughout Tradition, the Spirit arouses in the Church—Saint Teresa of Avila with her definition of contemplative prayer:

> Contemplative prayer in my opinion is nothing else than a close sharing between friends; it means taking time frequently to be alone with him who we know loves us.[16]

This definition is interesting because it underlines that one is not alone in prayer. Prayer is an exchange of love with God who loves us. The *Editio Typica* Latin text of the *Catechism* has translated *oratio* as "contemplative prayer." This choice can be debated; however, it requires us to look at the contemplative aspect of prayer which is considered its summit, to which other forms of prayer tend (cf. *Catechism*, no. 2708). Entry into contemplative prayer is already the work of the Spirit: "we 'gather up' the heart, recollect our whole being under the prompting of the Holy Spirit" (*Catechism*, no. 2711).

ACTIVE AND PASSIVE RECOLLECTION

"Recollection" can be active. I bring it about through my efforts to put into practice the words of Jesus: "but when you pray, go to your room and shut your door and pray to your Father who is in secret " (Mt. 6:6). The *Catechism* lists the places that are favorable to prayer: the church, a monastery, a prayer corner (cf. *Catechism*, no. 2691). These types of places favor active recollection, because we can withdraw from

---

15 See *Catechism*, nos. 2817, 2853.

16 Saint Teresa of Jesus, *The Book of Her Life*, 8, 5 in *The Collected Works of St. Teresa of Avila*, trans. K. Kavanaugh OCD and O. Rodriguez OCD (Washington DC: Institute of Carmelite Studies, 1976), 1, 67.

the noise of the world and enter into a silence which speaks of God; we close the door of our own room and we pray to the Father.

Recollection can also be the fruit of an action of the Spirit who "gathers up" my being through an interior call that is barely perceptable but efficacious, what Saint Teresa of Avila calls a "whistle by the good shepherd," [17] who has so much power over the senses and the faculties of the soul that they abandon the exterior things in which they were absorbed and return into recollection. The Spirit then acts through the gifts that were given to us at Baptism, the virtues which enable us to be docile to His promptings.

A GAZE IN THE SILENCE

Silence is not necessarily lazy passivity. It can be an interior focus fixed on the Lord in silent love. In an astonishingly simple way, this is what the peasant of Ars described to his parish priest, when praying in front of the tabernacle he said simply that he "looked" at Him and He, God, "looks at me." Far from being passive, contemplative prayer is a gaze of faith ("I look at Him") often supported by words, which are not a discussion but a kind of "kindling" to feed the fire of love. Far from being passive, contemplative prayer is a mysterious listening to Jesus, the Word of God.

A GAZE INTO THE DRYNESS

We remember that faith is at the same time full of light and yet obscure. Jesus lights up our hearts with such a light that we are dazzled by it, as dazzled as our eyes are when they want to stare at the sun which is too strong for us. And just as the eyes insinctively turn away from the sun which dazzles them with its light, though it is beneficial, in the same way our faith cannot stop staring at a divine mystery which floods the soul with a light that beatifies but is inaccessible and dazzling. The effect of God's action in contemplative prayer is quite often distraction, as we have said.

Distraction can become a state of prayer. It is then called "dryness," insofar as it is not the result of a half-heartedness which would then require conversion. The *Cathechism* warns us that dryness "is the moment of sheer faith clinging faithfully to Jesus in his agony and in his tomb" (*Catechism*, no. 2731). Dryness is thus the habitual state of contemplative prayer and the book, *I Want to see God*, makes explicit what the *Catechism* calls humble and persevering vigilance (cf. *Catechism*, nos. 2612, 2730). This dryness, while authentic, is allowed by the Spirit for an educational purpose. The *Catechism* cites Evagrius and Saint Augustine on the subject of the

---

17 See, Book IV *Demeures*, 3, 2.

prayer of request. We can apply it to dryness where, digging into our hearts, the Spirit hollows out in us a desire for Himself:

> Do not be troubled if you do not immediately receive from God what you ask him; for he desires to do something even greater for you, while you cling to him in prayer.[18]

DRYNESS IS A CONSEQUENCE OF THE SPIRIT'S INTERVENTION

Dryness also comes from the action of the Spirit Himself who comes to the help of our weakness; He constantly seeks to awaken us to keep watch, in His own way. The virtue of faith cannot remain for a long time with God because of the dazzling which represents "interior knowledge of the Lord." This transcends the natural capacity of our intelligence, accustomed to knowledge of the things here below. Our intelligence is dazzled, it is stripped and no longer able to sustain the act of faith. This is our "weakness." If we are faithful to finding again the presence of the Lord through a succession of acts of faith, the Holy Spirit sees our good will and "comes to the help of our weakness." That which we are incapable of doing, He does Himself, expressing "sighs too deep for words," that is, sighs which only God hears, who knows everything in our hearts and knows perfectly well what the Spirit means.

What are these "sighs"? It is the action of the Spirit who, through the mediation of the gifts of the Holy Spirit, substitutes for intelligence while itself supporting the virtue of faith being exercised. Theology says that the motive of faith becomes God Himself, and this perfects the exercise of faith. The Holy Spirit constantly perfects our faith by His gifts (cf. *DV* 5). The virtue of faith can then remain for a long time with God and drink long draughts of living water full of light and love.

But these realities happen in the "heart," that is, in our own deepest center, the center known only by the saints who have arrived at its summit. The *Catechism* definition, here, is truer than ever: "Faith is a filial adherence to God beyond what we feel and understand" (*Catechism*, no. 2609). "Beyond," means in the depths of our being which escape us, leaving us with "what we feel and understand" which, here, is the sad experience of weakness, sensitivity, and human faculties which do not succeed in fixing on God: this is dryness.

Contemplative prayer is a union with the prayer of Christ insofar as it makes us participate in His mystery. Without our realizing it, this dryness is praise of God. By agreeing to plunge freely into God's paternity in sheer faith with no thoughts,

---

18 Evagrius, *De Oratione* 34.

memories, or feelings, not even spiritual ones (cf. *Catechism*, no. 2731), such prayer, entirely for God's own sake, "gives him glory, quite beyond what He does, but simply because He is" (*Catechism*, no. 2639).

EXPERIENCE OF THE SPIRIT HIMSELF

As I have said, the saints who have arrived at the summit perceive something of these very profound realities, which Saint John of the Cross calls "*je ne sais quoi*," but, he specifies, "it is of the night." A passage from the book, *I Want to see God*, gives a good description of this quite supernatural experience, not only of the love which God infuses into us, but of the very source of that love: the Holy Spirit, a friendly and acting presence, a presence which teaches and transforms, a presence to which our contemplative prayer aspires.

Translated by Dr. Anne St. John-Hall.

PART 3

Considerations for Method

9

The Pedagogy of God: Source and Model for the Pedagogy of the Faith

Waltraud Linnig

In this short piece I would like to propose a few points to stimulate dialogue and reflection. The first one concerns the pedagogy of God more directly, while the second one sheds light on the link between the divine pedagogy and the pedagogy used by the Church: "How is the pedagogy of God the source and model of the pedagogy of faith?"

THE DIVINE PEDAGOGY AND ITS CHARACTERISTICS

When we speak of pedagogy, we speak of the *art of educating*, the art of knowing how to "lead the child" (this is the etymology of the word) so that he may reach adult maturity. Therefore, speaking of pedagogy involves speaking about a *journey* or a progression. The path along which the child travels in order to become an adult involves various stages where he advances progressively. This progression takes him from a state that can be called imperfect (childhood) to a perfect state (adulthood).

When we speak about the *divine* pedagogy, the pathway is the one that *God* proposes to the sinner in order for him to be saved and to benefit from the salvation given by Christ. The divine pedagogy refers, therefore, to a journey that concerns the relationship between man and God. It establishes a covenant; it reconciles man with God. Pius XI, in the encyclical *Mit Brennender Sorge*, spoke of a "pedagogy of salvation." The pathway, then, takes the sinner as its starting point; the stages are those of the progressive Revelation of God and of His salvation; the goal is the advent of the Savior and the full entry of the human person into the salvation of God.

We cannot, therefore, separate the pedagogy of God from the economy of salvation. The latter is the way by which God dispenses salvation, the progression in Revelation—His divine activity—taking place in words and actions (cf. *DV* 2). When we speak of divine pedagogy, we also underline the fact that this progression depends on the way by which man advances towards God. We can already see here the importance of Scripture, which witnesses to the economy of salvation, in focusing our attention upon the pedagogy of God. I will come back to this point at the end of the chapter.

Let us take up again the vocabulary of the "perfect" and "imperfect." According to Pius XI's encyclical, imperfection and perfection in the "pedagogy of salvation" concern Revelation itself. God's action is progressive because He must adapt Himself to the weaknesses and sins of mankind.[1] Man must be prepared little by little to receive the fullness and perfection of Revelation in Christ. The progression of divine pedagogy, therefore, concerns God's own action, but it is due to the state, the situation, and the dispositions of the person who is to be saved. In this sense, we are shown that the perfection of action in God is found in Christ,[2] linked to the perfection and effectiveness of His person. In Him, both divine and human action finds their summit.

The 1971 *General Catechetical Directory* refers to Hebrews 12:2 to underline the fact that progression in perfection does not only concern God's action, but also the advancement of mankind in the *Faith*: from no faith to an imperfect faith, man walks little by little towards a perfect faith thanks to Christ; it is Christ who leads mankind's faith to perfection.[3] It is interesting to note that the Church's documents speak of the *"pedagogy of faith,"* almost always linking it to the action of the Church. Now, the 1997 *General Directory for Catechesis* speaks of a pedagogy of faith as meaning first of all the pedagogy of *Christ*.[4] This is already an indication of

---

1 Cf. *Mit Brennender Sorge*, 19: "The sacred books of the Old Testament are exclusively the word of God, and constitute a substantial part of his revelation; they are penetrated by a subdued light, harmonizing with the slow development of revelation, the dawn of the bright day of the redemption. As should be expected in historical and didactic books, they reflect in many particulars the imperfection, the weakness and sinfulness of man. But side by side with innumerable touches of greatness and nobleness, they also record the story of the chosen people, bearers of the Revelation and the Promise, repeatedly straying from God and turning to the world."

2 "He brought to the world the supreme gift of salvation by accomplishing his redemptive mission in a manner which continued 'the pedagogy of God,' with the perfection found in the newness of his Person" (GDC 140).

3 Cf. GCD 33.

4 Cf. GDC 140: "Inviting his disciples to follow him unreservedly and without regret (cf. Mk. 8:34–38; Mt. 8:18–22) Christ passed on to them his *pedagogy of faith* as a full sharing in his actions and in his destiny" (emphasis added).

the link between the pedagogy of God and the pedagogy of the Church, to which we will be coming back later.

I have noted these aspects since it seems important that catechesis should encompass all the elements of the pedagogy of God. Man's progression, implied by the divine pedagogy, is very complex. It mirrors natural growth by the passage from the state of sinner to saved and by growth in the Faith. It is certainly one of the goals of catechesis to hold to these aspects and clarify them adequately. The *General Directory for Catechesis* proposes that a strong link be established between education in one's relationship with God and human education: "Evangelize by educating and educate by evangelizing" is the title given to this section.

> Being inspired by the pedagogy of faith, catechesis presents its service as a designated educative journey in that, on the one hand, it assists the person to open himself to the religious dimension of life, while on the other, it proposes the Gospel to him. It does so in such a manner as to penetrate and transform the processes of intelligence, conscience, liberty and action, making of existence a gift after the example of Jesus Christ. Thus the catechist knows and avails of the contribution of the sciences of education, understood always in a Christian sense. (GDC 147)

Starting from these very simple points on the pedagogy of God, here are some questions upon which we might reflect:

1. How should we distinguish and link the education of the human person in his or her natural growth—something which concerns the natural religious dimension of mankind—with the evangelization of the sinner called to salvation and called to growth in the Faith until he reaches the maturity of an "adult witness" of Christ? We need to accurately distinguish between the order of creation and the order of redemption.

2. If the divine pedagogy is a pedagogy of salvation, is it not the case that in our catecheses we have forgotten the subject of sin—forgotten original sin, for example, out of a concern to avoid provoking unhealthy notions? How should we speak about sin, so that those who are being catechized may advance towards salvation?

3. The *Catechism* provides us with a quotation from Saint Irenaeus that tells us the reason for this progressive divine pedagogy: it is so that God may become accustomed to mankind, and so that man may in turn become accustomed to God.[5] The progression, then, concerns the personal relationship between God and man; a *relationship* between persons takes time to build and has its own proper characteristics. Do we take this point sufficiently into account in our catechesis? If a relationship between persons is being built, we must be conscious that the catechist is dealing with two allied *freedoms:* divine freedom and human freedom. Neither of them may be forced. The "craft"[6] of catechesis consists precisely in this, of putting these two friendships in communion. How should we do this? In his book *I Want to See God*, Father Marie-Eugène underlines the fact that human reason is limited and that it cannot grasp completely the mystery of God's free action.[7] It is no less delicate a task to lead human freedom on its path to God.

4. The *Catechism* manifests the logic of divine pedagogy by means of a quotation from Saint Gregory of Nazianzen.[8] According to him, it is a question of prudence: "it was not prudent, when the divinity of the Father had not yet been confessed, to proclaim the Son openly and, when the divinity of the Son was not yet admitted, to add the Holy Spirit as an extra burden, to speak somewhat daringly." This quotation shows us that if, in His pedagogy, God must *adapt* to mankind, this adaptation does not only concern *language* (cf. *DV* 13 and also *GDC* 146), nor simply a *strength* that must be measured according to the weakness of man (see *GCD* 33), but it is also a question of the *logic of Revelation:* there is an order in the Trinity, there is an order in the knowledge and recognition

5 See the *Catechism*, no. 53. The quotation from Saint Irenaeus is taken from *Adv. Haer.* 3, 20, 2; cf. also 3, 17, 1; 4, 12, 4; 4, 21, 3.

6 This is the expression used by P. Willey, P. de Cointet, and B. Morgan in *The Catechism of the Catholic Church and the Craft of Catechesis* (San Francisco: Ignatius Press 2008).

7 See P. Marie-Eugene, O.C.D., *I Want to See God: A Practical Synthesis of Carmelite Spirituality* (Allen, TX: Thomas More Association, 1998), 136–150.

8 See the *Catechism*, no. 684. "The Old Testament proclaimed the Father clearly, but the Son more obscurely. The New Testament revealed the Son and gave us a glimpse of the divinity of the Spirit. Now the Spirit dwells among us and grants us a clearer vision of himself. It was not prudent, when the divinity of the Father had not yet been confessed, to proclaim the Son openly and, when the divinity of the Son was not yet admitted, to add the Holy Spirit as an extra burden, to speak somewhat daringly. ... By advancing and progressing 'from glory to glory,' the light of the Trinity will shine in ever more brilliant rays" (Saint Gregory of Naziansus, *Oratio theol.* 5, 26; PG 36, 161–163). Saint Gregory of Nazianzus, the theologian, then, explains this progression in terms of a pedagogy, of divine "condescension."

of the three divine persons by man. In catechesis, this order is not set in contradiction to the christocentrism, which is strongly required by the Church, but it is at its service. It is by respecting the order of Revelation that man is led to Christ who alone is able to lead the person into the mystery of the Trinity (cf. *CT* 5). Do we not sometimes present Christ too quickly, without having first set down the foundations of a sufficiently solid faith in God, Creator and Father, and without having educated the person in his or her own humanity, to enable him or her to enter into this faith in God? Who will Christ be for those who have been catechized, if faith in God the Creator is not anchored in their hearts?

To help us consider these questions, we can refer to the *three aspects* that characterize the divine pedagogy in the Old Testament according to *Dei Verbum* 15: the preparation for the advent of Christ, the declaration in prophecy of His coming, and its signification by means of symbols and types. These three aspects concern both the knowledge of Christ and also the action of man, who must also collaborate with His coming.

Some consideration in our reflections on these points should also be given to the "*evangelization of the heart*," which prepares the human person for faith in God, the Father, Son, and Holy Spirit. This "evangelization of the heart" is indispensable for catechesis; moreover, it is usually no longer assured through family life or through the immediate circle of the catechized, as it used to be, in a Christian society. It is very significant to realize that in *Catechesi Tradendae*, Pope John Paul II repeats an expression from *Presbyterorum Ordinis*, which is written about the priesthood, and applies it to all catechists saying that the catechist must be an "educator—of man and of the life of man—in the faith."

The *General Directory Catechesis* speaks of the "pedagogy of the Incarnation," saying that "the Gospel is to be proposed for the life and in the life of people" (*GDC* 143). Now, sometimes this expression is understood to mean that in catechesis, we have to "take charge of all the concrete circumstances, all the life, all the language, all the questions of men, in order to be able to announce the Gospel message in an adequate manner,"[9] as if we had to root ourselves in humankind and all its dimensions to the point that we would never be able to free ourselves from this situation. "Starting from life" is often a synonym for "staying" at the lowest point of man's

---

9 Andre Fossion, *La catechese dans le champ de la communication: Ses enjeux pour l'inculturation de la foi* (Cogitatio fidei 156), French Edition (Paris: Editions du Cerf, 1990), 207.

experience and forgetting the encounter with the Word of God, with all the new-ness of Revelation.

"Follow the way of man," counsels Saint Augustine, "and you will reach God."[10] Augustine is speaking here of the *humanity of Christ*, who is the way, the truth, and the life (cf. Jn. 14:6). E. Barbotin comments: "The catechesis of Jesus arises from humble daily realities in order to lead man from the experience of the world to the light of the revelation of the Kingdom of God."[11] The pedagogy of the Incarnation, then, does not mean simply that man should be met at the most concrete point of his life—which is necessary, as we know—but above all means al-lowing life to be transfigured by God's grace!

At present, there are few books on catechesis that pay much attention to divine pedagogy. On the other hand, the pedagogical sciences do play a significant part in them. This is sometimes linked to the fact that the divine pedagogy is under-stood as an analogy of the pedagogical sciences, rather than the reverse.[12] For these authors it follows that there cannot be a revealed pedagogical methodology which is applicable to all mankind, all cultures, and all time. However, spelling out the progressive levels in the divine pedagogy as we have sketched above could allow us to place the pedagogical sciences in relation to this very pedagogy of salvation and of faith. This question touches on the relationship between the action of God and that of man, between faith and reason.

THE DIVINE PEDAGOGY AND THE PEDAGOGY OF FAITH

In the Church's texts, many expressions are employed to qualify the link between divine pedagogy and the pedagogy of the Church. The *General Catechetical Directory* employs the expression "mindful of the pedagogy used by God" (GCD 33) without explaining how this *remembrance* of the divine pedagogy should influence the peda-gogy of catechesis.

Catechesi Tradendae proposes divine catechesis as a *model* for the pedagogy of the Church (CT 58). In saying "model," does it mean that we must "imitate" God's own way of doing things? In what way can God's action serve as a model for human action in the transmission of Revelation? Can man do the same thing as God?

---

10 *Sermo* 141, IV, 4.

11 Edmond Barbotin, *Catechese et pedagogie: Problemes actuels* (Le Sycomore), French Edition (Paris: Namur, Lethielleux/Culture et Vérité, 1981), 21.

12 For example, Emilio Alberich with the collaboration of Henri Derroitte et Jérôme Vallabaraj, *Les fondamentaux de la catéchèse* (Bruxelles/ Montréal: Lumen vitae/ Novalis, 2006).

Some authors understand the pedagogy of faith as if it were an *exterior imitation* of the pedagogy of God.[13] The Magisterium of the Church would here take the place of God to the point of substituting itself for Him. In this view, the Church, in its catechetical action, would be a sort of "intermediary" who would transmit Revelation, but without establishing a direct communication between God and the catechized. The Magisterium would thus be a sort of mediation, which would impede a direct relationship with God.

It seems to me that this last interpretation does not take into account the whole thought of John Paul II. For him, it is not a question of replacing the divine action in catechesis, as if God were delegating His power of action to the Church, while He Himself rested!

On the contrary! In *Christifidelis Laici*, God is recognized as "Father," and it is as Father that He is "the first and greatest teacher of his People" (CL 61). The divine pedagogy breaks with the Greek meaning of the word "paidagogos," which meant a child's supervisor (this task was often the duty of a slave); but above all, it was not the father's task (cf. Gal. 3:24–25; 1 Cor. 4:15). According to Scripture, the divine pedagogy is the work of a *loving father* (whether it be God or Saint Paul).

> God's work in forming his people is revealed and fulfilled in Jesus
> Christ the Teacher, and reaches to the depths of every individual's
> heart as a result of the living presence of the Spirit. (CL 61)

Only the divine action is able to touch from within the heart of every person! No one can replace God in this work, which concerns the deepest interiority of man.[14]

In this context, the Church is seen as *mother*: "Mother Church is called to take part in the divine work of formation..." (CL 61 and cf. GDC 141). The collaboration between God-Father and Church-Mother is expressed in Latin by the verb

---

13 For example, A. Fossion, *La catechese dans le champ de la communication*, 59–63.

14 Cf. also GDC 139, which presents God as a "*Father*" whose pedagogy is understood against a background of His *relationship* with His children. The *aim* of this pedagogy is the salvation of persons. The *stages* of the way towards salvation, of persons and of communities, are as follows: the point of departure is the condition in which the person finds him or herself; then, there is a liberation from the chains of evil, an attraction towards God through love, and a growth in this relationship of love for God, until the maturity of a free child, who is faithful and obedient to the Word of God, is reached. That is the pathway. The *means* that God uses in order to be effective are the *vicissitudes* of life which become lessons adapted to the various ages and life circumstances of people; that is, events in the life of the people where God has acted, and these are interpreted with words that will give their meaning. In order for them to be true lessons, these events must have been lived and understood in that sense. God also gives instructions that are to be transmitted to future generations through *catechesis*. He indicates the contents to be taught "when your son shall ask" what a rite means, for example (cf. Deut. 6:4 ff). God makes known the consequences of people's actions (reward or punishment), and He even makes *trials and sufferings* an element of formation—for example, a famine, which brings the people back to God (Amos 4:6), or the punishment of a son in order to educate him (Prov. 3:11–12), and so on. All these points are based on Scripture.

"to participate." Participation is not only an association, which could mean simply an exterior link. To participate in the action of the Father who touches the heart of man from within implies a close relationship, an intimacy with God, a communion, and a covenant. Paternity does not render maternity superfluous; neither does maternity render paternity superfluous. To speak of the divine pedagogy as the model for the pedagogy of the Faith of the Church is, therefore, more than a simple imitation of God's action. It is "participation," where both father and mother each have their own place and ways of acting. It is neither a question of substituting ourselves for God, nor of devaluing human action. It is, rather, a question of finding the right way to "collaborate."

THE PARTICIPATION OF MOTHER CHURCH
IN THE PEDAGOGICAL ACTION OF GOD THE FATHER

"From her very beginnings the Church, which 'in Christ, is in the nature of a Sacrament,' has lived her mission as a visible and actual continuation of the pedagogy of the Father and of the Son" (GDC 141). The maternity of the Church is completed with her "sacramentality": the pedagogy of faith must render the pedagogy of God *visible* and *present*. It must therefore inscribe the pedagogical action of God into the world of creation and into the daily life of every human being. The link to sacramentality allows us to understand that God inserts Himself into the action of the Church in order Himself to act through and in the action of the Church, the sign and instrument of divine action.

In this way the divine pedagogy is the "source and model" of the pedagogy of faith. The latter "finds its origin and its strength in God" (CL 61)—and this is meant literally. "I am the vine and you are the branches" (cf. Jn. 15:1 ff): the branches are given life by the sap that rises up from the stock. God is always at work in the action of the Church and feeds her from within. Other texts use still other expressions we can consider.

So, catechesis must be "radically inspired by the pedagogy of God" and from the pedagogy of God must "receive its constitutive characteristics" (GDC 143). Are we sufficiently conscious of the fact that we do not hold the first place in catechesis and that we are incapable of transmitting faith?[15] We can only transmit Revelation. Are we conscious of the fact that God is the inspiration and the first one to act in

---

15 Cf. M. Lena, "The Place of the Word," *Communio* VIII, 1 (January–February, 1983), 14.

catechesis and that the catechist must adapt him or herself to His action, giving it the first place, and entering into God's own way of doing things?

The *General Directory for Catechesis* explains the pedagogy of God and draws out a conclusion for the catechist: "Truly, to help a person to encounter God, which is the task of the catechist, means to emphasize above all the relationship that the person has with God so that he can make it his own and allow himself to be guided by God" (*GDC* 139). Catechesis, then, must establish such a link between the catechized person and God, that God may then act and display His own pedagogy towards the person, and the person may thus let him or herself be led by God—and this applies as much to the catechist as to the catechized person. All the methods used in catechesis find here their goal, but also their limitations. The principal agent of catechesis is God. The catechist must ordain all the catechetical activities in this way and create the right conditions so that God Himself may act in the heart of the catechized persons.

This makes us understand also that the delicate synthesis between *fides qua* (the adhering of man to God) and *fides quae* (the teaching of the contents of the Faith) (*GDC* 144) cannot be done through the simple rational work of man. Concretely, this synthesis is undertaken in reference to the mysterious action of God.

Catechesi Tradendae states:

> It is on the basis of Revelation that catechesis will try to set its course, and Pope John Paul explains that this Revelation is that of the "radical change of man and the universe, of all that makes up the web of human life under the influence of the Good News of Jesus Christ." We are dealing here with the demands of conversion linked to the gift of salvation. "If conceived in this way, catechesis goes beyond every form of formalistic moralism, although it will include true Christian moral teaching. Chiefly, it goes beyond any kind of temporal, social, or political 'messianism.' It seeks to arrive at man's innermost being." (cf. *CT* 52)

In concrete catechetical activity, are we sufficiently conscious of this "*originality* of the pedagogy of faith"? Catechesis is "an *active pedagogy* of the Faith" (*GDC* 144). It is not simply a question of transmitting a doctrine, a moral teaching or sacraments, but of transmitting Revelation in its entirety; in fact, the gift of God Himself, a life. In the light of this originality of the Faith, *Catechesi Tradendae* 58 makes a distinction between the pedagogy of faith and the contribution from the pedagogical sciences in catechesis. The pedagogy of faith is able to integrate the contribution of the pedagogical sciences in an appropriate way; the inverse is not possible. One consequence is that "[Catechesis] does not confuse the salvific action of God, which is pure grace, with the pedagogical action of man. Neither, however, does it oppose them and separate them" (GDC 144). Today, the risk may not be so much that of confusing the action of God with the action of man. The risk is that of forgetting the divine contribution in catechesis and of not knowing how to adapt to it and submit one's action, as a catechist, to it.

There is another, very instructive image: "The wonderful dialogue that God undertakes with every person becomes its inspiration and *norm*. Catechesis becomes an untiring *"echo"* of this. It continually seeks dialogue with people in accordance with the directions offered by the Magisterium of the Church" (GDC 144).

Are we conscious of the fact that the catechist must imitate and guide the dialogue of salvation that God Himself desires, gives rise to and makes grow between Him and the catechized? The image of the echo is very evocative! It is God who speaks; the catechist must be a sort of surface, which bounces back the Word of God onto the catechized so that the person may hear it as best as possible and respond to it. The dialogue that the catechist maintains with the catechized is for God a means for Himself to enter into a dialogue with the catechized person. This implies that the catechist him or herself is in communion with God, is in a dialogue with God in order to serve the dialogue between God and the catechized person.

CONCLUSION

Here are three keys to open the door for putting into practice a catechesis, which is in tune with the pedagogy of God.

1. Interiority

It is necessary to educate man in his interiority, where the dialogue of salvation with God takes place. "Help us to generate interiority ... to bring about the experiential dimension of the relationship with God, which allows one to touch or to feel his presence at the heart of this interiority."[16] Even if interiority cannot be "generated" but is discovered; even if the experience of God must not be reduced to a sensed and felt presence, to an "experiential" level—we must hear this cry!

16 Denis Villepet, *L'Avenir de la Catéchèse* (Paris: Editions de l'Atelier, 2003), 31–32.

Do we present teaching on the human person in catechesis in sufficient depth? This is indispensable for the discovery of this interiority. Do we really uncover for the catechized the depth of interiority?

Do we root vocal and liturgical prayer in a personal, intimate, and profound relationship with God? Does prayer come only at the end of the catechesis, simply to crown it? Do we not often forget that interior prayer is an indispensable condition for catechetical teaching to be received in the depths? Is it not the means, which allows one to listen and to respond to the Word of God?

2. The Holy Scriptures and the Word of God

In order to let God be the Pedagogue of people, the written Word of God is a privileged means in the hands of the catechist, for it is a living and effective Word through the inspiration of the Holy Spirit. It is not enough simply to make that Word of God known, or to limit us to a narration of the history of salvation. We must introduce persons into the history of salvation that God continues to write on human hearts. How do we do this? Here, intimate prayer plays a great role, for it allows us to listen to the Word of God in our hearts.

The catechist's saying with Christ that "my doctrine does not come from me" (cf. *CT* 6) does not reduce that person to being a simple spokesman for God or a purely passive tool.[17] Transmitting the Word of God does not mean rejecting the workings of any communication (which always implies some form of interpretation). The catechist *must* interpret the Word of God in order to transmit it! But what is interpretation? To interpret is not to change this Word, but it is to "play" it with all one's person, like a musical score. This musical score is the same for everyone, and it must be played faithfully, but each must play it with what he or she is, and make a wholly personal rendition. When, through the intimate relationship with God in the heart, we come to know God's "score," we can play it in our lives, in our behaviour, in our way of doing catechesis. In this "music playing" by the catechist, God slips in His voice in order to make the melody of happiness reach the ears of the persons to be catechized.

3. The Holy Spirit, the "Interior Master"

The *General Directory for Catechesis* never speaks of the "pedagogy of the Holy Spirit," though it speaks of the pedagogy of the Father and of the pedagogy of Jesus. The Holy Spirit is the one who brings about and *accomplishes* the pedagogy of the

---

17 Cf. A. Fossion, *La catechese dans le champ de la communication.*

Father and of the Son. The Holy Spirit becomes in man the "interior Master" (cf. GDC 288 and CT 72), which allows him to take in hand his own education in the divine pedagogy (GDC 142). To be an adult in the Faith is to know how to educate oneself, that is, how to recognize God's pedagogy towards us, and to be one's own catechist, so to speak. The human person no longer needs other pedagogues; he or she can advance towards his or her own full maturity as a witness to the Faith, always guided by God. The Holy Spirit renders man responsible for his own education and growth in the Faith. The goal is the state of the perfect man who "fulfills the plenitude of Christ," according to the *Letter to the Ephesians* (4:13; see GDC 142), who follows Christ to the point of sharing totally His cause and His destiny (cf. GDC 140). We can, therefore, ask ourselves if our pedagogy of the Faith allows the catechized person to live more and more from the breath of the Spirit, in order to become in his turn an adult in the Faith, a catechist "moved by the Spirit of God" (cf. Rom 8:14), a witness to the Faith for those who live around him.

Translated by Anne Harriss

10

Methodology in the Light of the Pedagogy of God

Caroline Farey

How does the pedagogy of God affect catechetical methodologies in practice? The *General Directory for Catechesis* indicates clearly that discerning and choosing the *method of communication* of the Faith needs special attention.

> The Church, in transmitting the *faith*, does not have a particular method nor any single method. Rather she discerns contemporary *methods* in the light of the *pedagogy of God*.[1]

This task depends not only on knowing the Faith to be transmitted but also upon knowing sufficiently what the Church means by the "pedagogy of God" so that one can give specific and deliberate attention towards evaluating catechetical methods in its light in order to discern better which methods more closely conform to God's own pedagogy.

Priests and catechists need formation, firstly in the deposit of the Faith, *then* in the pedagogy of God that is "universally valid" (GDC 10) and flows from Revelation, and *then* in how to examine methods and methodologies in its light in order to discern those methods that are suitable for communicating the Faith and those that are not.[2] We need, then, to work out *how* to place a method under "the light of the pedagogy of God" in order to discern and judge its suitability.

The *General Directory for Catechesis* explains that for *catechesis*, we are to turn to the pedagogy of God "as displayed in Christ and in the Church" (GDC 143), that

---

1   GDC 148 (emphasis added).

2   These opening paragraphs have been adapted from an article on a similar theme: Caroline Farey, "The Truth Will Set You Free," *Faith*, vol. 41, no.5 (September–October, 2009), 26–27.

is, the pedagogy of God once it has reached, in the fullness of time, the "perfection" of the supreme gift of salvation when God sent His Son, the Word, to become flesh in Mary.[3] The pedagogy of God for catechesis is, then, more specifically, the "pedagogy of the Incarnation" (GDC 143).

The infancy narratives in the Gospels of Saint Luke and Saint Matthew introduce us to the great mystery of the Incarnation. Amongst these accounts, the *Catechism of the Catholic Church* refers most frequently to the annunciation narrative of Saint Luke. It is here that we can turn, not only to contemplate the mystery, but also to discover the *pedagogy*, of the Incarnation. It is here that we can expect to find those "pedagogical instructions for catechesis … which permit the communication of the whole word of God in the concrete existence of people" (GDC 146)—in this case, in the concrete existence of the person of Our Blessed Lady.[4]

The closer and more fully a method follows the implications revealed by the light of God's pedagogy of the Incarnation, the richer and more effective the catechesis will be in nurturing and encouraging "a true experience of the Faith and thus a filial encounter with God" (GDC 143). Those methods that lack too many implications of this pedagogy will be least able to bring about that true experience and filial encounter and least suitable for catechesis. Most methods will lie somewhere between the two, and so this article hopes to clarify how any and every method, session, or resource used for catechesis might be guided and enriched. As we follow the account of the annunciation phrase by phrase, I hope we shall find new light, the light of the pedagogy of the Incarnation as outlined in a series of practical reflections, by which we might examine effectively our catechetical methods.

1. Transmission of the Faith takes place most effectively with the witness of life of "convinced and faithful disciples of Christ and his Church" (GDC 142).[5] Just as the angel Gabriel, is a personal, *named* messenger from God, so transmission of the Faith is most authentic when the *Faith* is known and lived personally by the catechist and when the *transmission* is personal. Catechesis is the work of the *persons* of the Blessed Trinity through the *person* of Christ and the *members* of His Church including the persons of priests, parents, and catechists.

---

3 Cf. GDC 140.

4 This idea draws in part from two articles by Petroc Willey on "An Annunciation Pedagogy" in the catechetical journal, *The Sower*, vol. 25, no. 4 (October 2004) and vol. 26, no. 1 (January 2005). These two articles are early attempts to bring pedagogy and method together and were written before the research undertaken for the conference in Rome from which this book is drawn.

5 Cf. GDC 142.

The light from this provides two key implications for any methodology; the first will always be for the person of the catechist, the second for the task and method of catechesis. Firstly, then, methods should always include support and formation of the catechist, with, for example, prompts for prayer, explanations of faith and morals, and references to sources in Scripture and Tradition. Any implication that catechists do not need formation for their own lives and for their catechetical work runs contrary to the personal nature of the Church and of catechesis.

Secondly, catechists and writers of catechetical materials need to be conscious of ensuring that their use of texts, power-point, worksheets for children, DVDs, and the internet, is undertaken in such a way that the transmission of the Faith as "personal" is *strengthened* by any media used rather than replaced, reduced, or obscured. The personal witness of faith, hope, and charity of the catechist should always be and remain evident.

2. Transmission of the Faith is a divine initiative motivated by the love of God. Just as the angel Gabriel was "from God," so the whole message is "from God." Revelation, the deposit of faith, and life of faith entrusted to the Church is from God. The whole catechetical endeavor is for the sake of communion with Jesus Christ, who is "God from God, Light from Light, true God from true God." Otherwise known as the "priority of grace," the divine initiative in Christ for man's salvation and beatitude should permeate all catechesis and every catechetical method.

The first implication of this for catechists is in their grasp and conviction that in catechesis there is a message to be delivered that does not belong to them but to the Church to which they belong. Nor is catechesis to be delivered as opinions amongst opinions, but as truth and grace "from God." As catechists, a life of grace is essential, that is, receiving "from God" in order to pass on what has been received. We need to check ourselves as to whether "who God is" and "what He does" always has priority or whether it is "who we are" and "what we do" that is given prominence in our catechetical sessions.[6]

A related implication for catechetical methodology and resources is the need to make evident and central who Jesus Christ is, and what He has done and is doing in and through His Church. The *General Directory for Catechesis* indicates in paragraph 98 four ways in which Christ should be central in catechesis and a fifth way, in paragraphs 99–100, as to how Christo-centricity should be Trinitarian.

---

6 See *The Sower*, for a series of articles on catechetical methodology by Marianne Cuthbertson and Caroline Farey, beginning with the first, "Teaching Gracefully," vol. 30, no. 1 (January 2009).

3. Transmission of the Faith takes place in specific places and within the context of specific cultures. The angel Gabriel went to a specific town "in Galilee called Nazareth,"—a town, which had a reputation because of its particular local culture.[7] A great deal has been written about "inculturation" of the Gospel message (cf. GDC 97). For the purposes of catechesis, the principle of double fidelity—fidelity to God and fidelity to man—is most helpful here. By "fidelity to God," what is clear is that inculturation does not imply, in any way, a reduction of the integrity, fullness, or purity of the Gospel message. "Fidelity to man," on the other hand, requires a close attention to the needs of the group to enable the fullest grasp of the Gospel message in the lives of the participants, to enable them each to progress on their journey towards maturity in the Faith within the context of their own people and parish.

Implications for methodology would include adaptations in the examples given of the work of the Holy Spirit in the Church, such as including local saints or saints relevant to the experiences of those being catechized (e.g., child saints for children, married saints for married catechumens) and also examples of the local "community experience of faith" (GDC 143). Published resources can only do this to a minor extent since, by their nature, they are generally for sale in a wide area. This means that catechists need to be especially aware of the issues in the local culture and parish that might hinder or help receptivity of the Gospel.

4. The great dignity of every human person in the eyes of God is manifested and acknowledged. The angel Gabriel greeted Mary in a manner indicating who Mary was in the eyes of God, "hail, full of grace." Mary's grace was uniquely hers but every person is to be greeted, or spoken of, in a manner indicating how precious they are in the eyes of God and every person is equally precious and desired by God for his or her own sake.

5. Opportunities for asking and answering questions of *meaning* are important in any catechetical method. Our Lady "asked herself what this greeting could mean"; she pondered, wondered, and questioned in order to gain deeper understanding. Questioning and pondering times are always valuable. Otherwise, it is all too easy to forget the depth of the mysteries that catechists have the privilege to share, that need "receptivity time," either as time for questions and answers or as time for silent pondering.

Catechist formation needs to go beyond immediate instructions of what to do, or that which is needed just for the delivery of certain truths; it needs to extend

7 See Jn. 1:45–46.

to greater depths of meaning for the sake of possible questioning and pondering by the participants. Catechetical methods need to include the Church's *reasons* for proclaiming what she believes as well as the truths themselves. The *Catechism* includes a great deal to help us appreciate the *coherence* of the Faith, how it links together, and how one truth depends on another.

6. Announcing the Good News of God is at the heart of every method. The angel Gabriel was quite clear in announcing God's plan to the Virgin Mary, of "handing over" the great treasure of His only Son to be born of her. At the heart of every catechetical method there must be a proclamation of some aspect of what God has revealed in His Son made man. When the *General Directory for Catechesis* says, "a good catechetical method guarantees fidelity to content" (GDC 149), it is the content of this announcement, proclamation, and explanation of divine truth that is involved. Every method is to be evaluated in the light of the pedagogy of the incarnation in terms of fidelity to delivery of the Gospel message, fidelity to the person Christ. The truth of Christ needs to be known, for Christ sets us free.

7. Telling the history of salvation. The angel Gabriel uses language and speaks of persons and events, from the Old Testament, uniting these in a single explanation to the work of God in the present, the future, and "forever." The whole process of salvation is historical and takes place in the lives of concrete historical figures. Catechesis should always include God's work of salvation starting with His covenants and promises in the Old Testament, the fullness of Revelation in Christ, and His continuing historical presence in the Church through history and Tradition.

Pope Benedict XVI has indicated that there is a tendency in the Church since the Second Vatican Council, and particularly in the field of catechesis, to follow a "hermeneutic of discontinuity." This manifests itself in catechesis in different ways, all of which "jump over" certain periods of history of the Church, thus also removing or obscuring much of Tradition—there can even be a certain tendency to ignore or play down the whole of history between the early Church and the Second Vatican Council itself! This is clearly contrary to the pedagogy of God.

8. "Life in Christ" is the goal of catechesis and needs time in every catechetical method. When Mary responds, having heard the angel Gabriel, she asks humbly "How will this be?" She seeks the way forward in the concrete experience of her life. There are two lessons to learn here for our catechetical work. Mary has heard something so beautiful and desirable that her response is to want what has been announced even though it sounds impossible to her. This is why she asks the angel how it can happen; she clearly doesn't expect to be able to bring about anything herself.

In the first place we can see that catechesis should present the fullness of the Faith in as attractive and desirable a manner as possible, even if it sounds impossible; a presentation can never do full justice to the beauty of the realities in which we believe. Secondly, whatever we announce is to be presented in such a way that there is time given also to a contemplation of its "embodiment" in the concrete circumstances of life.

9. Catechesis should always indicate the work of the Holy Spirit as the One who will bring about every desire for good. The answer to Mary's question is not a series of tasks to be done. Instead Mary is told that the Holy Spirit will achieve everything. Catechesis can sometimes be delivered in terms of a set of moral rules to follow. This can sound burdensome and restrictive, both to children and to adults alike, while the truth is in fact one that sets us free, bringing joy and peace.

What is essential in catechesis is to know that one can call on the Holy Spirit, that He has been promised and that He does not let us down. Catechesis that encourages this turning to the Holy Spirit as the answer to every desire for the good, to every call, to decision, and to every need to withstand temptation, will be one that follows the pedagogy of the Incarnation.

10. Every method should include visible signs by which to grasp invisible realities. The angel Gabriel immediately tells Mary of a real life situation where God has been indisputably active in someone's life—that of her cousin, Elizabeth. Stories of the saints are especially significant as lived evidence of the work of God in someone's concrete existence. The Holy Spirit is an invisible reality, but the fruits of the Spirit can be seen everywhere, wherever one sees or experiences a moment of "love, joy, peace, patience, kindness, gentleness, self-control" (Gal. 5:22) one sees the work of the Holy Spirit. Prayer and grace are invisible realities but the results of prayer and evidence of grace can be seen and recounted.

11. A good catechetical method will lead people to humble trust. A good catechetical method will be one that enables people to know and desire the work of God in their lives to the extent that they can say with Our Lady, "Be it done unto me according to your word." Catechesis should lead people to want not just an encounter with Christ, but even more the whole of life "in Christ" and "with Christ" in increasing trust in Him and reliance on Him.

12. A good catechetical method will respect freedom. We are told, in one of the shortest sentences in the New Testament, that the angel Gabriel left

Mary once Mary had given her response. An act of faith is interior and can never be forced. Allowing participants in catechesis to be free to make their own acts of faith, to make their own journey with God at their own pace, is urged upon all RCIA catechists but it is also right for all catechesis. The work of God with the soul of each person is to be treated with the utmost respect.

In conclusion, this set of meditations could be used perhaps as a means of shedding some "light" from the pedagogy of the Incarnation onto our catechetical methods. The purpose of all catechesis is for the Word of God to "take flesh" more and more in people's lives just as the Word was made flesh following the heavenly exchange between the Angel Gabriel, sent from God, and the virgin, Mary, who became the Mother of God.

170

11

The Ecclesial Vocation of the Catechist

Sr. M. Johanna Paruch, FSGM

Over the past few years, in my research and in my experience of speaking to catechists in the United States and Canada, I have arrived at some unfortunate conclusions about catechetical practice. Certainly many fail to follow the divine pedagogy in their teaching. I am not a "gloom and doom" observer of the situation, but I am a realist. Often even well meaning catechists, professional or volunteer, do not understand that what they do is not merely a job to teach religion, but a vocation, a special call to hand on the Faith. There are many reasons for this, but I want to focus on two.

The first is that they have not been trained properly in the Church's understanding of what it means to hand on the Faith, a faith that is both a body of truths that have been revealed to us by God, and particularly in the fullness of Revelation fulfilled in Jesus Christ (*fides quae*), and a faith that is a response to this revelation in love (*fides qua*).

The second comes from a rejection of the Church's understanding of what it means to hand on the Faith: the nature of catechesis, to echo, is denied and religious instruction is reduced to shared praxis, in which *our* stories are told but *The* Story is avoided, and no real response is elicited from the participants.

These, of course, are two extremes. There is a growing host of catechists who do understand their mission in the Church. They realize that we are in the new springtime of catechesis. As an American catechist, I want to take the opportunity thank the Bishops of the United States, and their committees on the *Catechism* and catechesis, who have labored so hard to spark and sustain a catechetical renewal in America.

We are concerned with the pedagogy of God—what it means in its essence and what it means in practice. I am looking at it here with regard to the ecclesial vocation of the catechist. Essentially, the catechist responds to the call of God to become a catechist. This resembles the dialogue of Revelation/response of faith. It also resembles the Annunciation/*fiat* dialogue between Gabriel and Our Lady. God calls the catechist to serve Him in the Church, to hand on what He has revealed to us, especially through His Son Jesus. He asks for an obedience of faith, both in the words and deeds of the catechist. And as is always implicit in His call, He provides the grace necessary for the catechist to live out that call. In this paper on the ecclesial vocation of the catechist, I want to emphasize what the Church teaches us in this regard. The catechetical program at Franciscan University owes its existence to this fundamental premise insisted upon by Msgr. Eugene Kevane, one of the few voices in the post-conciliar Church in the United States that sought assent, both the assent of faith and religious assent. Barbara Morgan brought this to Franciscan University.

THEOLOGY AND CATECHESIS

The first two paragraphs of the *Instruction on the Ecclesial Vocation of the Theologian*[1] resound with the relationship between Revelation and the response of faith to what has been revealed. The then Cardinal Joseph Ratzinger wrote:

> In the Christian faith, knowledge and life, truth and existence are intrinsically connected. Assuredly, the truth given in God's revelation exceeds the capacity of human knowledge, but it is not opposed to human reason. Revelation in fact penetrates human reason, elevates it, and calls it to give an account of itself (cf. 1 Pet. 3:15). For this reason, from the very beginning of the Church, the "standard of teaching" (cf. Rom. 6:17) has been linked with baptism to entrance into the mystery of Christ. The service of doctrine, implying as it does the believer's search for an understanding of the faith, i.e., theology, is therefore something indispensable for the Church.
>
> Theology has importance for the Church in every age so that it can respond to the plan of God "who desires all men to be saved and to come to the knowledge of the truth" (1 Tim. 2:4). In times of great spiritual and cultural change, theology is all the more important. Yet

---

1 Available at http://www.vatican.va/roman_curia/congregations/cfaith/documents/
rc_con_cfaith_doc_19900524_theologian-vocation_en.html

it also is exposed to risks since it must strive to "abide" in the truth (cf. Jn. 8:31), while at the same time taking into account the new problems which confront the human spirit. In our century, in particular, during the periods of preparation for and implementation of the Second Vatican Council, theology contributed much to a deeper "understanding of the realities and the words handed on." But it also experienced and continues to experience moments of crisis and tension. (Introduction, no. 1)

If the Congregation for the Clergy, which oversees catechetics, was to write a document called *Instruction on the Ecclesial Vocation of the Catechist*, what could it say? Could the word "catechesis" be exchanged for the word "theology" in the above passage? As we know, catechetics is clearly distinct from theology. However, it too, is at the service of Revelation, at the service of truth, at the service of doctrine, as the text states. Strikingly, Pope John Paul wrote in *Fides et Ratio*, "Theological work in the Church is first of all at the service of the proclamation of the Faith and of catechesis. Proclamation or *kerygma* is a call to conversion, announcing the truth of Christ, which reaches its summit in his Paschal Mystery: for only in Christ is it possible to know the fullness of the truth which saves" (cf. Acts 4:12; 1 Tim. 2:4–6) (*FR* 99). Earlier, in *Catechesi Tradendae*, John Paul expressed concern for the effect theology has on catechesis:

> This point must again be insisted on. Aware of the influence that their research and their statements have on catechetical instruction, theologians and exegetes have a duty to take great care that people do not take for a certainty what on the contrary belongs to the area of questions of opinion or of discussion among experts. Catechists for their part must have the wisdom to pick from the field of theological research those points that can provide light for their own reflection and their teaching, drawing, like the theologians, from the true sources, in the light of the magisterium. (*CT* 61)

We are only too aware of the skepticism, deconstructionism, and dissent practiced by many theologians, leading to confusion concerning God, Revelation, Jesus Christ, Sacred Scripture, and the Church. Because this is indeed the case, it is no wonder that many catechists find themselves in one of the two groups mentioned above.

ECCLESIAL AS CHRISTOCENTRIC

The placing, in the *General Directory for Catechesis*, of the discussion of the pedagogy of the Church is interesting. It lies in between the section on the pedagogy of Christ and the pedagogy of the Spirit. At first glance, it may seem odd that the, usually indivisible, treatment of the Trinity is interrupted, so to speak, by the Church.

However, the *General Directory for Catechesis* states that

> From her very beginnings the Church, which "in Christ, is in the nature of a Sacrament," has lived her mission as a visible and actual continuation of the pedagogy of the Father and of the Son. She "as our Mother is also the educator of our faith." (GDC 141)

This, of course, is accomplished through the power of the Holy Spirit. *Lumen Gentium* spoke of the Church as the sacrament of Christ. The mystery of the Church resides in the mystery of Christ. "To carry out the will of the Father, Christ inaugurated the Kingdom of heaven on earth and revealed to us the mystery of the kingdom. By His obedience He brought about redemption. The Church, or, in other words, the kingdom of Christ now present in mystery, grows visibly through the power of God in the world" (*LG* 3).

Reflecting on *Lumen Gentium*, the *Catechism of the Catholic Church* reminds us that we cannot speak of the Church unless we speak of Christ (see *Catechism*, no. 748). It is only with this understanding that we can come to understand the function of catechesis in the Church and the vocation of those who are truly called to hand on the Faith. We are familiar also with Pope John Paul's profound statement that we teach in essence the Person of Christ, and that, "the primary and essential object of catechesis is, to use an expression dear to Saint Paul and also to contemporary theology, 'the mystery of Christ'" (*CT* 5).

Later, John Paul wrote,

> The Christian, having accepted by faith the person of Jesus Christ as the one Lord and having given Him complete adherence by sincere conversion of heart, endeavors to know better this Jesus to whom he has entrusted himself: to know His "mystery," the kingdom of God proclaimed by Him, the requirements and promises contained in His Gospel message, and the paths that He has laid down for anyone who wishes to follow Him. (*CT* 20)

Frequently in post-Vatican II catechesis, the Kingdom of God has been emphasized, but its emphasis has been on the "here and now," rather than the "here and not yet." Often, that narrow understanding led to a focus only on themes of justice and peace for its own sake rather than the mandate of Jesus and one of the means by which one comes close to Him in order to enter the eternal Kingdom. Pope Benedict has warned that in this "regnocentrism" as he coined it, the kingdom is "simply a name for a world governed by peace, justice, and the conservation of creation. It is by no means this. ... Jesus himself is the Kingdom: the Kingdom is not a thing. It is a person; it is a he." [2] Recall that the definitive aim of catechesis is to put people in touch, intimacy, in union with Jesus Christ.

In order to understand the true nature of the Kingdom, and of the Church, we must fundamentally understand Christ. Often, in post-conciliar theology and catechesis, Jesus Christ, true God and true man, was redefined. In theology a low non-ascending Christology led many theologians, and thus many catechists, to make Jesus in their own image. Once this occurs the Church can be redefined in the same way. Pope Benedict had refuted this so clearly in Jesus of *Nazareth*.

Caroline Farey has this to say:

> The vocation of the catechist is fundamentally pedagogical, as we have seen from the very origins of the word. The catechist is called, however, to a unique form of pedagogy because what is taught is not just knowledge but a person, a divine person with a divine purpose, the purpose of uniting the listener to himself in his people, in his Church. No human pedagogical system can do this. What the catechist needs to learn is the pedagogy of God himself. How then does God teach? We can see God's way of teaching, of revealing himself, in the Scriptures. In fact God uses all that is human. All that is good in human pedagogical methods can be drawn into his way but no human system is sufficient in itself.[3]

In 1957, Msgr. Rudolph Bandas wrote *Contents and Method of Catechization*, explaining catechetical methodology from a Christocentric perspective. Much of his thinking is found in the post-conciliar catechetical documents. He affirmed that the Church's catechetical methodology has been abiding. "He who created the human soul and determined the laws according to which the mind assimilates and attains

2 Benedict XVI, *Jesus of Nazareth* (San Francisco: Ignatius Press, 2007), 53.
3 Caroline Farey, "The Vocation of the Catechist" in *Hear, O Islands*, ed. John Redford (Dublin: Veritas, 2002), 311.

truth must of necessity be the pedagogue and educator *par excellence*."[4] Thus his first chapter is dedicated to Christ the divine Teacher. Bandas wrote that, "As head and Redeemer of the human race Our Lord had a perfect knowledge of all the truths necessary for salvation. Whenever Christ taught these supernatural truths He at the same time aided the hearer's mind by illuminating it with grace."[5]

He also wrote that, "The Teacher and Educator of all mankind knew all truths and ways of knowing and actually experienced the manner in which the human mind functions in acquiring truth. His method of imparting truths to the human mind, consequently, must necessarily excite our interest and reverent curiosity."[6]

In *Evangelii Nuntiandi*, Pope Paul VI observed that, "during the Synod [on evangelization], the bishops very frequently referred to this truth: Jesus Himself, the Good News of God, was the very first and the greatest evangelizer; He was so through and through: to perfection and to the point of the sacrifice of his earthly life" (EN 7). We can then construe that since catechesis is a moment of evangelization, Jesus was the very first and greatest catechist.[7] However, John Paul made it very clear in *Catechesi Tradendae* 5–9 that Jesus is the source, the content, and the goal of catechesis. He is the ultimate teacher, the unique teacher. "This teaching is not a body of abstract truths. It is the communication of the living mystery of God. The Person teaching it in the Gospel is altogether superior in excellence to the 'masters' in Israel, and the nature of His doctrine surpasses theirs in every way because of the unique link between what He says, what He does and what He is" (CT 7).

Subsequently, the catechist must be Christ-like. We were all created in the image of God. We were baptized into the Father, the Son, and the Holy Spirit. We were anointed to share in the three-fold mission of Christ as priest, prophet, and king. Pope Paul VI told us that the Church exists in order to evangelize. Thus, all the baptized are called to evangelize. We know that catechesis is a moment of evangelization (see CT 18), and while all the baptized are called to evangelize, only a few are called to catechize. Our American bishops have written,

---

4 Rudolph Bandas, *Contents and Methods of Catechization for the Use of Lay Teachers of Religion, Sisters, Seminarians and Priests* (St. Paul, MN: The Confraternity of Christian Doctrine of the Archdiocese of St. Paul, 1957), 126. Bandas served as the archdiocesan director of the Confraternity of Christian Doctrine and the Rector of St. Paul Seminary in St. Paul, Minnesota. He served as a peritus at the Council, attending all sessions.

5 Bandas, *Contents and Methods of Catechization*, 126.

6 Bandas, *Contents and Methods of Catechization*, 126.

7 See CT 18.

The apostolic work of the catechist springs from the Sacrament of Baptism through which all believers come to share in the prophetic ministry of Christ and the evangelizing mission of the Church. It is strengthened by the Sacrament of Confirmation. The call to ministry of the catechist is a vocation, an interior call, the voice of the Holy Spirit. ... Their commissioning by the Church is a participation in the divine calling to teach as Jesus did. Their personal relationship with Jesus Christ energizes their service to the Church and provides the continuing motivation, vitality, and the force of their catechetical activity. Christ invites all catechists to follow him as a teacher of the faith and a witness to the truth of the faith.[8]

Hence, if one understands that the mission of the catechist comes ultimately from Christ, that it must be carried out with Christ, and is carried out to lead those being catechized into intimacy and union with Christ, and they understand truly who Jesus Christ is, they will understand the ecclesial vocation of the catechist. John Paul made very clear what this means:

Whatever be the level of his responsibility in the Church, every catechist must constantly endeavor to transmit by his teaching and behavior the teaching and life of Jesus. He will not seek to keep directed towards himself and his personal opinions and attitudes the attention and the consent of the mind and heart of the person he is catechizing. Above all, he will not try to inculcate his personal opinions and options as if they expressed Christ's teaching and the lessons of His life. (CT 6)

When the Church celebrated the Pauline year in 2008, I celebrated that year as a year of the catechist, for Paul was the ultimate catechist, who truly understood his vocation to *preach Christ* as coming from Christ and brought the Church to place after place, regardless of hardship, opposition and ultimately death. Pope Benedict wrote, "For Paul, adherence to the Church was brought about by a direct intervention of Christ, who in revealing himself on the road to Damascus identified himself with the Church and made Paul realize that persecution of the Church was persecution of himself, the Lord."[9] Paul had to prove himself as a member of the Church.

---

8 United States Conference of Catholic Bishops, *National Directory for Catechesis* (Washington DC: USCCB Publishing, 2005), 228–229.

9 Benedict XVI, *General Audience*, Saint Peter's Square (Wednesday, November 22, 2006).

To accept the persecutor as brother would require deep faith on the part of the early Christians. In some ways Paul had to evangelize the evangelizers; he had to convince them that he was also chosen to proclaim the Good News to all nations. Bandas constructed a profile of the catechist, which reflects the life and teaching of Paul (see 2 Cor. 5:20).

> Christian teachers are ministers of Christ and the dispensers of the heavenly mysteries. They are the ambassadors of Christ; God as it were exhorting by their mouths. They have the honor of collaborating in the spread of the Gospel in virtue of a divine power. Their office is derived not from men but from God through Jesus Christ. They are the depositories of a divine doctrine which they must preserve unaltered.[10]

We should also note an unusual and entirely humbling correlation between the work of Christ and the work of the catechist in the *General Directory for Catechesis*. The *General Directory for Catechesis* boldly writes, in the face of Scriptural passages on Christ as the one mediator,[11] "The catechist is essentially a mediator. He facilitates communication between the people and the mystery of God, between subjects amongst themselves, as well as with the community," then adds as a caveat, "For this reason, his cultural vision, social condition and lifestyle must not be obstacles to the journey of faith" (GDC 156). The catechist must be Christ-like and ensure that "his activities always draw support from faith in the Holy Spirit and from prayer" (GDC 156).

THE CATECHIST, PRIESTHOOD, AND THE MAGISTERIUM

The catechist, called by Christ to serve in His Church, must have a real and loving relationship with the Magisterium of the Church. *Dei Verbum* taught (and the *Catechism* reiterated) that the Magisterium itself is the servant of the Word of God, and teaches only what was handed on to it (DV 10; Catechism, no. 86). *Dei Verbum* notes that the Magisterium listens devotedly, guards with dedication, and expounds faithfully. We see again the movement of the divine pedagogy—Revelation and response. As catechists, we respond to the Magisterium and in turn we listen, guard, and expound the Word of God found in the Deposit of faith, in Scripture and Tradition.

---

10 Bandas, *Contents and Methods of Catechization*, 126.
11 See 1 Tim. 2:4; Heb. 9:15.

In the same vein, I would like briefly to look at assent. I am convinced that the dissent found so embedded in the hearts of many from 1968 onwards is the seminal act that caused the rupture in religious education after the Council. *Lumen Gentium* 25 speaks of assent given to the Roman Pontiff and to the bishops who act in union with him. The Profession of Faith, found in the *Code of Canon Law* makes it very clear.

> With firm faith I believe as well everything contained in God's word, written or handed down in tradition and proposed by the church—whether in solemn judgment or in the ordinary and universal Magisterium—as divinely revealed and called for faith.
>
> I also firmly accept and hold each and every thing that is proposed by that same church definitively with regard to teaching concerning faith or morals.
>
> What is more, I adhere with religious submission of will and intellect to the teachings which either the Roman pontiff or the college of bishops enunciate when they exercise the authentic Magisterium even if they proclaim those teachings in an act that is not definitive.[12]

I have spoken about the Magisterium. Let me now speak about the link between the priesthood and the ecclesial vocation of the catechist. The *Code of Canon Law* (773–780) makes it very clear that the Bishop, whom *Lumen Gentium* calls the "herald of the faith"[13] and then the pastor are responsible for catechesis. The catechist, then, works under the authority of the bishop and more commonly the pastor.

The *General Directory for Catechesis* states,

> The function proper to the presbyterate in the catechetical task arises from the sacrament of Holy Orders which they have received. … In virtue of this ontological configuration to Christ, the ministry of the priest is a service which forms the Christian community and co-ordinates and strengthens other charisms and services. In catechesis

---

12 Cf. *Ad Tuendam Fidem*. See also the text of the "Oath of Fidelity" in the appendix.

13 "For the bishops are heralds of the faith, who draw new disciples to Christ; they are authentic teachers, that is, teachers endowed with the authority of Christ, who preach the faith to the people assigned to them, the faith which is destined to inform their thinking and direct their conduct; and under the light of the Holy Spirit they make that faith shine forth, drawing from the storehouse of revelation new things and old (cf. Mt. 13:52); they make it bear fruit and with watchfulness they ward off whatever errors threaten their flock (cf. 2 Tim. 4:14)" (*LG* 25).

> the sacrament of Holy Orders constitutes priests as "educators of the faith." They work, therefore, to see that the faithful are properly formed and reach true Christian maturity. (GDC 224)

Frequently, since the Council, the catechetical function of the priest has been forgotten. The reasons for this are legion, but the fault lies both on the part of priests and the laity alike. In the Council's Decree on the Laity, and in John Paul's post-synodal exhortation, *Christifidelis Laici*, the diversity and complementarity of all the members of the Church is made clear. "Indeed, the Church is directed and guided by the Holy Spirit, who lavishes diverse hierarchical and charismatic gifts on all the baptized, calling them to be, each in an individual way, active and coresponsible" (CL 22).

Nevertheless, the exhortation makes clear that all the apostolates in the Church must be carried out under the direction of the pastor. This is not an imposition of a hierarchical bureaucracy, but an invitation to work with he who is the *alter Christus capitis*. John Paul added, "pastors must always acknowledge that their ministry is fundamentally ordered to the service of the entire People of God (cf. Heb. 5:1). The lay faithful, in turn, must acknowledge that the ministerial priesthood is totally necessary for their participation in the mission in the Church" (CL 22).

Pope John Paul II also desired that we rediscover the true meaning of the parish. In my experience the parish can often be divided up into little "kingdoms": the RCIA kingdom, the Youth Ministry kingdom, the Religious Education kingdom, and so on. Pope John Paul reminded us that it is necessary "that in light of the faith all rediscover the true meaning of the parish, that is, the place where the very 'mystery' of the Church is present and at work" (CL 26). If a catechist works under the notion, implicit or explicit, that the parish is merely a sociological configuration, that catechist has not truly grasped the ecclesial nature of his vocation. Pope John Paul also stressed the Eucharistic bond that holds the parish together and the *Catechism* teaches a related point: that the Eucharist is not only the source and summit of Christian life, but that all apostolates in the Church come from it and lead back to it (cf. *Catechism*, no. 1324).

Saint Augustine, as Bishop of Hippo, gave us the text *De Catechizandis Rudibus*, which reads as if it were written today. In his letter to the deacon Deogratius, who asked the busy bishop for assistance in this catechumenal work, Augustine wrote,

As for myself then, if, in the exercise of those capacities which through the bounty of our Lord I am enabled to present, the same Lord requires me to offer any manner of aid to those whom He has made brethren to me, I feel constrained not only by that love and service which is due from me to you on the terms of familiar friendship, but also by that which I owe universally to my mother the Church, by no means to refuse the task, but rather to take it up with a prompt and devoted willingness.[14]

For the Year of the Priest, Pope Benedict XVI called our attention to the life of Saint John Vianney, the Cure of Ars. We know well his pastoral work, especially in the confessional, but he also took catechesis very seriously. Pope John XXIII wrote of Saint John Vianney,

It is said that Saint John M. Vianney lived in the Church in such a way that he worked for it alone, and burned himself up like a piece of straw being consumed on fiery coals. May that flame which comes from the Holy Spirit reach those of us who have been raised to the priesthood of Jesus Christ and consume us too.

We owe ourselves and all we have to the Church; may we work each day only in her name and by her authority and may we properly carry out the duties committed to us, and may we be joined together in fraternal unity and thus strive to serve her in that perfect way in which she ought to be served.[15]

May all catechists share in that same zeal for the Church, working with the Bishops and priests whom they serve.

In the Rite of Ordination of Deacons, the Bishop hands over the Gospel saying, "Believe what you read. Teach what you believe. Practice what you teach." In the Rite of Ordination of Priests, the Bishop hands over the chalice and paten to the priest and says,

"Accept from the holy people of God the gifts to be offered to him. Know what you are doing, and imitate the mystery you celebrate: model your life on the mystery of the Lord's cross."

---

14 Saint Augustine, *De Catechizandis Rudibus*, 2.

15 Pope John XXIII, Encyclical on St. John Vianney *Sacerdotii Nostri Primordia* (August 1, 1959), 33, 34.

Through their ordination, priests, from the Supreme Pontiff to our local pastor, make real the pedagogy of God in the life of the Church. Our call to be catechists is both validated and nourished by priests, by Scripture, and the sacraments, especially the Eucharist. May we respond to our ecclesial vocation by teaching what we believe, modeling *our* lives on the mystery of the Lord's cross. In our fervent prayers and sacrifices offered for priests, let us, as catechetical leaders in the Church, ask that both priests and catechists may fully carry out their unique but complementary work in handing on the Faith.

Let us return to the discussion of the pedagogy of the Church.

> Throughout the centuries the Church has produced an incomparable treasure of pedagogy in the faith: above all the witness of saints and catechists; a variety of ways of life and original forms of religious communication such as the catechumenate, catechisms, itineraries of the Christian life; a precious patrimony of catechetical teaching of faith culture, of catechetical institutions and services. All of these aspects form part of the history of catechesis and, by right, enter into the memory of the community and the praxis of the catechist. (GDC 141)

None of these would have been possible had not the Church been directed and inspired by the divine pedagogy. And let us note that the witness of the saints and catechists is primary. Catechists are truly called to be saints.

In conclusion, let us turn to Mary, Mother of the Church and model of catechists. She is Mother and teacher.

> She was the first disciple above all else because no one has been "taught by God" (cf. Jn. 6:45) to such depth. She was "both mother and disciple," as Saint Augustine said of her, venturing to add that her discipleship was more important for her than her motherhood (cf. *Sermo* 25, 7: PL 46, 937–938). There are good grounds for the statement made in the Synod Hall that Mary is "a living catechism" and "the mother and model of catechists." (CT 73)

Through her response of faith, her *fiat*, which the *Catechism* calls the most perfect embodiment of the obedience of faith (cf. *Catechism*, no. 144), the Word was made flesh, and dwelt among us. As catechists, our response, our assent, our own personal *fiat*, brings those we are catechizing into intimacy, into union with Jesus Christ and the fullness of His Church.

About Our Contributors

DR. CAROLINE FAREY has responsibility for catechist formation at Maryvale Institute.

REV. DR. WOJCIECH GIERTYCH OP is theologian to the papal household.

REV. PROFESSOR MANUEL DEL CAMPO GUILARTE is the Director of the Higher Institute of Religious Science of San Damaso, Madrid, Spain.

DR. WALTRAUD LINNIG is the Director for the program of formation for the transmission of the Faith at Studium of Notre Dame de Vie (Venasque, France), aggregated to the Pontifical Faculty of the Teresianum.

ANTONIO CARDINAL CAÑIZARES LLOVERA is Prefect of the Congregation for Divine Worship and the Discipline of the Sacraments. He previously served as Archbishop of Toledo and Primate of Spain from 2002 to 2008.

BISHOP RICHARD J MALONE, STL, ThD is Bishop of the Diocese of Portland in Maine and Chairman of the United States Bishops' Committee on Evangelization and Catechesis.

REV. DR. LOUIS MENVIELLE is a priest member of Community of Notre Dame de Vie in Venasque, France. He works at the Congregation for the Clergy in Rome.

SR. M. JOHANNA PARUCH, FSGM, PhD is a member of the Sisters of St. Francis of the Martyr St. George and is Professor of Catechetics at Franciscan University, Steubenville, Ohio, USA.

MSGR. PAUL J. WATSON is the Director of Maryvale Institute in Birmingham, England.

DR. PETROC WILLEY is the Dean of Graduate Research at Maryvale Institute.

Appendix

Oath of Fidelity on Assuming an Office to Be Exercised in the Name of the Church

(Formula to be used by the Christian faithful mentioned in Canon 833, nos. 5–8.)

I, N., in assuming the office of _____, promise that in my words and in my actions I shall always preserve communion with the Catholic Church.

With great care and fidelity I shall carry out the duties incumbent on me toward the Church, both universal and particular, in which, according to the provisions of the law, I have been called to exercise my service.

In fulfilling the charge entrusted to me in the name of the Church, I shall hold fast to the deposit of faith in its entirety; I shall faithfully hand it on and explain it, and I shall avoid any teachings contrary to it.

I shall follow and foster the common discipline of the entire Church and I shall maintain the observance of all ecclesiastical laws, especially those contained in the Code of Canon Law.

With Christian obedience I shall follow what the Bishops, as authentic doctors and teachers of the faith, declare, or what they, as those who govern the Church, establish.

I shall also faithfully assist the diocesan Bishops, so that the apostolic activity, exercised in the name and by mandate of the Church, may be carried out in communion with the Church.

So help me God, and God's Holy Gospels on which I place my hand.